DATE DUE

MAY 0 7 1999		
OCT 27 2000		
OCT 24 2002		
MAY 15 2007		
GAYLORD		PRINTED IN U S A

Family Abuse

Tough Solutions to Stop the Violence

Family Abuse
Tough Solutions to Stop the Violence

CAPTAIN ROBERT L. SNOW

Foreword by
Dr. David Ford

PLENUM TRADE • NEW YORK AND LONDON

Library of Congress Cataloging-in-Publication Data

Snow, Robert L.
    Family abuse : tough solutions to stop the violence / Robert L.
Snow ; foreword by David Ford.
        p.   cm.
    Includes bibliographical references and index.
    ISBN 0-306-45560-9
    1. Domestic violence--United States--Prevention. 2. Conjugal
violence--United States--Prevention. 3. Child abuse--United States-
-Prevention.   I. Title.
HV6626.2.S56   1997
362.82'927'0973--dc21   96-39662
                                                                  CIP

ISBN 0-306-45560-9

© 1997 Robert L. Snow
Plenum Press is a Division of Plenum Publishing Corporation
233 Spring Street, New York, N.Y. 10013-1578
http://www.plenum.com

10 9 8 7 6 5 4 3 2 1

Printed in the United States of America

To my wife, Melanie
God's gift to abused children

Foreword

One of the great ironies of human life is that the family—our primary source for love, support, and security—can be the most abusive of any group to which we belong. Official records do not document all acts of intrafamilial abuse. Underreporting, misclassification, and difficulties in identifying victim–offender relationships serve to conceal the problem from public view. Nevertheless, we know from national surveys that violence alone is remarkably high—in a given year, the average American is nearly as likely to be assaulted by a member of his or her own family as by anyone else. The risk is especially severe for women, children, and the elderly by virtue of their economic and emotional dependency on their abusers.

Those of us who study and advocate for victims of family abuse rarely observe firsthand the acts we seek to describe and explain. Apart from our personal experiences, few of us witness the varieties of criminal acts that family members commit against one another. The police, on the other hand, are routinely called to intervene in family crises as they occur. Police officers see the anger, the terror, the anguish, and the injuries. No doubt they witness the worst of family abuse. What they see may not represent the full nature of the problem, but their observations provide a window onto details otherwise hidden.

Captain Robert Snow opens the curtains for us to appreciate

what the police encounter. *Family Abuse* reveals the big picture of physical, emotional, and economic abuse prevalent in the family. It documents his experiences as witness to and interpreter of events. Using both true-life examples and publicized cases from around the country, he describes family abuse as an alarming source of pain for those victimized. At the same time, he helps us understand police concerns and frustrations, and, without excuse, he tells us how it is that the police response to family abuse falls short of citizen expectations.

Captain Snow clearly believes that family abuse can be remedied through criminal justice intervention. He sees that police need to understand the dynamics of family abuse to shape an appropriate response, and that prosecutors and judges must do their part to coordinate the system's response. But he argues that criminal justice, alone, will not prevent family abuse. At best, it may deter some perpetrators while signaling a community's intolerance of crimes within the family. Ending abuse requires commitment from all sectors of the community. Captain Snow concludes *Family Abuse* with provocative ideas for training, for law enforcement policy, and for public policy—ideas on which police, politicians, and ordinary citizens can find common ground for organizing communities to end abuse.

David A. Ford, Ph.D.
Chairperson, Department of Sociology
Indiana University at Indianapolis

Acknowledgments

A book on a subject as complex as family abuse could never be written without assistance from many people. I especially want to thank the editors I worked with at Plenum, both Senior Editor Linda Greenspan Regan, who saw the worth of this book and acquired it, and Assistant Editor Melicca McCormick, whose insightful editing and thoughtful suggestions contributed significantly to making the book what it is. I also want to extend my gratitude and thanks to my agent, Fran Collin, for her consistent hard work on my behalf.

Although I received advice and assistance from many experts and authorities in the field of family abuse while writing this book, I want to particularly acknowledge two people who very patiently and methodically critiqued my manuscript. I offer my deepest thanks to both Dr. David Ford of Indiana University, a nationally recognized expert in the field of conjugal violence, and my wife, Melanie, a child abuse detective for the Indianapolis Police Department. Their help was immeasurable.

While in the writing of this book I used real-life incidents, and readers will undoubtedly recognize the names of some of the people in a few of the more famous and newsworthy cases, a condition I agreed to for most of the incidents was that I would change the names so that the identities of the victims would be protected. While I believe bringing the problem of family abuse out into the open is crucial if the problem is ever to be solved, I also feel that the victims have already suffered enough without having to worry about their victimizations being exposed to public scrutiny. So while I can't personally thank all of the victims here for their assistance, I want to express my heartfelt gratitude to them.

Lastly, I want to thank Warren and Bobbi Morphew for their help in giving me the time to write this book.

Contents

Family Abuse

Tough Solutions to Stop the Violence

1

Family Abuse in America

Saturday; 5 April 1969; 10:00 P.M.

It was the night before Easter Sunday, an evening many people spend in quiet reflection and joyful expectation of the upcoming holiday. For me it became a night of violence and bloodshed.

The night before Easter 1969 was to be my first night ever as a police officer, and I had hoped it would be an evening of chasing criminals and solving crimes. Instead it became an evening when the startling extent of family abuse in American society was revealed to me for the first time. I passed the night racing from one family abuse case to another, trying to use what I found were very limited resources to stop this abuse. During the night I witnessed family members using their fists, blunt objects, and firearms on each other. I saw family members forced to live in constant fear and dread, and I spoke with weak and helpless family members who had been sexually abused, terrorized, and brutalized by other family members. By the end of my eight-hour shift I felt defeated, heartbroken, and frustrated. We had solved very little because we had no true weapons to fight with, and we could only put a Band-Aid on what I would later discover was one of America's major wounds.

❖ ❖ ❖ ❖ ❖

1

It had rained earlier in the day, and everyone coming out of
the chilly night and through the revolving door tracked puddles of
water into the Police Headquarters building on North Alabama
Street in Indianapolis. I and eleven other new police officers, all
of us dressed in the distinctive gray uniform of a recruit trainee,
marched anxiously along a hallway of the headquarters building.
I could hear a steady hum of conversation coming from the Roll
Call room as we stepped up to the door and stopped, no one
seeming to want to be the first one through. We all looked at each
other for several seconds, and then finally one brave recruit officer
took the lead, and we filed into a room full of veteran officers
dressed in light blue uniform shirts. The conversation seemed to
dim a bit as many of the officers looked over at us, and made not
so under-the-breath comments about how the quality of recruit
officers seemed to worsen every year. This was a tradition born
many years before and is still practiced to this day.

I walked over and stood with my fellow trainees against the
wall, anxious and excited. We had been at the Police Academy
now for two months, learning the academic side of police work.
Tonight, we would learn the practical side, and see police work as
it really was. We were going on street patrol for the first time.

The Police Academy had issued our guns—Smith and Wesson
.38 caliber revolvers—earlier that week and, as we waited against
the wall for roll call to begin, I brushed my arm self-consciously
against mine, unused to the weight on my right side. Tonight, each
recruit trainee was scheduled to ride with a veteran officer and to
actually see and experience what he had been hearing about in
class for the last two months. We still had a month and a half left
in the Police Academy and we would ride with a veteran officer
now every Saturday afternoon or evening until we graduated.

The room almost immediately quieted when a captain, wearing the white uniform shirt of a command officer, stepped up to
the lectern. In the silence, two officers unwittingly continued what
now sounded like a very loud conversation at the back of the
room. The captain looked at them for a second and then tapped
the bottoms of a stack of papers on the lectern. Someone nudged

the officers and the room went silent. Clearing his throat, the captain read off a few announcements, gave out information on the various suspects the police were looking for (which everyone dutifully copied down in their notebooks), and then began calling roll.

Interestingly, I found as I attended my first police roll call, rather than answering with a "here" or "present," the officers answered with a number. What I didn't know then was that the response given to their names was the number of traffic tickets the officers had written during the previous day. In the late 1960s there was a quota system for traffic tickets in Indianapolis (in those days the police department received a portion of the fines paid for traffic tickets), and woe to any officer who would answer roll call with a "here" or "none."

As we trainees stood against the wall waiting and not really understanding what was going on, the captain, after writing down the number the officer responded with, would occasionally respond back with the name of one of the recruit officers. The captain first called roll for Adam sector, Boy sector, Charles sector, and then David sector, all of the quieter, outlying sectors. When the captain finished with David sector, eight of the recruit trainees had been assigned to one of the officers, and only four of us remained yet unassigned. Four officers and three inner-city sectors left. I could suddenly feel my heart thumping against my rib cage. I couldn't believe my luck. I was going to get one of the good sectors.

"Edward sector," the captain said, shuffling the stack of papers on the lectern, and then running his finger down the new top sheet. "Alford, Terry," he called out.

"Three, sir!" shouted a voice from the back of the room.

The captain wrote down the number, and then added, "Snow, Robert."

I looked over and tried to see who had just responded to the captain, but I hadn't been paying close enough attention, and wasn't sure who Officer Terry Alford was. The captain called roll for Frank and George sector, assigning the three remaining recruit officers, and then finally dismissed the roll call. As soon as the captain stepped away from the lectern, a huge buzz of conversation began again, and, after several minutes of standing around and apparently catching up with the latest gossip, the officers finally began walking over to pick up their recruit trainees.

An officer I guessed to be in his middle forties, which I, at the age of twenty-one, then simply classified as old, lumbered over. Sporting a full head of unruly gray hair, and dressed in a poorly fitting uniform that hung loosely on his body, Officer Terry Alford certainly didn't look to me like the stereotyped police officer seen on *Adam-12* or *Dragnet*. He gave me a smile and stuck out a huge, calloused hand.

"Hi, I'm Terry Alford. I guess we're riding together tonight."

"Bob Snow," I answered, shaking his hand. "You're assigned to Edward sector, huh?"

The instructors at the Police Academy had talked a lot about Edward sector during the last two months. It was, in 1969, the poorest and most crime-ridden of the police sectors. It was the sector on which an officer was most likely to get into a fight, most likely to have to chase someone, and most likely to see some serious crime. Although electricity filled my stomach, I couldn't have felt luckier. I knew all of the other recruit trainees envied me.

"Yeah, you'll like Edward sector," Terry said. "It's where all of the young guys want to ride because there's so much action."

Five minutes later, after Terry had given me a crash course on how all of the equipment on the police car worked and where the first-aid kit and fire extinguisher were—just in case—we cruised up College Avenue and into Edward sector. Our unit number was Edward Nine, and Terry assigned me the job of answering the radio and making all of the reports. I couldn't believe my good luck. On his instruction, I pulled the radio microphone off the dashboard clip, cleared my throat, and then signed us into service. Only seconds, it seemed, after I hung up the microphone, the dispatcher came back with: "Edward Nine, domestic disturbance at 2312 North Carrollton."

After writing down the address on the run sheet, my palms

suddenly sweaty and tingling, I pulled the microphone back off the dashboard clip and answered: "Edward Nine's clear."

"Edward Nine," the dispatcher responded, "your time out is twenty-two twenty-five."

I wrote the time, 10:25 P.M., down on the run sheet, and barely concealed my excitement as I wiped my palms on my slacks. I quickly reviewed everything I had learned in the Police Academy about proper procedures when responding to a run where there might be violence. I didn't have long to do this, though, because, as it turned out, we were only a few blocks from the address, and soon turned onto the 2300 block of North Carrollton.

We had been taught in the Police Academy that when an officer responds to a run where there might be violence he should never park his vehicle directly in front of the address, but down the street a bit. That way, if there happened to be any firearms involved, the officer wouldn't be an easy target as he stepped out of his car. Also, the instructors had told us, parking down the street gives an officer the opportunity to assess the situation, from a safe distance, as he is walking up to the address. Terry, I noticed, however, parked directly in front of the house, stepped immediately out of the car, seemingly didn't stop to assess the situation, and walked directly up a half-dozen steps and onto the porch, knocking on the door. The cold night air suddenly seemed to go right through my jacket as I walked dutifully behind, looking into all of the dark areas and trying my best to assess the situation, all the while carrying the report pad in my left hand so that my gun hand would be free.

A woman I guessed to be in her middle to late twenties answered the door, and even in the dim light of the porch I could see that her left eye was already bruised and swelling. A stream of blood ran down her chin.

"Evening, Betty," Terry said. "I see you and Jim have been at it again."

The woman, who was sobbing, nodded and stepped back, waving us into the house. Walking inside, I saw sitting on the landing of a stairway two children, a boy and a girl about five and six. Both children were crying as they clung to each other. When Terry said hi to the children, calling them by name, I wondered if perhaps the family was friends of his since he seemed to know all of them on a first-name basis. (I later found out that there were about a dozen families in Terry's district that he knew on a first-name basis, not because they were friends, but because he had been on dozens of calls to their homes about family abuse.) As we stood in the living room, I noticed that a strong odor of bourbon hung in the air, and I spied a smashed whiskey bottle in the doorway leading to the kitchen, and also noticed a lamp in the living room lying on its side.

"Betty," Terry said as he took her over to a light and examined her eye and chin, "how many times have I told you that Jim's not going to change on his own? Somebody's going to have to make him change. You didn't go down to the Prosecutor's Office last time like you promised me, did you?"

Now standing under a bright light, Betty appeared haggard and aged far beyond her twenty-five or twenty-six years. She shook her head. "He's really not a bad man when he's not drinking," she said between sobs. "He's only mean when he's had a few. He's really not a bad man when he's sober. Really, he isn't."

"Where's he at now?"

"He's out in the garage. I thinks he's got another bottle out there."

"Come on." Terry waved for me to follow as he started for the garage. I stuck the report pad up under my left arm, and then brushed my right hand across my revolver, why I'm not sure, probably just to be certain it was there, and then fell in behind him. I tried to quickly review everything we had learned in our defensive tactics class. She had said he was mean when he was drunk.

"Please don't hurt him!" Betty called after us. "Just make him leave for awhile. Please! Don't hurt him!"

Terry and I walked into the kitchen, carefully avoiding the broken whiskey bottle, and, a moment later, stepped through a door at the rear of the kitchen and into what looked less like a garage and more like a flea market that had been closed for years. No vehicles sat parked there, just piles and piles of dust-laden junk. A man, wearing a wrinkled and soiled blue work uniform with patches saying "Well's Heating and Air-Conditioning" over one breast and "Jim" over the other, sat in a rickety-looking, grease-stained lawn chair and swigged from a pint bottle of Old Crow whiskey.

"Well, Jim, I see you and Betty have been into it again," Terry said with a tone of resignation.

Jim looked up at us with glassy eyes for a few seconds, then finally seemed to recognize Terry, and pulled himself up straight in the chair. "Yes sir," he said. "But it wasn't my fault this time. Really, it wasn't. The damn woman just won't quit nagging me. But believe me, officer, it's over for the night. Really, it is." The odor of whiskey, along with droplets of saliva, sprayed from his mouth as he talked.

Terry didn't seem impressed. "Jim, you know the routine. You're going to have to go somewhere for the night. You can come back tomorrow. Maybe you and Betty can talk it out then. But not tonight. If you come back tonight, I'll have to lock you up."

Jim appeared for just a moment as if he wanted to protest, but then apparently thought better of it and pushed himself up out of the chair. "Yes sir, I'll walk over to my brother's house. He always lets me spend the night there whenever Betty and I get to fighting."

I tensed my body, ready for him to suddenly and unexpectedly strike. However, when we escorted Jim out of the garage and into the kitchen, he simply grabbed a jacket off the back of a chair and then left through the rear door of the house without saying anything more to us or anything at all to his wife or children. Once he had left, I turned to Terry. "Do you think he'll really stay away?"

"Oh yeah," Terry said with a nod. "He's been through this a lot of times. He knows all of the right moves."

Surprised at Jim's docility, I walked back into the living room with Terry, where Betty still stood, the two children now clinging to either side of her. Terry shook his head.

"Betty, how long you planning on putting up with this? How many more years are you going to let Jim beat on you?"

She seemed to try to bring a reasonable expression to her face, but failed. "He's really not a bad man when he's sober. Really, he's not." Betty then attempted to look Terry in the eyes, as if to give credence to what she had just said, but after a moment glanced down at the carpet, and sighed. "I know. I ought to do something. But where would I go if I didn't have this place? If I leave him what will I live on? I've never worked before. I can't get a job that'll pay anything."

While Terry was talking with Betty, I noticed that one of the children, the little girl, had a red streak across her cheek, as though she had been struck with something. When the little girl saw me looking at her, she gingerly fingered the injury. Terry then also seemed to notice it.

"Oh great!" Terry said, throwing up his hands, "now he's started on the kids. I've been telling you for years that this stuff never gets any better. One of these days he's going to go too far and then I'll be taking one of you, or maybe all of you, out of here in a body bag. Now listen to me, Betty, you need to go down to the Prosecutor's Office first thing Monday morning and file a warrant for him. That's the only way this stuff's ever going to stop. I'll be there with you and we'll have the judge make him get some help for his drinking."

Betty didn't say anything for a few moments as she continued to look down at the carpet, but then finally nodded. "Okay," she said in a barely audible voice, "I will. I promise. First thing Monday morning."

I pulled the report pad out from under my arm and started the paperwork for an assault report, but Terry shook his head and motioned for us to leave. Once we were outside, my mind swirling with confusion, I grabbed Terry's arm as he started down the steps to the sidewalk.

"Wait a minute. Don't I need to get some information from her for the report? The instructors at the Academy told us that the Prosecutor's Office won't do anything if there's not a report on file."

Terry didn't answer until we had gotten back into the police car. Then he let out a breath and shook his head. "She won't be at the Prosecutor's Office. Trust me, she won't. I've been coming here probably every other weekend for the last three or four years. Hell, tonight was minor compared to most times. One weekend, a year ago or so, he hit her with a chair and fractured her skull. I arrested Jim that time, but after she got out of the hospital Betty changed her mind and wouldn't testify against him. Hell, a couple months ago he knocked out a tooth and broke her nose. And there was this one time I remember when he took after her with a fiberglass fishing pole. There wasn't a spot on that woman's body that wasn't covered with welts. You'd think she'd want to do something. But it's the same thing every time. She promises she'll show up at the Prosecutor's Office, but then she never does."

At this time in my career I didn't know much about family abuse and the police role in dealing with it, but would soon find that in the 1960s and 1970s each officer handled family abuse cases in whatever way he wanted. The Police Academy gave no training in crisis counseling or in the appropriate method for talking with people involved in family abuse situations. Terry did not want to file a report in the case of Betty and Jim, and probably would have been reprimanded by his sergeant for clogging up the system if he had. In later years, however, I would find that reports made on incidents such as these can be very beneficial if I later needed to show a pattern of continued abuse (in the event a serious crime developed from the abuse or the victim decided she did want to prosecute after all). Although Terry did all he could that night with the resources available to him in 1969, twenty-eight years as a police officer has taught me that whenever the police come to the scene of a family abuse situation and do nothing substantial, as in the case of Betty and Jim above, all this does is tell the abusers that their behavior is acceptable and that continuing it will have no bad consequences for them.

That night, as we pulled away from the curb, I felt as though we were leaving a door open that should be closed, but not knowing then what I could do about it, I signed our unit back into service. Five minutes later, we answered the report of a burglar alarm going off at a warehouse. Terry, however, said we didn't need to be in a big hurry because it went off on a regular basis. Soon after this run, I heard our unit number again.

"Edward Nine, domestic disturbance, 1001 East 19th Street."

Terry stuck out his bottom lip as he looked over at the police radio. "Hmm, that's a new one. People must've just moved in."

I okayed the run, and several minutes later we pulled to the curb on East 19th Street, but this time several houses down from our address. Terry climbed out of the car and looked around as we walked slowly up to the house. When we stepped onto the porch, Terry directed me to stand over past the left side of the door (just like they taught us in the Police Academy, a safety measure in case someone fires a shot through the door), and then he reached over from past the right side and knocked. My stomach knotted up and pulled tight as we waited.

"Who is it?" a voice finally called from inside.

"Police!" Terry called back.

A thin, dark-eyed woman with gray-streaked hair squeezed tightly into a bun opened the door, then looked over her shoulder when someone behind her shouted: "Stella, you tell them son-of-a-bitches that this is my house, and I don't want them in here!"

"What's the problem, ma'am?" Terry asked the woman.

Her hands clenched into fists, Stella looked back at us. "It's my mother. I think Ewell's hit her, and he might've hurt her bad. I need you to look at her."

When we walked into the living room I could hear the muted sound of screaming coming from somewhere, while on a couch a few feet away, Ewell, obviously intoxicated, sneered at us through watery, bloodshot eyes.

"This is my fucking house," the man told us, "and I said I want you sons-of-bitches out of here!"

Terry acted as though he hadn't heard the man, and simply followed Stella to a closed door off the living room. At the door Terry turned and whispered to me, "Look at his knuckles." I turned and examined Ewell as Stella opened the door. I could see that the knuckles of the man's right hand were skinned and had been bleeding.

As soon as Stella opened the door the muted screaming I had heard when we stepped into the house started again, but now teeth-clenchingly loud. Inside the room, a thin, elderly woman I guessed to be at least in her eighties lay in bed, blood streaming down from her mouth. According to Stella, the woman in the bed, her mother, was an invalid and senile. The elderly woman, I quickly found, didn't seem to know we were there. She lay in the bed and continued screaming.

"I think Ewell hit her," Stella told us, her expression becoming stern. "I was upstairs a little while ago and I heard mother start screaming. I'm positive he hit her. I just know he did. He's been threatening to do it ever since she moved in with us. You know, he tried that stuff with me a long time ago, and I told him what I'd do if he ever tried it again. And I meant it!"

Blood rose to Stella's cheeks as Terry told her about Ewell's skinned knuckles. For a few seconds she simply stood inhaling and exhaling loudly through her nose. "You know, I probably shouldn't have, but I've let him get away with a lot of mean, hateful talk over the years," Stella said. "But I told him what I'd do if he ever used his fists again. Well, now he's going to have to learn that I wasn't joking. I want him to go to jail! Do you hear me, I want him to go to jail!" Stella had worked herself up into a fury, and now stood looking at us with clenched fists and labored breathing. "I told him I'd have him locked up if he ever tried that stuff again. And I meant it! I want him to go to jail!"

"Well, ma'am," Terry explained, "there's not a whole lot we can do tonight other than make a report. This is only a misdemeanor. You'll have to go down to the Prosecutor's Office Monday morning and swear out a warrant."

What differentiates a misdemeanor (minor crime) from a felony (serious crime) varies from state to state. In 1969 in Indiana Ewell's battery of his mother-in-law would have to have been life-threatening to be a felony (which would then have made him eligible for arrest on the scene without a warrant). Fortunately, today most police officers around the country can arrest in family abuse situations without a warrant even if the battery is only on a misdemeanor level.

"He hit her and I want him to go to jail tonight!" Stella insisted, looking back and forth from me to Terry as though not sure who was in charge.

"I'm sorry, ma'am," Terry went on explaining, "I'm sure he did hit her. But like I told you, this is only a misdemeanor. We have to *witness* a misdemeanor before we can make an arrest. You'll have to get a warrant."

"I think he might've also stolen some of Mom's pension money to buy whiskey," she added, looking quickly back and forth between Terry and me.

Terry shook his head. "I'm sorry, ma'am, but—."

At that moment, Ewell, smelling of very cheap bourbon, staggered into the bedroom and pointed a stubby finger at us. "I told you sons-of-bitches that I wanted you out of my house! Now get your asses out of here!" Ewell then staggered back into the living room.

Terry squeezed his lips together for a second as he looked at the elderly woman, who had finally stopped screaming, and then at Stella. "You're right, ma'am. I think I need to take your husband to jail."

Although I was a brand-new officer and didn't know it at the time, the police in 1969 usually performed an attitude check whenever they went to a domestic disturbance, and gauged what actions they would take based on the attitudes of the people involved in the disturbance. While Jim at our earlier run apparently passed, Ewell obviously failed the attitude check. Fortunately, changes in the training police officers receive and the laws available for dealing with family abuse have done away with this attitude check. Police officers today are trained that the safety of the victims is what they should gauge their response on when dealing with family abuse situations.

That night in 1969, though, I wondered what charge Terry planned to use. While Ewell was obviously rude and intoxicated, I hadn't observed him breaking any laws. In Indiana it was only against the law to be drunk in a public place, and a disorderly conduct charge required that a person disturb the peace and quiet of a neighborhood. So far, I hadn't seen any evidence of Ewell violating either law.

What I wasn't aware of at the time, and they certainly hadn't taught us this at the Police Academy, was that there was an informal, unwritten law that Ewell had broken, the FWP law, which is an acronym for Fucking with the Police. It was a law that in the 1960s and 1970s I would see hundreds of people arrested for. Most police officers back then really became upset when someone treated them with disrespect. That person usually went to jail. And while I found Terry to be particularly inventive in his use of the law that night, most officers at that time didn't bother with legalities but just simply arrested the disrespectful person on a variety of charges, even though they had, at the very best, shaky grounds for doing so. Most of the judges in the 1960s and 1970s, I was also to find, would usually go along with FWP arrests in family abuse situations if the officers made the judge aware that the family abuse was a recurrent problem or that there had been a second or third run to the same address that night.

Again, like the attitude check, law changes and an increased emphasis on public relations have reduced the use of the FWP law. While I certainly wouldn't say that no one is arrested any longer for violating the FWP law, much fewer certainly are because police departments and the courts no longer permit or support it.

"What are you planning on charging him with?" I asked, nervous about being involved in a possible false arrest.

"Drunk," Terry answered.

"But you can't," I said, remembering my criminal law class. "It's not against the law to be drunk in your own house." I could feel little beads of perspiration forming on my forehead and back.

Terry winked at me. "I know. Watch this."

Stepping out of the bedroom, Terry led me and Stella across the living room, out the front door, and then down the steps to the police car, completely ignoring Ewell, who shouted over and over for Stella to get back in the house.

"Now don't anyone look at Ewell until I say so," Terry said as he opened the car door and pulled the radio microphone off the dashboard clip, asking for an ambulance to be sent for the injured woman. Afterward, we stood for several minutes in the street behind the police car as I gathered the information I would need for my report.

"All right," Terry said, "now everybody look up at the house for a second."

When I turned my head up toward the house I saw Ewell now standing just inside the front door looking down at us. He yelled something at us, but because of the distance I couldn't understand what it was.

"Don't anyone look at him again," Terry said as I continued gathering information from Stella for my assault report. A minute or so later, I heard the door of the house slam. Out of my peripheral vision I could see Ewell now at the top of the half-dozen steps that led down to the sidewalk.

"Stella, I told you to get your ass back into the house! I ain't scared of those sons-of-bitches. They ain't got no business here. This is my house!"

"Don't look at him," Terry instructed the woman in a low voice. "Act like he isn't there."

We continued standing in the street behind the police car for another minute or so, and Ewell called out several more times for Stella to get back into the house, but no one looked at him or even acted as though we had heard him. Finally, he came down the concrete steps and walked out onto the sidewalk. I tensed, not knowing what to expect, but prepared to defend myself.

"Stella, I ain't telling you again! You get your—."

What occurred next happened so quickly that all I could do was just watch with my mouth open. Before Ewell had time to finish his sentence, Terry was up on the sidewalk, had grabbed Ewell, threw him up against the police car, and handcuffed him. "You're under arrest for public intoxication," he told him.

Twenty minutes later, after the paddy wagon had carted Ewell off to jail, the med tech from the ambulance had checked Stella's mother, and Terry had instructed Stella on how to go about obtaining a warrant for the beating of her mother, Terry and I marked back into service. While for the 1960s Terry's handling of this incident struck me as impressive, such would not be the case today. In the 1960s the laws in the United States still considered most cases of family abuse, except under the most drastic or life-threatening circumstances, to be private family matters that should not be addressed or interfered with by the legal system. Even in the above case, in which Stella and her mother were obviously in danger, the law provided no method of resolution for the police. Police officers in those days were forced to seek alternate methods, as Terry did, to correct what they saw as serious matters. Fortunately, the last decade has seen dramatic changes in the law, and today Ewell would have been arrested at once.

Within ten minutes of leaving Stella's house we received another run, this one, the dispatcher said, a woman threatening her boyfriend with a gun. When we arrived at the address a few minutes later, it turned out to be another location Terry wasn't acquainted with, and we again practiced all of the proper safety procedures. I wondered how police officers ever managed to eat since, at the thought of facing someone brandishing a gun, my stomach immediately knotted up again. We soon found, however, that the woman's brother had already taken the gun away from her, and that the boyfriend had then immediately left. It took us several minutes to quiet the woman down enough to get the specifics of what had happened. For the first few minutes she stormed around the house, going back and forth from the kitchen to the living room, knocking over anything within an arm's reach, and screaming: "That son-of-a-bitch has been fucking my daughter!"

We finally found out that the woman's boyfriend, who apparently had no job and baby-sat for the woman's children while she worked, had been sexually molesting the woman's nine-year-old daughter for over a year. The woman told us that she'd found out about it because she hadn't felt well that night and had come home early from work, catching the boyfriend on the couch with the little girl. Since the boyfriend wasn't there, we took a report and marked it to the attention of the Sex Crimes Branch.

When we marked back into service I looked at my watch. It

wasn't quite midnight and already we had been to three family disturbances. Before I went home the next morning at 6:00 A.M. we would also take the report of a robbery at a filling station, bandage up a drunk who had been hit in the head with a rock thrown by another drunk, and respond to four more family disturbances. In the case of two of the family disturbances Terry knew the participants by their first names, including one in which the husband and wife were still swinging at each other when we got there. In this case both people had refused to stop fighting, and my stomach, rather than knotting up, filled with hot acid when Terry and I had to jump in and physically restrain them. Eventually we sent them both to jail since twice while we were talking to them they leaped up and went back at each other. At another of the disturbances, we were met by a woman who had a huge gash on her head that was bleeding so badly we sent her to the hospital. Her husband, she said, hit her with a hammer, then fled the house before we got there.

Around 3:00 A.M., contrary to what Terry had predicted, we were called back to Jim and Betty's. Jim had returned and was causing more problems. He claimed he had only come back for some of his clothing, and, even though he remained respectful to us throughout the incident, Terry arrested him anyway for disorderly conduct. Terry later told me that while he knew he didn't have the legal grounds he needed to make the arrest he still had to do it. It was important, Terry said, that the people on his district knew he wasn't bluffing when he told them not to come back that night. If he let someone get away with something like this, he said, then he'd lose all control. (The judge went along with Terry the following Monday morning and found Jim guilty, but only sentenced him to probation.)

Fortunately, today's laws would have made this arrest unnecessary since the police could have arrested Jim on the first run to his house. But in the 1960s the police lacked any such legal support.

In addition to all of these runs, we also wrote two traffic tickets and were dispatched to Methodist Hospital on the report of a man shot by his live-in girl friend. Almost before I could pick up the radio microphone to acknowledge the run, we were disregarded by another unit that was closer to the hospital. Terry, however, apparently taking his responsibility as a trainer very seriously, drove by there anyway. Yet, even though we went to the hospital, I still didn't see very much. The emergency room was packed with sick and injured people and everything seemed totally confused. The noise level of the place made it impossible to hear a conversation unless you were right up next to the other person. All I saw was a shock room (the room in which emergency room personnel perform the immediate life-saving work) with a lot of people working feverishly on a patient, and what seemed to me like an awful lot of blood, a sight that left me cold.

At the end of my shift I thanked Terry for a very instructive evening. I would ride with him again before I got my own car and district, and we would eventually become good friends after I was permanently assigned to Edward sector; and, later, after my promotion to sergeant on Edward sector. No matter how long I was a police officer I always felt that Terry could teach me something new about police work.

Terry died in the mid 1970s and consequently did not see the changes in family abuse laws and training that would have made his job easier and certainly more satisfying. Looking back from my twenty-eight years as a police officer, I find that, even with the lack of laws and training, Terry was still a compassionate man who did all he could within the legal framework available at the time to deal with family abuse.

Today, police officers find dealing with family abuse a bit easier. In most states, for example, police officers can now arrest for misdemeanor assaults not witnessed by them but committed during family abuse incidents. In many states these arrests are strongly encouraged and even mandated. While I don't support mandatory arrests (for reasons I will go into later), I do after twenty-eight years believe that arrests should be made in the large majority of cases where an assault has taken place during a family abuse incident. Abusers must be shown that their actions are a crime and will be treated as such. Abusers must be shown that society considers their behavior unacceptable and will not tolerate it.

In 1969, though, police work was still very new and confusing to me. After driving back to my apartment, I found I was too tense from the excitement of the evening to sleep. I sat up for awhile and thought about what had happened that night. Besides being confused, I was also a bit disturbed. What had happened certainly wasn't what I had expected police work to be, and it certainly wasn't what was portrayed on TV. We hadn't chased or apprehended any bad guys. We hadn't solved any big crimes. Mostly we had just tried to keep the peace and settle family fights. We had spent the biggest part of the night trying to keep family members from bludgeoning, knifing, and shooting each other, or dealing with the consequences of it when they had. The amount of family abuse I had witnessed truly disturbed me. Was there really that much of it in the community? If there was, how come I hadn't seen it before? Was I really that naive? Had I gone through my life with blinders on?

I tried to recall if maybe I had witnessed some family abuse in the past, but simply hadn't recognized it for what it was. Although my brothers and I had always thought that our father was overly strict, I knew I had never really experienced any family violence or abuse of the kind I had seen that night. And my mother and father, while I'm sure they must have had their disagreements, had never displayed any of the open aggression I had seen during the previous eight hours. I did remember hearing that the man who lived next door to us when I was growing up liked to beat his wife when he got drunk, but I had never actually witnessed it. Until that night I had never really witnessed any true family violence or abuse, and had never really suspected its extent or prevalence in our society.

The following Monday the instructors at the Police Academy held a debriefing session to discuss our experiences while riding with veteran officers. Every single trainee had a story similar to mine. After graduation from the Police Academy, I became a street officer, eventually got my own beat, and also began knowing my abusive families by name. I quickly learned that family abuse is widespread in our society, and occurs many more times than most members of the public would ever suspect.

❖ ❖ ❖ ❖ ❖

Anna Quindlen, who was at the time a syndicated columnist for *The New York Times,* called family abuse "the quiet crime."[1] This seems to me to be a very appropriate name for a brand of deviant behavior few people in America realize is occurring all around them, even when it is affecting other family members or close friends. Few members of the American public realize the widespread nature and extent of family abuse in their community, and most probably would be stunned if they did. Even those of us who work regularly with the victims and perpetrators of family abuse know only of the cases that come to our attention, but no one really knows how many victims of physical, sexual, emotional, and financial abuse simply suffer in silence, and never come to the attention of anyone outside their immediate family.

In the last ten years or so, however, the seriousness of family abuse as a major social problem has finally become recognized. More and more people have come to realize that family abuse is not just a family problem, but rather a national concern. Dozens of talk shows in the last decade have featured family abuse victims and perpetrators, many magazines in the last ten years have contained articles about family abuse, and even the daytime soap opera *The Young and the Restless* did a number of segments about a battered wife who killed her husband. But it is not just the media that has become aware of how serious the family abuse problem is in America.

"Violence in the home is so common," said Dr. Robert E. McAfee, president of the American Medical Association, "that every practicing physician sees cases. Even those who don't realize it."[2] "In this country, domestic violence is just about as common as giving birth," said Health and Human Services Secretary Donna E. Shalala at a Washington, D.C. symposium on violence.[3]

United States Surgeon General C. Everett Koop, in an article in the *Journal of the American Medical Association,* stated that family violence is the leading cause of injury to women between the ages of 15 and 44, causing more injuries than automobile accidents, muggings, and rapes combined. The National Coalition Against

Domestic Violence states that their research shows that half of all women will experience some form of violence from their husbands during their marriage. The *Journal of the American Medical Association* states that from 22 to 35 percent of all the visits by women to hospital emergency rooms in this country are the result of family abuse. According to the *Journal of Elder Abuse and Neglect*, one in every twenty-five elderly people in this country will be abused each year.[4]

Sadly though, along with adults, the victims of family abuse are often those who can least defend or protect themselves—children. The United States Advisory Board on Child Abuse and Neglect, a panel established by Congress to evaluate the scope of child abuse and neglect in the United States, stated that a two-and-a-half-year nationwide study found that abuse and neglect in the home are leading causes of death for young children, greater in number than deaths from accidental falls, choking on food, suffocation, drowning, or fires. The Board also found that 50 percent of the homes with adult violence also have child abuse and/or neglect.[5] Even more alarming, according to a Carnegie Corporation study released in 1994, one in every three child victims of physical abuse is an infant.

These very alarming statistics come from what I consider very reliable sources. However, I found while doing research for this book that I had to be very careful about the facts and statistics quoted in certain sources. A number of writers, I discovered, are so committed to the cause of fighting and exposing the brutal truth about family abuse that they often misrepresent or distort facts and statistics in order to stress their point about the seriousness of this problem. For instance, a number of writers I came across in my research, no matter what the source of their facts and statistics said, refuse to acknowledge that there is any family abuse or violence in this country initiated by women. (As a police officer I can assure you there is, though certainly not to the level of male-initiated abuse or violence.)

An example of female-initiated family abuse is that which was perpetrated by Guinevere Garcia, who in January of 1996 sat on Death Row in Illinois. This thirty-six-year-old woman has admitted to killing her eleven-month-old daughter by placing a plastic bag over the infant's head, to tying up, pistol whipping, and robbing her first husband, and to murdering her second husband. "I killed George Garcia, and only I know why," she said from Death Row.

As occurs with most prisoners who are sent to Death Row, Guinevere Garcia's sentence has been the subject of protests by those opposed to the death penalty. "This is not a suicide," she told opponents of the death penalty, who unsuccessfully urged her to appeal to the governor for clemency. "I am not taking my own life. I committed these crimes. I am responsible for these crimes."[6]

On 18 April 1996, federal authorities charged Rita Gluzman under a 1994 interstate domestic violence law. She is accused of hacking her estranged husband, Yakov Gluzman, to death with an ax and then arranging for her cousin to drop her estranged husband's remains, which had been cut into more than sixty-five pieces, into a New Jersey river. The Gluzmans were reportedly going through a bitter divorce after twenty-seven years of marriage. Violence and abuse by women is not as uncommon as we like to believe.

Another "fact" I ran into constantly while doing research for this book was that men who killed their wives were treated more leniently by the criminal justice system than were women who killed their husbands. Actually, the opposite is true. According to the U.S. Department of Justice research paper *Violence between Intimates*, 94 percent of the men convicted of killing their wives were sent to prison, while only 81 percent of the women convicted of killing their husbands were sent to prison. On the average, for spouse killers sent to prison, men received sentences almost three times as long as those given to women.[7] A further study of murder, this one in America's seventy-five largest counties and conducted by the Bureau of Justice Statistics, along with confirming the above findings, also found that only 2 percent of the husbands charged with killing their wives were acquitted by a court, while 14 percent of the wives charged with killing their husbands were acquitted.[8]

Even though stressing this point about the existence of much more female-initiated family abuse than most would suppose, I don't want readers to think that violence is evenly distributed between men and women, because it is not. There is much more male-initiated family abuse. For example, in 1994, the police arrested 1348 men for murdering wives and girlfriends, while arresting only 574 women for murdering husbands and boyfriends.[9] In addition, hundreds of thousands of assaults also take place each year between intimates, occurring in about the same percentages as murders. Also, investigators find that most, but not all, intra-familial child sexual abuse is initiated by men.

The most important point that must be stressed is that any abuse in the home, no matter who initiates it, affects all family members. Everyone in the family becomes caught up in the whirl-wind of anger, fear, violence, and pain. Everyone becomes a victim, and the entire family suffers, no matter who is the perpetrator.

Still, a number of other writers, I also found, insisted that women who kill their mates or physically abuse their children are not responsible for their acts, but are instead only reacting to severe abuse by a man (which is sometimes true, but certainly not always). One writer who particularly sticks in my mind concluded a book with the demand that all women now imprisoned in this country for killing or attempting to kill a spouse or boyfriend be pardoned because they undoubtedly did so only in response to years of abuse. This may seem to many readers like a wild, unrealistic demand, but in 1990, Ohio Governor Richard F. Celeste did indeed grant clemency to twenty-six women who had killed or tried to kill a man they said had battered them. Soon after this, Maryland Governor William D. Schaefer followed suit and granted a similar clemency to ten women. These actions strike me as setting a dangerous precedent, as the following incident shows.

❖ ❖ ❖ ❖ ❖

One afternoon, while working as a uniformed district sergeant on Edward sector, I heard two officers being dispatched to a man shot, the location of which happened to be only a few blocks from where I was, and so I headed that way. When I arrived at the address, I found a man lying in the street with four bullets in him. He was still conscious and told me that he had come home unexpectedly and found his wife in bed with another man. Before he could do anything, he said, his wife grabbed a pistol and shot him. We sent him to the hospital and, of course, arrested his wife. Upon questioning at the Homicide Office, the victim's wife readily admitted shooting him, but when asked by the detectives if she had shot her husband because she feared he would do something violent upon discovering her having sex with another man, she simply shrugged.

"I wasn't sure what he'd do," she told us. "He's usually a wimp, but I couldn't be sure what his reaction might be when he caught me like that."

The detectives learned that she had pretty much controlled the couple's marriage, and she admitted to them that she physically abused her husband quite often, hitting him with whatever happened to be close. The man, fortunately, didn't die from the bullet wounds, but did experience some serious complications from the shooting that required a long hospitalization. When the case went to trial several months later, I was amazed at the story the woman told. She painted a picture of herself to the court as a battered wife who had lived in constant fear of her husband, and, neglecting to mention the affair her husband had discovered her involved in, told the court that she had shot her husband because she feared he was about to batter her again. The court, fortunately, didn't believe her story and convicted her of assault and battery with intent to kill. The point of this anecdote is that before embarking on a course of freeing all people who claim to have been abused by a spouse or intimate partner, there should be a careful examination of each case. At the same time, the court must continue to take every accusation of violence (male or female) seriously so that the few who abuse the system do not prevent those truly in crisis from getting help or justice.

❖ ❖ ❖ ❖ ❖

At bottom, there is no need for any distortion of the facts and statistics about family abuse. I can attest (as can probably every other police officer in the United States) that family abuse is a critical problem with devastating effects on its victims. According to the National Institute of Justice's Assessment Program, 99 percent of the police chiefs polled said that domestic violence contributed significantly to their workload, while 91 percent said the same thing for child abuse.[10] Family abuse, as these chiefs of police know, is a problem that pervades every level of our society, rips apart families, and destroys any chance for children to lead safe and healthy lives. It also costs billions of dollars every year. According to a recent study by the National Institute of Justice, child abuse and domestic violence cost the United States nearly $150 billion a year in medical expenses, lost wages, public services, and other costs.[11] In addition to this monetary cost, family abuse also represents a serious threat to our future generations.

The National Institute of Justice's March 1995 *Research in Brief* states that several studies have shown that a childhood history of physical abuse and neglect makes it more likely that person will be arrested for violent crimes later in life. Other studies have shown that boys who witness a father's violence against their mother are ten times more likely to be wife abusers than those from nonviolent families. A study reported in the journal *Psychosomatic Medicine* found that children living in stressful family situations (such as those where family abuse is present) had an increased risk of respiratory illnesses, while an article in the *American Journal of Psychiatry* stated: "The group of adolescents who attempted suicide differed ... in that they had experienced more turmoil in their families, starting in childhood and not stabilizing during adolescence."[12] An article in the journal *Child Abuse and Neglect* said: "Child victims (of abuse) show greater feelings of sadness, lower self-esteem and self-worth, and they perceive the adverse events in their lives as unpredictable, which generates helplessness."[13]

These studies alone should convince any reader that family abuse is a significant problem with far-reaching effects on our society and its future. But while researching this book, I also found that there are a number of writers who have gone in the opposite direction, attempting to find fault with any facts or statistics that show family abuse to be a huge and critical problem in our country. For example, an article in the *National Review* by Cathy Young attempted to refute the enormity of certain family abuse statistics by stating that the findings of one study "included such acts as shoving, slapping, or throwing things in its definition of battery."[14] I'm always amazed that acts people would find reprehensible (and criminal) if committed by strangers are apparently acceptable, or at most should only be winked at by the authorities, if they are committed by a family member. I'm certain that if Ms. Young were shoved, slapped, or had something thrown at her by a stranger, the police would hear about it. A person should have the same amount of safety and security in his or her own home.

The most heavily cited numbers one finds when researching family abuse are that there are three to four million people a year being abused by their spouses or intimate partners, two to three million children abused or neglected annually by their parents, and one and a half to two million cases of elder abuse each year. From my experience as a police officer, I believe that these figures are on the conservative side.

"How many more cases (of family violence) never come to police attention," says researcher Lawrence Sherman in his book *Policing Domestic Violence*, "is almost impossible to say, since not even survey research can overcome some people's reluctance to talk about the problem with strangers."[15]

"Domestic violence flourishes because of silence, because the problem stays hidden and, in a subtle but powerful way, acceptable," said Esta Soler, Executive Director of the Family Violence Prevention Fund, quoted in an article in the September 1994 issue of *Ebony*.[16]

"[E]lder abuse is far from an isolated and localized problem involving a few frail elderly and their pathological offspring. The problem is a full-scale national problem which exists with a frequency that few have dared to imagine." Quote from *Elder Abuse: An Examination of a Hidden Problem* by the Select Committee on Aging of the United States House of Representatives (1981).[17]

Police officers usually don't get involved in this battle over how much family abuse there is in America. They know that family abuse is probably the most prevalent crime committed in the United States. Family abuse has been called "the common cold of police work," because police officers are so very often sent on family abuse runs. Like the common cold, even though stopped temporarily, family abuse seems to recur with regularity.

Being the common cold of police work, family abuse runs are disliked by most police officers. The officers often feel that their work is futile because the legal system seldom recognizes the seriousness of family abuse, and consequently doesn't treat the cases with the same concern as other crimes. The abusers, seeing this, then feel no fear about going back and continuing their crimes. Police officers also fear such calls because family abuse runs can be dangerous.

In his book *Policing Domestic Violence*, Lawrence Sherman, a critical pioneer in the search for the most productive police response to domestic violence runs, points out that between 1973 and 1982 only sixty-five police officers in the United States were killed while responding to domestic violence runs.[18] While Dr. Sherman presented this information with the intention of showing that family violence runs are really not as dangerous as most police officers believe they are, and consequently police officers should not fear to get more involved in their solution, I know sixty-five police officers who would disagree with that. But besides the perhaps small danger of being killed while responding to a domestic violence run, police officers more often don't like domestic violence runs because they must confront the very real threat of serious injury. The most seemingly reasonable and rational people can, when involved in family abuse situations, become suddenly, and unpredictably, violent. Of course, readers must realize that if there is this much danger to police officers, individuals who are armed and trained in self-defense, imagine the danger level to unarmed and usually helpless victims.

Like most police officers, I have had my share of family abuse runs that have suddenly, and unpredictably, turned violent. Two in particular still raise goose bumps when I think about them. In one of them, I was sent with another officer to assist a woman who said she wanted us to stand by and protect her while she moved her things out of an apartment she and her boyfriend had shared.

The boyfriend, she told us, had been very abusive to her, and she was frightened of him. What we didn't know at the time was that the woman was mentally unbalanced and prone to extreme violence on the slightest provocation.

The woman's boyfriend met us at the door and was immediately very cooperative, raising no objection to us standing by as she collected her clothing and personal items. Everything went fine for the first fifteen minutes or so, but then she said she wanted half of the light bulbs, half of the magazines lying on the coffee table, and finally began going through the food in the refrigerator, dividing everything, down to a moldy head of lettuce. After we had been there for about a half-hour and the woman was taking her share of an opened box of laundry detergent, the other officer told her that she needed to hurry because we had to get back into service.

For some reason this infuriated the woman. Without warning, she grabbed a large, two-pronged meat fork from a box she had packed and attacked the other officer, driving the prongs deep into a forearm he threw up to protect himself. After a moment of shock, I leaped to his assistance and grabbed the woman, pulling her away from him. She immediately turned and sunk her teeth into my arm, tearing into the flesh. It took both of us (and her boyfriend) several minutes to finally subdue and handcuff her. I still carry a scar from this attack.

As a side note to this case, a judge sentenced the woman to 180 days in jail for her attack on us. She served the entire sentence, apparently not being able to build up any "good time" for an early release. However, on the very day she finished her sentence and was released from jail, an unknown assailant mysteriously murdered her boyfriend. Although the homicide detectives never arrested anyone for this murder, I and the other officer have always suspected she was the killer.

In another family abuse case, this one just as deadly and unpredictable, I received a radio run described by the dispatcher as a person having trouble with his brother. Having been assigned to the sector for only a few months, and finally operating as a one-officer unit, I wanted to impress the other officers. I happened to be only a block or so away from the run, and so I sped to the address. Then, contrary to police department policy and proper procedure, but being a new, brash officer, I went up to the door before my backup arrived. A man met me at the door, thanked me for coming, and said that he was having a problem with his brother, who lived in another apartment in the house. The man would not be specific about what the problem was he was having with his brother, but insisted that I speak with him. I, of course, agreed to, and followed the man to a door at the back of his apartment. He opened the door for me and I stepped through into a small hallway, immediately finding myself facing what appeared to be a very angry man holding a shotgun aimed at my chest.

Suddenly, I heard the door behind me shut and lock. With nowhere to go, and no place even to seek cover, I stood facing the man with the shotgun for several seconds. The man didn't say anything, but simply stared at me with his face glowing red and his body trembling. Since I still had my revolver holstered and the door behind me was locked, I had no choice but to bluff him, hoping he wouldn't notice the sweat on my face or how my left knee shook. In the sternest voice I could muster I told the man to put the shotgun down right now or else (what else I'm not sure). After a few tense moments, the man apparently realized that holding the shotgun on me wasn't accomplishing anything since I wasn't the one he wanted to shoot. He put the gun down. I was so angry (mostly at myself for allowing myself to get caught in this kind of situation) that I arrested both the man with the shotgun and the brother who had locked me in the hallway. Even though the judge eventually convicted both of them, they received only suspended sentences.

While family abuse runs like these are unquestionably dangerous to police officers, they are many times more dangerous to those against whom the abuse is directed. Confirming this and what I said earlier about the larger percentage of male-initiated family abuse, according to the U.S. Department of Justice's report *Violence between Intimates*, serious injuries to a woman are twice as likely when the assailant is an intimate as when he is a stranger. Also, compared to men, women experience over ten times as many violent incidents by intimates. The Department of Justice in addition found that living in the suburbs or rural areas does not decrease a woman's risk of attack by an intimate. *Violence between Intimates* reports that from 1987 to 1991 intimates committed an annual average of over 621,000 reported rapes, robberies, and assaults against each other. Divorced or separated women, the report said, were twice as likely as women never married, and over ten times as likely as married women, to report a violent victimization by an intimate.[19] Confirming this last statistic, the U.S. Justice Department's *Special Report: Family Violence* by Patsy Klaus and Michael Rand reports that while divorced and separated women make up only 7 percent of this country's population, they account for 75 percent of all battered women.[20]

Along with injuring each other, every year thousands of men, women, and children are also killed by spouses, ex-spouses, parents, siblings, children, boyfriends and girlfriends, and other intimates. In 1994, according to the FBI's *Crime in the United States*, 3368 men, women, and children in the United States were murdered by a family member or an intimate partner. According to the United States Advisory Board on Child Abuse and Neglect: "More babies and young children die at the hands of their parents than in car accidents, house fires, falls, or drownings." Along with these deaths (most of which occur before the child is four years old), every year 18,000 children are permanently disabled, and 142,000 seriously injured through abuse and neglect.[21]

Even in the face of these startling and disturbing figures I'm sure there are still a number of readers who will remain unaffected because, since they have no abuse in their own families, they feel sure they will suffer none of its effects. These readers couldn't be more wrong. They are affected very directly. Besides the problem of family abuse creating millions of future citizens (some of whom these readers will undoubtedly come into contact with) who will have significant adjustment problems that will lead to criminal and antisocial behavior, a recent study by the Washington State

Institute for Public Policy found that 60 percent of the women in America on *tax-supported* public assistance have experienced some type of family abuse as adults, abuse that often led to the need for this public assistance.[22]

In addition to costing taxpayers, the effects of family abuse inevitably spill over into the public at large and endanger, and occasionally even kill, people who are not a part of, or even know, the family involved in the abuse. Many innocent people in this country, for example, are struck every year by stray bullets fired at a family member, many innocent co-workers are killed when someone with murderous intentions storms a workplace looking for a spouse or intimate partner, and many people are taken hostage simply by having the bad luck to be nearby when someone decides to take a spouse or intimate partner hostage. On 28 October 1995, in Indianapolis, a man jumped onto the hood of a car driven by his live-in girl friend, apparently in an attempt to keep her from leaving their home. The woman, with her fifteen-month-old baby in the car, drove the vehicle on city streets at speeds between 55 and 65 miles an hour, ran through several traffic lights, and swerved back and forth across the traffic lanes, seriously endangering innocent pedestrians and other drivers. The man was eventually thrown from the car and died of massive head injuries. A check of the couple's history found that the police knew them well, having been sent to their home numerous times because of family abuse runs.

I hope I have given enough facts, anecdotes, and statistics in this chapter to demonstrate what every police officer already knows: family abuse is a disease that is eating away at the body of our country. It is a disease that is much more widespread and serious than most people would suspect, and it is nearing epidemic levels.

The good news is that family abuse is not an incurable disease. There are solutions, albeit tough solutions, that can cure it. There are solutions that family abuse victims can personally initiate. There are solutions that can be initiated by a victim's family members, friends, and even neighbors. There are also solutions that can come from enacting new laws and more vigorously enforcing existing ones. There are solutions that can take family environments that are brutal, demeaning, and deadly, and change them back into their intended purpose of being loving, nurturing, and supportive.

2

Child Sexual Abuse

The February wind, hitting exposed skin with a sting like hurling steel needles, sent little bursts of dry snow slithering across South Rural Street in Indianapolis, making Officer Ronald Kemper reluctant to get out of his police car again. He had hoped when he came to work that morning that, since it was so bitterly cold, all of the people on his district would behave themselves and allow him to stay in the comfort of his warm car. But no such luck. He let out a sigh as he glanced over at the site of his fifth run already that morning, a two-story, wood-frame house badly in need of some paint. A few moments before, the dispatcher told him that a Mr. Charles Decker had called from this address, saying he wanted to talk with an officer about a crime he had committed. Although someone wanting to confess to a crime wasn't an everyday occurrence, it certainly wasn't unheard of. As Officer Kemper turned up his collar and climbed out of the white Caprice, all the time wishing he was in Florida, he hoped this wasn't another nut who wanted to confess to being on that grassy knoll in Dallas.

"Mr. Decker?" The door was opened by a man Officer Kemper guessed to be about thirty-five.

The man nodded. "Come on in, officer."

Officer Kemper stepped into the living room, but didn't sit down, even though Mr. Decker offered him a seat. He could see dust bunnies nesting under all of the tables and chairs, but though he looked closely for movement he didn't see any active roaches or other insects. Still, Officer Kemper knew from experience that a smart police officer never sat down on unfamiliar furniture. You never knew what might jump on you or crawl up your pants leg. It had happened to him before, and just the thought of it made him itch.

"Mr. Decker, the dispatcher said you wanted to talk to the police about a crime you've committed."

The man nodded and then started to speak, but Officer Kemper raised a hand. "Look, before you say anything, sir, I have to warn you that you don't have to talk to me if you don't want to." Officer Kemper then went on and explained to Mr. Decker his constitutional rights against self-incrimination.

All of the time Officer Kemper was talking, though, he could see Mr. Decker nodding and licking his lips, looking like the only kid in class who knows the answer to the teacher's question, and seeming hardly able to wait until he could speak. "I understand all of that," he said the moment Officer Kemper finished, "but I just can't stand it any longer. I really can't. I mean, it's really been bothering me lately because she's just a young girl. I mean it. I just can't stand it any longer."

Stopping for a second, Mr. Decker wet his lips again. "And the more I think about it the more it really hurts me. I mean, she's my daughter, not some stranger. I tell you, I just can't believe I actually did it. But you're a man. I don't have to tell you how it is when a man does something like that. I mean, a man's not usually in his right mind at the time. You know what I mean?" He looked at Officer Kemper as if he expected him to nod in agreement. Officer Kemper's expression didn't change. "But I can't deny that I did it," Mr. Decker continued, "and sometimes I feel like I'm going to go crazy because I just know somebody's going to find out."

"What exactly is it that you've been doing?" Officer Kemper asked, already knowing the answer. He did his best to keep his face impassive, his stomach suddenly feeling queasy.

Mr. Decker began not only licking his lips again, but now also rubbing his hands together, as though not so certain any longer about the wisdom of what he was doing. "Well, I've … I've been, you know, molesting my daughter."

"You've been sexually molesting your daughter?"

His hands stopped moving and now gripped each other tightly. Suddenly, Mr. Decker couldn't meet Officer Kemper's eyes any longer, and he simply stared at the floor and nodded.

"How old is your daughter, Mr. Decker?"

"Uh, she's twelve now."

"Has this been going on for a while?"

Again, Mr. Decker looked at the floor and nodded.

Officer Kemper realized immediately it was time for him to stop and turn this case over to a detective from the Family Advocacy Center. In Indiana, child molesting becomes a much more serious crime, with severe penalties, when the victim is under twelve years old.

"Excuse me, Mr. Decker, I'll be right back."

Giving a nod, Officer Kemper walked back outside and then down to the sidewalk, shivering from the steady blast of icy wind that came out of the northwest, feeling the moisture immediately freezing on his moustache. He pulled the microphone of his walkie-talkie off the Velcro patch on his shoulder, and contacted the dispatcher, asking her to get in touch with the Family Advocacy Center and to have one of the detectives there contact him on the radio.

On that morning, Detective Monica Styles sat at her desk in the Family Advocacy Center and heard the call on the police radio for any child abuse detective. Detective Styles talked for a moment with the dispatcher, then switched channels on her walkie-talkie and contacted Officer Kemper. After listening to Officer Kemper's description of Mr. Decker's confession so far, Detective Styles asked him to bring Mr. Decker down to the Family Advocacy Center.

The Family Advocacy Center is a facility in Indianapolis that houses not only child abuse detectives from both the Indianapolis Police Department and the Marion County Sheriff's Department, but also workers from the county's Child Protective Service and representatives from the Marion County Prosecutor's Office. Concentrating all of these professionals in one facility makes handling child abuse cases in Indianapolis much more efficient, since everyone involved in the process knows everyone else, and obtaining help in a child abuse case from another agency is as simple as walking down the hallway and asking. Even more important than this, the facility was designed to give detectives, prosecutors, and child protective service workers a location that wouldn't be cold and intimidating when they needed to talk with child abuse victims.

Child abuse detectives know that talking with a young victim in the home, where either a horrified parent or, just as often, the stony-faced perpetrator, is standing nearby, many times keeps the child from opening up and telling about what has happened. Likewise, questioning child abuse victims in the sterile and official-appearing atmosphere of most police facilities also usually stifles any inclination to talk. The Family Advocacy Center, on the other hand, is located in a downtown office building, and with its colorful wallpaper, child-size furniture, and piles of toys, looks more like a day care center than a law enforcement facility. Since its creation over a decade ago, detectives have found that children feel much more relaxed and unafraid in the atmosphere of the Family Advocacy Center, and are much more likely to talk about what has happened to them.

But in addition to talking with the victims, the Family Advocacy Center is also used for questioning suspects. The atmosphere fostered there also usually tends to relax the suspects, and make them more willing to talk.

After Officer Kemper had brought Mr. Decker to the Family Advocacy Center and told Detective Styles what he'd found out so far, Detective Styles took Mr. Decker back to one of the interview rooms, which to most victims and perpetrators looks more like a small sitting room. She again advised him of his rights, and then turned on the tape recorder. Detective Styles knew that, on the surface at least, this was a fairly unusual situation. Although she had questioned many child abuse suspects during her years as a detective, she didn't see many who, out of remorse, wanted to come in on their own and confess. In the cases she had seen during her time as a child abuse detective there was almost always an ulterior motive for this sudden drive to confess, a motive that usually had very little to do with remorse. Regardless, though, Detective Styles knew she needed to keep Mr. Decker cooperative and willing to talk, and so she decided it was time to put on her friendly, helpful face.

"All right, Mr. Decker, why don't we start at the beginning. I understand you have a daughter."

He nodded. "Meredith, she's twelve."

"Okay, why don't you just fill me in on what you were telling Officer Kemper."

"Well, first off, it's important for you to know that this isn't totally my fault. Really, it's not. Not totally. My wife, it's her that lets Meredith wear short shorts and halter tops. Really, I tell my wife not to let her do that because it's temptation, but she says, no, she makes the money and she'll raise Meredith the way she wants." (Mrs. Decker's job, Detective Styles found, kept her away from home most of the day, and so Meredith was watched over by Mr. Decker, who was unemployed.)

"So anyway," Mr. Decker continued, "one day Meredith came home from school and I told her to go in and take a shower and change her clothes. So she did, and she put on a see-through top. So there you go. Don't you see? There's temptation." (Detective Styles found out later that Meredith was eight years old at the time of this event.)

Mr. Decker cleared his throat, and seemed to think for a moment. "So this goes on for awhile, and then finally I started looking at her and seeing that she was developing. It was like I couldn't help myself. But look, before we go any farther, it's important for you to know that as far as anything I did I just rubbed on her. Okay? Nothing else. I just rubbed on her. That's it." Mr. Decker made motions of rubbing on his chest and groin. "I did it the first time, and then I said no, I'd better not do this anymore. It's wrong. Afterward, I got real shaky and scared and nervous, but then maybe a week later or so I did it again. And then I said, 'Oh my God, what am I doing?' But then I did it a third time."

Detective Styles fought to keep up the friendly, understanding expression when she felt the muscles around the base of her neck pull tight, as they always did at this point in any confession. "How long has this been going on?"

Mr. Decker now wrung his hands. "I don't know. I really don't. But I've stopped. I swear, I really have. I got to thinking about it and I said to myself, 'God, that's wrong!' So you see, that's why I'm here talking to you, because I want to get some help, to get it off my mind. I mean, I've got a lot of pressure on me, what with just knowing that somebody's bound to find out. But I swear to you that I've stopped." (Detective Styles would learn later that indeed he had stopped, but only because his wife had moved out on him recently and had taken Meredith with her.)

"Yes, I'm sure the pressure's been pretty bad," Detective Styles said as sympathetically as possible. "Can you tell me when this all began?"

Shrugging, Mr. Decker seemed to have to think for a few moments. "I don't know, in the summer maybe. Really, I don't know. But look, this ain't all my fault. If you could see the way she wiggles her butt, the way she carries herself, you'd understand why I did it. I mean, the temptation's just always there."

"Yes, I'm sure there's been a lot of temptation. But look, since we're here talking, and you've already told me this much, is there anything else you want to tell me? Anything else you want to get off your chest? You know that if there's anything else I'll find out about it eventually, and, believe me, it'd be a lot better if you tell me yourself." Detective Styles knew from her years of experience as a child abuse detective that Mr. Decker was much too nervous and stressed for just rubbing on his daughter. There was more. She was certain of it.

Mr. Decker sat for several seconds chewing on his lips. "Well yeah, I guess there is, but this is the hard one." He was now visibly sweating, and he swiped at his forehead. "Well, you see ... well ... she's been doing me."

"Okay. Now when you say she's been doing you, what do you mean?"

He again swiped at his face. "Oh Lord, this isn't good. No, it isn't. It's really bad. But I guess you're right, I can't stop now." Mr. Decker took a breath. "She's been doing my penis."

"What exactly has she been doing?"

"Well, you know, sucking it." His face was now a sheen of sweat.

Detective Styles did her best to hide the wave of disgust that surged through her, and she fought to keep up the helpful, friendly expression. "How many times has this happened?"

"I don't know. Probably five or six. But look, there's something else you need to know. I don't think I'm the only one she's doing it to. The way she does it she knows exactly what she's doing. You understand what I'm saying? From the start she knew exactly what she was doing. But somebody else taught her, not me."

Giving a nod of what she hoped would appear to be understanding, Detective Styles continued, "Okay, did you ever do anything to her vagina besides rub it?"

Mr. Decker jerked his head up and then shook it violently, sending little droplets of sweat flying. "No! I swear to God, no! I'm crazy, I know, but I wouldn't do that!"

Detective Styles finished the questioning soon afterward, and asked him for his estranged wife's new address and telephone number. Then, with as friendly a tone as she could muster up, she told Mr. Decker to just go on back home and that she would contact him later that day. She knew it was important for her and Mr. Decker to part on friendly, cordial terms because she didn't want him to suddenly become frightened and decide to take off. Detective Styles figured she would likely have to go out that afternoon and arrest him. But before she could, she had to first talk to the other people involved in the incident. In any criminal investigation a confession alone, without corroborating evidence, is not enough to obtain a conviction on. This need for additional evidence has come about because police officers have found far too many times that people with mental problems will want to confess to crimes that either were never really committed or were not committed by them. Detective Styles contacted Mr. Decker's estranged wife, explained to her that she was investigating a possible molestation, and asked her to please bring Meredith down to the Family Advocacy Center.

After listening to Mr. Decker's description of his daughter, and expecting an early bloomer, Detective Styles was a bit taken back when she met Meredith. In a room full of twelve-year-olds, she realized, Meredith would not have stood out. Thin, with long brown hair and a clear complexion, Meredith spoke with the soft, and still childlike voice of a youngster just entering puberty. While Detective Styles had often found that child abuse victims are reluctant to talk about what has happened, this wasn't the case with Meredith. She spoke with a soft, almost timid, voice, but she didn't hesitate when asked about the abuse. It seemed to Detective Styles that Meredith had just been waiting for someone who seemed interested and concerned about her.

"Meredith," Detective Styles asked after taking her to one of the comfortably outfitted interview rooms in the Family Advocacy Center, and trying to put her at ease, "have you had problems with somebody touching you in a bad way?"

She nodded. "My dad."

"Do you remember how old you were when it first started?"

"Uh huh, I was eight. I know because I was in the third grade."

"Okay, when he touched you in a bad way, what parts of your body did he touch?"

Without hesitation, Meredith answered, "My chest, my behind, and my vagina."

"When he touched you, what did he use?"

"His hands and his mouth."

"What parts of you did he touch with his mouth?"

Meredith finally hesitated and appeared embarrassed. At last, though, she whispered, "My vagina."

"Were your clothes on or off?"

"He made me take them off."

Detective Styles felt her pulse quicken and she glanced over to be certain the tape recorder was operating. She knew she now had the corroboration she needed. Mr. Decker was going to jail. "Did your dad ever take his clothes off?"

She nodded. "He'd pull his pants down."

"After he pulled his pants down, then what would happen?"

"He would ... He would ..." Meredith stopped and looked down at the floor, seeming unable to go on.

"Just go ahead and say it, Meredith," Detective Styles said in a soothing and reassuring voice, "whatever it is." Detective Styles knew well the importance at this moment of being both supportive and nonthreatening. Meredith had to feel she could talk about whatever had happened without worrying about being ashamed or judged. "Believe me, Meredith, you won't shock me, no matter what you say. None of this is your fault, so you can tell me what happened, no matter how bad you think it is." She reached out and touched Meredith's hand, who looked up at her with the expression of a mistreated puppy, tears welling in her eyes.

"He would ...," Meredith started again, but then stopped. After a few seconds, she finally took a deep breath. "He would make me suck it."

"What did he make you suck?"

"His penis," she said, looking down again at the floor.

"How old were you when this started?"

"I was nine. I know because I was in the fourth grade."

"Did your dad ever talk to you about what would happen if you told anyone?"

Meredith wiped at the tears now running down her cheeks as she nodded. "He said that if I ever told anyone I'd get into big trouble."

"Have you told anyone besides me what your father's been doing?"

She shook her head.

"Not even your mother?"

Again, Meredith shook her head.

Detective Styles glanced over to be certain the tape recorder was still rolling, feeling the adrenaline tingling in her fingertips. Molestation cases, she knew, seldom fell together this well.

During their following lengthy conversation, Detective Styles found that Meredith had an unusually accurate memory for dates, addresses, schools, and other important items, and she knew that if it ever came to it Meredith would probably be a good witness in court. Detective Styles also knew that she now had more than enough evidence to arrest Mr. Decker, but first she had to talk with Mrs. Decker.

With just the information she had gathered so far, Detective Styles felt certain that the reason Mr. Decker had suddenly decided he wanted to confess had nothing at all to do with any remorse he felt. Detective Styles suspected it had more to do with the fact his wife had recently left him and filed for divorce, taking Meredith with her, and putting her out of his control. Mr. Decker had probably begun worrying that she would tell her mother about what had been happening for the past four years.

After speaking with Mrs. Decker, Detective Styles found that, true to what Meredith had said, she didn't know anything about her husband's molestation of their daughter, and appeared stunned by the revelation. However, when asked if she had seen any behavioral changes in Meredith since leaving her husband, Mrs. Decker said, yes, she certainly had.

"I've noticed a real improvement," Mrs. Decker said. "I mean, she's changed a whole lot. It's like she's a completely new child."

"Have you noticed any difference in her grades at school," Detective Styles asked.

Mrs. Decker gave a nod. "The grades on all of her papers and homework have really jumped up. I mean, it used to be all C's, D's, and F's, and now she's jumped up to all A's and B's. I've talked to her teachers and they say it's amazing how much she's changed."

After a few more questions concerning her awareness of the molestation, Detective Styles thanked Mrs. Decker for coming in and bringing her daughter, and told Mrs. Decker that she would be hearing from her soon. Detective Styles then took all of the information she had collected down the hallway to one of the prosecutors assigned to the Family Advocacy Center. The prosecutor, after reviewing the material, approved warrants for Mr.

Decker on five counts of child molesting, which covered incidents
that occurred both before and after Meredith had turned twelve.

Detective Styles, after obtaining the necessary arrest warrants, took another child abuse detective along and then drove out
to South Rural Street and placed Mr. Decker under arrest. Mr.
Decker, still cooperative, thanked Detective Styles, saying how
much he hoped he would now get professional help.

The next day, at Mr. Decker's arraignment, the judge entered
a plea of not guilty for him, which is standard procedure since Mr.
Decker did not yet have an attorney. Mr. Decker thanked the judge
and repeated how much he hoped he would now get some professional help.

Within a few days of Mr. Decker's arrest and incarceration,
however, his sister contacted Detective Styles and demanded her
brother's release. The sister insisted to Detective Styles that, without the slightest doubt, the police had been wrong for arresting
her brother. She insisted her brother was totally innocent and that
Meredith was obviously lying. The sister didn't seem the least bit
flustered or rattled when Detective Styles told her that it had been
her brother who had brought the case to the attention of the police,
and that it had been her brother who had come in and confessed.
After only a second or so, the sister again began demanding her
brother's release. In a complete turnabout, she now based the
demand not on the claim that her brother was innocent, but on the
fact that it had obviously been Meredith who had initiated everything.

This type of illogical behavior displayed by Mr. Decker's
sister is very common in family abuse cases, both sexual and
physical, and is one of the major reasons family abuse is so difficult to prosecute. Not only do the individuals committing the
abuse usually try to hide it out of fear of public exposure and
arrest, and the victims out of fear of shaming themselves and their
family, but often family members not even connected with the
abuse try to deny its existence, even in the face of incontrovertible
evidence. On those occasions where the evidence is so great that
the abuse can no longer be denied, it is not unusual at all for these
same people to absolve the abuser of all blame and instead place

the responsibility for the abuse totally on the victim, as Mr. Decker's sister did. In addition, even when abusers like Mr. Decker admit their actions, they still many times try, as Mr. Decker did, to shunt at least part of their responsibility by blaming other people for giving them the opportunity or causing them the temptation or frustration that led to the abuse.

A few days later, once Mr. Decker had gotten himself bailed out of jail, he underwent a change of heart about his confession. Detective Styles found out that Mr. Decker had been under the impression that if he confessed everything and asked for psychological counseling, that counseling would be the only consequence of his crime. When he discovered, however, that the state intended to criminally prosecute him for child molesting, he recanted his confession, and finally insisted that he had been under the influence of something (he never did say what) when he made his confession.

In May 1993, three months after Mr. Decker had made his call to the police about wanting to confess, the prosecutor offered him a plea bargain through which he would get the psychological counseling he wanted, but also six years in prison, followed by three years of probation. Mr. Decker refused the offer, still believing that all he should receive for what he had done was a bit of counseling. After a number of delays, the case finally went to trial in May 1994. Mr. Decker, however, didn't show up for his trial. The judge immediately revoked his bond and issued a rearrest warrant.

The police arrested Mr. Decker soon afterward, and he remained in the Marion County Jail until his case again went to trial in September 1994. A jury, after hearing all of the evidence, found Mr. Decker guilty of nine counts of child molesting (several more counts had been added after further investigation of the case). The judge sentenced him to 92 years in prison. In Indiana, this means Mr. Decker, if he behaves himself, will have his first parole hearing in 46 years, or in the year 2040.

As a footnote to this case, following her husband's sentencing and incarceration, Mrs. Decker found a new job that allowed her to spend more time with her daughter. Meredith is still doing well in school, and is now a high school cheerleader. The first Christmas after Mr. Decker's trial and sentencing Detective Styles received a Christmas card from Meredith and Mrs. Decker, thanking her for her concern and hard work, and telling her that they felt she was now part of their family.

❖ ❖ ❖ ❖ ❖

According to the National Institute of Justice's *When The Victim Is A Child*: "On average, each incest pedophile (child sexual abuser) commits from 35 to 45 acts against one or two children."[1] This means that the sexual abuse of a child by a family member often goes on for many months or years, as it did in Meredith's case.

"Growing up I thought maybe one family in a thousand would have sexual abuse," said child abuse Detective Michael Duke. "But I've found that it's much, much worse than that. I had no idea how prevalent it was."

Even the case of Meredith above, though, while certainly serious in its level of abuse, is actually only a little over halfway up the spectrum of seriousness of intrafamilial child sexual abuse. Intrafamilial child sexual abuse can include:

- Exhibitionism, in which the adult exposes him or herself to the child.
- Voyeurism, in which the adult watches a child bathe or change clothing.
- Kissing, which is not the customary peck usually given by a relative but a passionate kiss.
- Fondling, which can include the adult fondling the child or the adult forcing the child to fondle him or her.
- Pornography, which can involve simply showing the child pornographic material or, much more serious, taking pornographic pictures of the child.
- Oral sex, either perpetrated on the child or by forcing the child to commit oral sex on the adult.
- Intercourse, which can be either vaginal or anal.
- Sadism, in which the child is battered or in some other way seriously injured by the molester during the sex act.

❖ ❖ ❖ ❖ ❖

While most people visualize child molesters as degenerate old men who hang around schoolyards wearing dirty trench coats, this is usually far from the case. A number of studies have been conducted to find out just who child molesters are. One such study, conducted by the American Humane Association, found that 42 percent of all sexual molesters of children were the natural parents, while other relatives made up an additional 22.8 percent of all child molesters. These totals, incidentally, did not include adoptive, step, or foster parents.[2] Dr. Diana Russell in her book *The Secret Trauma: Incest in the Lives of Girls and Women* stated she found that 38 percent of the women she surveyed said they had been sexually abused before their 18th birthday. Almost half of these molestations were by a family member.[3]

Just how common, though, are these acts of child sexual abuse by family members? They are much more common than most of the American public would suspect, though no one knows the actual number. Studies have found that, in groups of adults who admit to being sexually molested as children, from 7 to 50 percent say they have never told anyone else about the abuse. It must be remembered, incidentally, that these groups are made up of adults who have admitted to being sexually molested as children. Many adults will never admit this to anyone, and in many cases victims block out entirely the memories of the incest. But the true number of intrafamilial child sexual abuse victims is undoubtedly huge. It is so huge that there are even several large organizations that promote sex between adults and children. The North American Man Boy Love Association and the Rene Guyon Society both advocate sex between adults and children, and both claim that the only harm that comes from this is the stigma that society places on the participants. This, of course, is self-serving nonsense.

"In all of the cases I've investigated where an adult says he or she was just trying to teach the child about sex or give the child pleasure," said Detective Styles, "inevitably the sexual gratification of the adult turns out to be the real, and only, motivation."

Yet, of all these sexual molestations by family members, how many are reported to the authorities? A study reported in the *Journal of the American Academy of Child and Adolescent Psychiatry* found that 30 percent of the women questioned in the study said they had experienced some type of sexual abuse before age sixteen. In almost 40 percent of these cases the abusers were family members. However, an important finding was that only 7 percent of these child sexual abuse cases were ever reported.[4] A *Los Angeles Times* poll of 2627 men and women discovered sexual abuse among 27 percent of the women and 16 percent of the men. Extrapolating from other studies, it can be assumed that about half or more of this abuse was committed by family members. A third of the victims in this poll, however, said that they had never told anyone about the abuse.[5] One must wonder how many of the 73 percent of the women and 84 percent of the men who claimed that they had never experienced sexual abuse actually had, but just wouldn't tell.

While conducting research for a previous book, I attended a child sexual abuse prevention seminar given to adults (to make them aware of what was being taught to the children). The seminar presenter, police sergeant Terry Hall, had been sexually molested as a child by his uncle and he talked freely to the audience about his experiences of attempting to deal with the molestation and trying to make other family members believe it actually happened. At the end of his talk two adults in the audience, a man and a woman, came forward and wanted to speak with Sergeant Hall about their own intrafamilial sexual molestations as children. Both said they had never told anyone about the abuse, but after hearing Sergeant Hall talk of his own sexual abuse by a family member it gave them the courage to speak up. Unfortunately, Sergeant Hall told me, in addition to almost always having adults come forward like that, whenever he gives his talk to children he usually also finds several never-before-reported cases.

"Out of a school of 500 children, I usually have three or four previously unknown cases come forward," said Sergeant Hall. "I have had as many as fifteen children in one school at last find the support and encouragement to tell about their abuse for the first time."

Why don't these victims of intrafamilial child sexual abuse

tell anyone about the abuse? There are a number of reasons. The perpetrator may threaten the victim. A father in Wytheville, Virginia, hanged his young daughter's cat by the neck from a tree, telling his daughter that the same would happen to her if she ever told anyone about his incest with her. Victims also often fear that they won't be believed or that no one will care. In an article in *The Washington Post*, columnist Donna Britt relates a young incest victim's description of what happened when she finally told her mother that she had been repeatedly raped by her stepfather. The victim told the columnist that her mother listened to her story, then went into her room and went to sleep. The next day, her mother got up and went to work as if it had never happened.[6]

Molestation victims many times don't report their abuse because they feel ashamed and fear that they will be blamed for what happened. In another case reported in *The Washington Post*, a thirteen-year-old girl, pregnant with her stepfather's child, was rejected and abandoned by her real mother, and left to live with the stepfather. Also, many molestation victims don't tell because they have been bribed to keep quiet. Consequently, parents and others should be alert to and cautious of a family member who seems to always be showering a child with gifts. Here in Indianapolis we recently had a case in which it was discovered that an uncle had been sexually molesting his niece for years. The family members said they thought the number of gifts the uncle had been giving the niece seemed excessive, but they just figured he was a good uncle.

Finally, victims often fear telling of their molestation because they don't know what will happen when they do tell or what everyone's reaction to the disclosure will be. Dr. Ronald Summit in his article "The Child Sexual Abuse Accommodation Syndrome" gives an excellent description of what often occurs when a child discloses intrafamilial sexual abuse: "In the chaotic aftermath of disclosure, the child discovers that the bedrock fears and threats underlying the secrecy are true. Her father abandons her and calls her a liar. Her mother does not believe her or decomposes into hysteria and rage.... The girl is blamed for causing the whole mess, and everyone seems to treat her like a freak."[7]

Usually, police officers find, the reaction to disclosure of incest is at one of two ends of a spectrum: either total disbelief and denial that it could have happened or total belief and a desire to kill the abuser. And while some readers might wonder how parents could disbelieve a child who discloses sexual abuse by another family member, an act that usually takes tremendous courage on the child's part, a study of sexually abused children reported in the journal *Child Abuse and Neglect* found that 35 percent of the mothers of sexually abused children chose to believe and support the accused molester over their own children.[8]

Along with children not reporting the abuse, often families of the child abuse victims don't report it either. Besides refusing to believe that an accused abuser could do such a thing, many families don't report child sexual abuse, because they fear that if the abuser, a family member, is arrested and imprisoned, the repercussions would tear the family apart. Other families don't report intrafamilial child sexual abuse because they feel that this is a shame they simply cannot bear to have exposed by the incident being tried in an open court. In addition, many parents worry that if they report intrafamilial child sexual abuse then the abused child will only suffer more by being forced to go through the trauma of a police investigation and an open trial. Studies show, though, as I will discuss in the chapters on family abuse prevention, that this is usually a baseless concern.

While most descriptions of incest use the feminine pronoun for the victim, boys are also often victims of intrafamilial child sexual abuse. Many of the studies I have reported on above include a large percentage of male child sexual abuse victims, though not as large a percentage as females. Kathleen A. Kendall-Tackett and Arthur F. Simon found in their study of people sexually molested as children that an equal number of boys and girls were sexually molested by their natural fathers, while stepfathers tended to molest mostly girls.[9]

Although this smaller percentage for males may represent a true picture of the number of victims, it must also be remembered that boys are less likely than girls to report sexual abuse because of the fear of being labeled a homosexual, even though a certain amount of intrafamilial male child sexual abuse cases involve adult female perpetrators. For example, in Johnson City, Tennessee, a woman recently received a 10-year prison sentence because she joined her husband in sexually molesting their own sons. Female perpetrators of family sexual abuse, however, rather than the actual molesters, are often instead accessories. In January 1995, a Virginia women pleaded guilty to supplying her two daughters, ages 7 and 8, to her boyfriend for sex. In return, the boyfriend gave the mother money and crack cocaine. Regardless of these two examples though, fathers, stepfathers, and live-in boyfriends far outnumber adult females in intrafamilial child sexual abuse cases. Police detectives usually find that mothers are more often guilty of criminal neglect: they know about but ignore the sexual abuse of their children, allowing it to happen even though they don't actually take part in it.

For various unfounded reasons, there is a common belief that intrafamilial child sexual abuse occurs only in poorer, lower-class families. "I never thought child sexual abuse went into the upper socioeconomic classes, but it does," said Lieutenant Deborah Saunders, head of the Indianapolis Police Department Child Abuse Unit. "Also, being Black, I always thought there wasn't much sexual abuse among Black children, but there is."

In *The Los Angeles Times* poll quoted above it was found that white youths from the suburbs *were the most likely* victims of sexual abuse. The problem with many studies of intrafamilial child sexual abuse is that the studies only use victims who have come to the attention of the authorities, and few cases of abuse among upper-class youth ever reach the authorities. In addition, victims have a much harder time making believable accusations against an upper-class intrafamilial child molester. Most of these incest perpetrators function very well in the world outside the family, and are usually very successful both financially and socially. Also, juries are more likely to believe a denial by one of these upper-class perpetrators of incest than a denial by a lower-class, uneducated person. In Carmel, Indiana, a very affluent suburb of Indianapolis, Phillip Quillen was accused by his daughter, Chaucie, of subjecting her to years of sexual abuse, including intercourse. He denied everything, and the first trial for this sexual abuse ended, likely because of his stature in the community, in a hung jury. However, in 1995, two years later, Mr. Quillen pleaded guilty to sexual battery in the case and was sentenced to a suspended three-year prison term and six years' probation. The truth is that child sexual abuse in middle and upper class families is simply not that unusual.

Victims of intrafamilial child sexual abuse, regardless what class they come from, often face a lifetime of psychological problems. Child sexual abuse has been found to be associated with such problems as depression, low self-esteem, sleep and somatic disorders, hyperactivity, eating disorders (anorexia nervosa and bulimia), personality disorders, and suicide attempts. An article in the journal *Addiction and Recovery* states that of the clients an addiction counselor sees it is not unusual at all for 40 to 50 percent to have been sexually abused as a child. The topics recovering chemically dependent women most often discuss, according to the article, are child sexual abuse, incest, and rape.[10] Just as bad, women who were sexually abused as children are much more likely to be arrested for prostitution, according to a study reported in a National Institute of Justice research paper.[11]

Whenever violence accompanies intrafamilial child sexual abuse, the problems for the victim become even more pronounced. This occurs because the violence violates all expected norms of family life. Family is where the child should feel safe and protected. In cases of violent sexual abuse, not only is the child being brutally victimized by someone who should be expected to protect him or her, but the violence dangerously shapes the child's future interactions with others. The book *Violence Against Women* states: "Research shows that victims of sexual violence, especially child-incest victims, often become victims of sexual violence in later life. The most common explanation is that they have learned to value themselves so little—and understand abuse as so ordinary and non-escapable—that they fail to implement ordinary measures of self-protection."[12]

Because intrafamilial child sexual abuse is abhorrent to most people and violates all societal norms, it is a crime few people want to hear about or deal with. For this reason many people refuse to believe that it happens. This attitude causes considerable problems for the criminal justice system. The police often find that, because of it, people refuse to give the evidence or statements necessary for a molestation arrest, and often the only evidence available is the child victim's word against that of the adult. And even when an arrest is made, prosecutors find that, because of public disbelief, juries often refuse to convict, even when the evidence is there. Consequently, many prosecutors will only try specially selected child sexual abuse cases, and some will not try any cases at all. This, of course, is totally unacceptable since it means that intrafamilial child sexual abuse in that community goes unpunished, and, because of this, usually unstopped. Just as bad, even when the police arrest and prosecutors obtain a conviction, many judges, often because of their own ignorance about child sexual abuse, do not impose sentences that represent the seriousness of the crime.

None of this is acceptable. The criminal justice system is meant to protect citizens, and children should not be excluded from this protection. The laws in America dealing with child sexual abuse don't need changing so much as America's attitude toward it. It is a crime that happens often and in every type of family. Americans must open their eyes and realize this.

Although I will give more detailed advice in later chapters, from my years as a police officer I would advise parents who want to prevent child abuse to be alert to what is happening around them. Be cautious and suspicious of what appears to be unusual and inappropriate behavior between an adult and a child. Don't believe that any person could not be a molester, and listen to your children when they want to talk about someone acting funny. But most important, act immediately if it appears child abuse has occurred. Child abusers should never be allowed the secrecy that allows them to continue with their crimes.

3

Spousal and Elderly Sexual Abuse

In the early morning hours of 23 June 1993, twenty-four-year-old Lorena Bobbitt, a manicurist originally from Ecuador, lay asleep in her bed. According to the testimony she gave at both her own and her husband's trial, she was awakened when her husband, John Wayne Bobbitt, returned home to their apartment in Manassas, Virginia, after being out drinking with a friend. Her husband, she claimed, a twenty-six-year-old part-time cab driver and bouncer at the Oldies Music Legends nightclub in Manassas, woke her up and demanded sex.

"I said I didn't want to have sex," she told the packed court-room during both trials. "He pushed me and held my hands. I said no twice."[1]

But still, she testified, her husband forced her to have sex. Afterward, she said, he told her that "forced sex excites me."

Once her husband had fallen asleep, Lorena went to the kitchen to get a drink of water. This wasn't the first time forced sex had happened in their marriage, she told the court. He had raped her a number of times before. While in the kitchen she saw a twelve-inch, red-handled filet knife. Grabbing the knife, Lorena returned to the bedroom, pulled back the sheets, and used the knife to cut off two-thirds of her husband's penis.

"I kind of felt a jerk," John told the court during his testimony. "That hurt real bad and I sprang up—like, silent pain. I grabbed my groin and held myself."[2]

Immediately after the amputation, Lorena fled the couple's apartment, carrying both the knife and her husband's severed penis with her. Lorena would later say that she didn't realize what she had done until she was driving away in the car. It was then that she discovered she was carrying her husband's penis, which she flung out the car window into some weeds.

John, after the attack by his wife, raced into the adjoining room and awoke the friend he had been out drinking with, who was sleeping over at his apartment, and asked the friend to take him to the hospital. At around 5:00 A.M., John showed up at Prince William Hospital, where hospital personnel, upon examining John's injuries, immediately notified the police and asked them to go to Mr. Bobbitt's apartment and search for the severed penis. The police, of course, found nothing there.

At a little after 5:00 A.M., Lorena called the police from a pay phone. She told them that she had been raped and had fled her apartment in a panic. She also told them that she had unknowingly taken her husband's severed penis with her and had thrown it out the car window at Old Centerville Road and Maplewood Drive.

"She knew where it was and was kind enough to tell us," a Manassas police officer told *Washington Post* reporters.[3]

After finding the severed penis, police officers wrapped it in ice and had it taken to the hospital. Dr. David Berman, a reconstructive plastic surgeon, and Dr. James T. Sehn, a urologist, performed a delicate nine-and-a-half-hour operation and reattached the severed organ. While at first the doctors weren't sure how much recovery of use Mr. Bobbitt would have, the operation was successful enough that John eventually appeared in an X-rated movie.

Soon after the incident, John and Lorena both filed for divorce. Each claimed physical abuse.

Then, in a situation that certainly made the local prosecutor's office feel very uncomfortable, charges were brought against both parties. What made the prosecutor's office feel uncomfortable was that in the first trial they would have Lorena Bobbitt as the chief prosecuting witness and John Bobbitt as the accused, and then in the second trial the Bobbitts would switch roles.

In John's trial, which was held first, he stood accused of marital sexual assault. Under the law in Virginia, a married man could only be charged with the rape of his wife if the couple was living apart at the time or the victim was seriously injured. At his trial, John portrayed himself as a victim of marital abuse, telling the jury how his wife would often hit him if something didn't go her way. He also had a number of witnesses who appeared in his behalf and said that Lorena had a bad temper. As to whether or not he raped his wife on the morning of 23 June 1993, John was a bit evasive. One time he said he did not recall if he and his wife had had sex. But another time he told a police detective that "if he had had sex with his wife, he may have done it while he was asleep, that he did those things very often."[4]

The jury, which initially split six to six on his guilt, eventually voted unanimously to acquit John Bobbitt. "If someone had heard her scream," said one of the jurors after the trial, "or if there had been some sort of bruising, that would have been more substantive evidence. Everything was pretty circumstantial, and could be interpreted several ways."[5]

Julie Blackman, a social psychologist and forensic consultant, told *New York Times* reporter Jan Hoffman that: "Mr. Bobbitt's wound made his conviction on a marital assault charge less likely. Even if the jury believed that he raped his wife they may have found him not guilty because they felt she had already sufficiently punished him."[6]

Two months later, with John Bobbitt now sitting on the prosecution side and Lorena Bobbitt on the defense side, a trial was held charging Lorena with malicious wounding. At her trial Lorena described her and John's marriage as four years of escalating violence that had begun just a few months after she and John were married. He would, she claimed, kick, punch, and slap her. He would also use, she told the court, what he called "Marine Corps torture techniques" to inflict pain on her. And, she said, he forced her to have sex a number of times against her will, including forced anal sex.

A few days before the rape that resulted in her husband's mutilation, Lorena testified at her trial, she had gone to court to obtain a protection order against John, but left when she was told it would take some time to get the protection she was requesting. At her trial, a psychiatrist testified that Lorena's years of abuse had led her to a near psychotic breakdown, and that her actions on the morning of June 23rd were the result of an irresistible impulse brought on by the years of abuse. The psychiatrist told the court that Lorena's mind went blank after the rape, and only later in the car did she realize what she had done.

During the trial, even the prosecution's own expert witnesses concluded that John had abused his wife and likely raped her on the morning in question. In the case two months earlier against John Bobbitt, the same prosecutor who was now prosecuting Lorena Bobbitt had then portrayed her as a victim of her husband's abuse. Several defense witnesses said that John had bragged to them that he liked "rough sex," and a number of Lorena's co-workers testified that they often saw her with bruises. Lorena's doctor told the court that a week before the rape which resulted in the cutting off of her husband's penis, Lorena had told her that John often forced her to have sex. Despite all of this testimony, however, the prosecution still contended that what Lorena did was not the result of an irresistible impulse, but simply an impulse she didn't resist, and that she should be convicted.

However, like the outcome of her husband's trial several months earlier, a jury found Lorena not guilty, though in her case it was because of temporary insanity, brought on by the rape and abuse. As required by law, the judge sent Lorena to a mental hospital for forty-five days, in order for the court to ascertain whether she presented any danger to herself or others.

Because of the worldwide publicity generated by the case, both John and Lorena hired agents to handle requests for interviews and to negotiate book and movie offers. Lorena Bobbitt, when eventually released from the mental hospital, went back to work. John Bobbitt went on a publicity tour. While in Las Vegas,

John met and eventually moved in with twenty-one-year-old Kristina Elliot, a former topless dancer. In May 1994, the police responded to a call at the couple's apartment in Las Vegas, where the officers arrested John for domestic battery against Kristina. A court later found John guilty, and the judge, who said he felt Mr. Bobbitt had an "attitude problem," sentenced John to sixty days in jail, with forty-five of the days suspended.

❖ ❖ ❖ ❖ ❖

In the aftermath of all the publicity about the alleged crimes and the acquittal of both parties, many people wonder what really happened in the Bobbitt case, with the exception, as one reporter said, of making the town of Manassas "a town where the men now sleep on their stomachs." The prosecutor in both cases, Prince William County Commonwealth Attorney Paul B. Ebert, was quoted in an article in *The New York Times*: "She says one thing, he says another, and the truth lies somewhere in between."[7]

In police work you almost always find that when two people tell a story, seldom does either party, even when one party is totally innocent, ever tell the complete, total, and unvarnished truth. Instead, people usually only tell what they feel will present them in the best possible light. This is likely what occurred in the Bobbitt case. In my opinion, the likely facts of the case are that John was an abusive husband, he came home drunk, and he raped his wife. On the other side, Lorena, rather than being temporarily insane, was more likely simply furious at her husband's sexual assault, and, being tired of all the abuse she had suffered in the marriage, struck back at her abuser in a way she knew would have a tremendous impact.

Interestingly, while the details of this case were so gruesome that they attracted media attention from all over the world, the penis amputation, bizarre as it was, is the only thing that really sets this case apart from the thousands of other cases of sexual abuse between intimate partners that occur every year in our country. In the book *It Could Happen to Anyone*, the authors tell of a study done in 1989 which showed that in a sample of ninety-seven physically battered women almost 45 percent of them had also suffered sexual abuse at the hands of an intimate partner.[8] As further evidence of the widespread prevalence of sexual assault by an intimate partner, according to statistics gathered by workers at the Austin, Texas, Family Violence Diversion Network, 51 percent of the women referred to the program because of physical abuse said they had also suffered forced sex at the hands of their husbands or live-in boyfriends.[9] In a study reported in the book *Rape in Marriage*, 37 percent of the physically battered women who were interviewed also reported being raped by their husbands.[10] According to the Bureau of Justice Statistic's research paper *Violence between Intimates*, 23 percent of the men incarcerated for violent offenses against an intimate partner were sentenced for rape or other sexual offenses.[11]

While the above statistics are impressive by themselves, they are even more impressive when the number of intimate partner rapes are compared to stranger rapes. In a random sample of 930 women in San Francisco, a researcher discovered that 14 percent of the women interviewed said they had been raped by a husband or ex-husband. This was twice the number of women, the researcher found, who reported sexual assaults by strangers. A similar study conducted in Boston discovered that 10 percent of the women interviewed reported being raped by a husband or intimate partner, again twice as many women as those who reported being sexually assaulted by a stranger.[12]

A research paper by Louis J. Shiro and Dr. Kersti Yllo, published in the Maine State Bar Association's *Bar Bulletin*, stated that from their investigation they estimate that between 10 and 14 percent of all married women have been raped by their husbands. Half of the women the researchers interviewed who said they had been raped by their husbands claimed they had been raped twenty times or more. The researchers divided these marital rapes into three categories: (1) battering rapes, in which the women were beaten until they submitted; (2) nonbattering rapes, in which just enough force was used to accomplish the act, which the researchers found occurred mostly in middle-class couples; and (3) obsessive rapes, in which the husbands had unusual demands, often involving other men and women or devices.[13]

While this last type of rape might sound a bit bizarre to many readers, it occurs more often than most people would suspect. I recall a case I had once in which the dispatcher sent me to a phone booth near a residential area, where, upon arriving, I found a woman hiding behind a nearby bush wearing only a torn T-shirt. She had bloody scrapes on her face, and I could see that her right eye was already dark and puffy. She told me that her husband, to whom she had been married only a few months, had been out drinking that night. When he came home, she said, he brought two friends with him and wanted her to have sex with all three of them. When she refused, her husband beat her until she agreed to go along with his demands. Although I made a report, took her to the hospital, and had a warrant issued for her husband, the case never went to court. Once she had obtained a divorce, the woman apparently (and certainly understandably) decided she didn't want to have to tell in open court what had happened.

Being raped by a stranger is a horrible enough situation for any woman to have to deal with. Being raped by your own husband or intimate partner, though, makes it doubly so. Researcher David Finkelhor stated it best when he said: "When you're raped by a stranger, you have to live with a frightening nightmare. When you're raped by your husband, you have to live with your rapist."[14]

Incidentally, the numbers from the research findings above of sexual assaults by husbands or intimate partners are thought by many researchers to be very conservative estimates of the actual numbers. According to many researchers, getting women to speak about forced sex in marriage or between intimate partners is extremely difficult because the victims feel intense shame and humiliation about it.

Indeed, many victims of sexual abuse by a husband may not want to talk about it because they may not realize it is a crime. And actually, up until about twenty years ago, the rape of a woman by her husband was not a crime in the United States. Women, by taking marriage vows, were until fairly recently considered to have given consent to engage in sexual relations with their husbands whenever the husbands wanted. For example, a law from this time (Pennsylvania) stated: "A person commits a felony of the first degree when he engages in sexual intercourse with another person *not his spouse* [emphasis mine]: (1) by forcible compulsion; (2) by threat of forcible compulsion that would prevent resistance by a person of reasonable resolution; (3) who is unconscious; or (4) who is so mentally deranged or deficient that such person is incapable of consent."

While spousal rape is now against the law in all fifty states, some spousal sexual abusers claim a religious right to rape their wives. In January 1996, Ramiro Espinosa of Los Angeles received a one-year jail sentence for spousal rape. As his defense, Espinosa told the court that his Roman Catholic faith gave him the right over the body of his wife.

In answer to these kind of claims, the nation's Catholic bishops issued a statement approved by the Administrative Committee of the United States Catholic Conference saying that there is nothing in the Bible requiring women to submit to abusive husbands or to remain in abusive relationships. "Violence in any form—physical, sexual, psychological or verbal—is sinful," the bishops' statement said.[15]

Yet, even though marital rape is both condemned by the church and now a crime in all fifty states, it is still often looked upon by many people as a less serious violation. For example, in a study titled "Spouse Abuse in Texas: A Study of Women's Attitudes and Experiences," which was conducted by the Criminal Justice Center of Sam Houston State University, researchers found that 91 percent of the women polled considered forced sex as abuse. However, only 51 percent of these women thought that rape by a husband which occurred only once was a "very serious offense." When it was committed more frequently, the percentage of women who thought it was a "very serious offense" rose to 70 percent.[16] I find it more interesting that 30 percent of the women polled didn't believe forced sex to be a very serious offense, even when it occurs regularly.

I suspect that this 30 percent are those women who have never experienced such a thing, and have no concept of the anguish it would cause. I witnessed a bit of this lack of understanding recently when I went to a Sports Bar to watch Mike Tyson's first fight after being released from prison for rape. I was amazed by the large number of women who were there and by the number who swooned over the image of Mike Tyson on the television screen, even though they were all aware that he had been convicted of rape and just released from prison, since the announcers mentioned this at least a dozen times. A number of the women even made openly sexual remarks about him, regardless of the fact that Tyson has been quoted as saying: "I like to hurt women when I make love to them ... I like to see them scream with pain, to see them bleed.... It gives me pleasure."[17] I think these women must have felt what Mike Tyson's former wife, actress Robin Givens, felt when asked what attracted her to Mike. She said it was the excitement of the danger. Of course, part of this attraction likely comes from society's stereotyped image of a sexually appealing man: a powerfully built, macho-acting, and potentially dangerous person.

Why women are attracted to a certain type of man, however, is not the question here. The overriding question is why certain men feel the need to sexually abuse their wives and intimate partners. According to the book *The Violent Couple*: "Frequently (forced sex) happened after a violent incident. A man's violence pushed a woman away emotionally; therefore his dependency was threatened, and he forced sexual intercourse between them as a way of restoring his own sense of emotional closeness."[18] According to a number of experts, violent men are often very emotionally dependent on the women they abuse. And so, after physically abusing them, the men many times begin fearing the consequences of their actions and worrying about losing the women. Therefore, these men will often force the women to have sex, illogically believing that if they have sex the women will no longer hate them.

The elderly can also often be the victims of sexual abuse by intimate partners or other family members. Much of this abuse, many researchers believe, is simply a continuation of spousal sexual abuse that began many years before. But this is not always the case. Sometimes the sexual abuse of elderly people is a continuation of parent–child incest, or revenge by the child for this incest. In the book *Elder Abuse and Neglect* the authors cite several examples of sexual abuse of elderly mothers by their sons, which the authors believe was just an outgrowth and reversal of earlier incest.[19]

How much elder sexual abuse actually does occur in the United States? No one really knows the exact numbers for sure because, like most kinds of sexual abuse, this is not something that many people will talk about freely. In addition, many people have the mistaken belief that the elderly are not likely to be the targets for sexual abuse, and so they don't look for, or ignore, signs of possible sexual abuse.

The Police Executive Research Forum, in its book *Improving the Police Response to Domestic Elder Abuse*, states: "Some people in the field of elder abuse believe that many cases of sexual abuse go unreported because professionals fail to recognize or identify sexual abuse. They attribute this oversight to the misperception that the elderly are not likely targets for sexual abuse and, consequently, fail to investigate situations in which sexual abuse is likely to have occurred."[20]

But roughly how much elder sexual abuse actually does occur? According to the *Summary of the Statistical Data on Elder Abuse in Domestic Settings for FY90 and FY91*, by the National Aging Resource Center on Elder Abuse (NARCEA), less than 1 percent of all elder abuse each year involves sexual abuse. However, since NARCEA estimates that there were over 735,000 cases of elder abuse in domestic settings in 1991, this still places the number of elder sexual abuse cases well into the thousands.[21]

While the true extent of the sexual abuse of people, both young and old, by spouses, intimate partners, and family members will likely never be known since so many victims never come forward, it comprises a critical problem in this country that often causes more emotional scars and hatred than physical battering. One researcher found that women who had been raped by an intimate partner were more likely to attempt to leave the relationship than those who had only been physically battered. The rage involved in such relationships can be explosive. Lenore Walker in her book *Terrifying Love* states that 87 percent of the 90 women she studied, women who had attempted to kill an intimate partner, had been sexually abused by that partner. In another study, this one of 42 women who had been charged for the homicide or attempted homicide of an intimate partner, 75 percent report being raped by that partner.[22]

Spousal sexual abuse, like child sexual abuse, continues to occur, and occur in huge numbers, not because of an absence of laws, but because of the public's attitude about it. While every state has a law against spousal rape, not everyone (including many in the criminal justice system) believes it is a crime. Consequently, as in the Bobbitt case, juries often won't convict for spousal rape, regardless of the evidence. This flies in the face of everything our Constitution stands for. The American public (including those working in the criminal justice system) must recognize that no one is another person's property, and that every person has the right to decide what is done to his or her body.

To stop sexual abuse of spouses and the elderly, these crimes must be addressed, like child sexual abuse, at the first instance or first indication they have occurred. The perpetrator must never believe that he or she can do this and get away with it. Perpetrators of spousal or elderly sexual abuse, if they are to be stopped, must be exposed and suffer negative consequences. While this will naturally cause a certain amount of embarrassment for the victim, the alternative is increasing and more frequent abuse.

All of the statistics and anecdotes I have presented in this chapter, along with the studies mentioned above concerning women's attitudes and actions after being sexually assaulted by an intimate partner, should make the reader aware of how life-shattering being sexual abused by an intimate partner can be. It is a crime that few can forgive or ever forget.

4

Physical Abuse

Lonnie Dutton, most of the people in Grady County, Oklahoma, claimed, was a mean man. Few people liked him—and most went to lengths to avoid him.

"Lonnie was a belligerent, obnoxious, spiteful person whose only goal seemed to be how many people he could make hate and fear him," a cousin of Lonnie's told *Los Angeles Times* reporter Louis Sahagun.[1]

A large man at over 200 pounds, and usually unemployed, Lonnie reportedly always kept a 9 mm pistol tucked in his bib overalls. And he wasn't reluctant to use it. He once shot his own father when his father tried to intervene in the nearly constant physical abuse Lonnie heaped upon his wife and children, and he reportedly put the gun up to his mother's head several times when she also tried to stop the abuse.

Almost daily, the authorities later discovered, Lonnie inflicted his own brand of physical abuse on his wife and children. He would beat his sons with his fists, and he would kick them with steel-toed boots. One time, he made his two sons throw darts at their sister and mother, and then he brutalized his wife by pouring hot sauce in her eyes when she complained. Neighbors reported often seeing his wife, Maria, with a black-and-blue face or a swollen and busted lip.

Lonnie's father tried several times to stop the family violence.

Although Lonnie punched, stabbed, and shot him when he intervened, the father never called the police. "Lonnie would have killed me and my wife," his father said. "He was a monster."

Along with the almost daily beating and brutalizing of his family, Lonnie also forced his children to shoplift, and would soundly beat the child who came back with the least amount. In addition, he regularly gave his sons the warning: "If anyone ever messes with Sissy, shoot them behind the ear or in the head! Kill them!" This advice would prove fatal for Lonnie.

On 12 July 1993, the boy's ten-year-old sister told them that Lonnie, their father, was messing with her. The boys, following their father's advice, took a stolen rifle Lonnie had given them for Christmas and shot Lonnie behind the right ear, killing him.

❖ ❖ ❖ ❖ ❖

Lonnie Dutton was an extremely vicious and dangerous man, and, unfortunately, the physical abuse he inflicted on his family is not that uncommon in America. A very similar case occurred in Tyler, Texas, where Donna Marie Wisener killed her father, Glenn Wisener, a forty-nine-year-old truck driver. A court, however, later acquitted Donna Marie for her father's killing. According to court testimony, Glenn would throw logs at his wife and daughter, beat his stepson with anything he could get his hands on, would handcuff his daughter to a chair, and would beat her unconscious. At the same time, he would also send his daughter sexually suggestive cards and would give her groping-type "rubdowns."

While the level of violence in these two cases may strike some readers as incredibly brutal, in other families it is even worse. Physical abuse many times becomes a form of terrorism practiced in the home. Recently in Saginaw, Michigan, a father put his twenty-two-month-old daughter in a microwave oven. He told the police he did it to discipline her. An article in the May 1992 issue of *Pediatrics* carries a warning to pediatricians to be on the lookout for a grisly new form of physical child abuse: shocking children with electric stun guns. Two pediatricians in Arizona reported treating an eight-year-old boy who had been shot with a stun gun fired at him by his mother's boyfriend.

Everyday the police in America see thousands upon thousands of family members who have been physically abused by other family members. Just from my own experiences as a police officer I have seen family members who have been shot, stabbed, slugged, slapped, had bones broken, had scalding liquids thrown on them, been run over by cars, run over by lawn mowers, hit with ball bats, hit with shovels and rakes, beaten with an electrical cord, assaulted with chain saws, and thrown from moving cars. I'm sure if I referred back to my old notebooks I could undoubtedly find even more ways in which family members have brutalized each other. Clearly, in this country family members regularly inflict serious physical abuse on each other.

National estimates of the physical abuse of just spouses is four million cases a year. It is believed that there is probably at least half this amount of both physical abuse of children and physical abuse of the elderly. At an American Medical Association symposium on family violence, Health and Human Services Secretary Donna E. Shalala told participants that one out of four women will be assaulted by a household partner in her lifetime, and that 20 to 30 percent of the injuries which send women to hospital emergency rooms each year are the result of physical abuse by a husband or boyfriend. She also stated that 17 percent of the women interviewed in public prenatal care clinics report being physically assaulted by a partner during pregnancy.[2] According to Dr. M. Roy Schwarz, American Medical Association senior vice president for medical education and science, the percentage of pregnant women assaulted by intimate partners is closer to 23 percent.[3] A study published in the June 1995 issue of the *Journal of the American Medical Association* said that a survey of 833 women in Denver found that half reported being the victim of family violence, while according to a 1992 hearing of the Senate Judiciary Committee, 1.37 million family violence incidents were reported to the police in 1991, and it must be remembered that reported cases are usually only a fraction of the actual numbers.

"Physical abuse is much more common than I thought before I took this job," said police detective Michael Duke, who investigates child abuse. "I had no idea how prevalent it was."

As with sexual abuse, no one really knows just exactly how much intrafamilial physical abuse occurs each year because families usually try to hide it from outsiders. Many victims of family abuse, especially spouses and intimate partners, blame themselves for the violence and are ashamed to admit to anyone that it occurs. Also, many victims of spousal abuse are afraid that if anyone finds out about the physical abuse it will harm the abusing spouse's reputation, and consequently his or her career and money-making ability. This holds true particularly in military families, where a recent study of 55,000 soldiers at forty-seven bases suggested that violence is present in one out of three military families. Child and elderly victims of intrafamilial physical abuse often don't report the abuse because they fear that if they do it will only result in more, and even worse, violence. No matter how carefully constructed surveys and polls are, and no matter how much the polltakers insist they will keep the information confidential, many people simply refuse to admit to anyone that their marriage or family is not what it should be.

Regarding this point, but talking specifically about the physical abuse of children, the authors of the book *Domestic Violence: No Longer Behind the Curtains* state: "even when guaranteed anonymity, and even when the survey questions are professionally prepared to approach the question several different times from several different directions, it is very likely a significant proportion of those surveyed do not admit to child abuse or neglect." The authors then go on to say: "this growing awareness of the social unacceptability of child abuse might have led some of those interviewed to deny that they violently assaulted their child."[4] This same reasoning applies to the physical abuse of spouses and the elderly. In all of my years of responding to family disturbances as a police officer I have found that the perpetrator of the physical abuse nearly always, no matter who the victim was, tries to deny any involvement, or, if this isn't possible, tries to at least mitigate his or her responsibility for any physical abuse. In addition to all of this, many surveys and polls about family violence are flawed because their focus is on criminal assaults. Often, victims of family abuse don't consider intrafamilial violence to be a crime. They have many times been raised in families where this type of violence was common, and while they may think it's wrong, they don't necessarily consider it a crime.

In "Battered Women and the New Hampshire Justice System," Dr. Murray Straus, a respected researcher in the area of family abuse, states: "My real feeling, though I don't have the statistics to prove this, is that there's been at least one violent incident in the majority of all American marriages." Dr. Straus then goes on to state: "You can say that for a typical woman the problem of violence is not the violence in the streets we hear about all the time, but it's the violence in her own home. That is the place where a typical woman is the most likely to be assaulted."[5]

❖ ❖ ❖ ❖ ❖

When I was a uniformed district sergeant on Edward sector, I was asked by Dr. David Ford, an Indiana University at Indianapolis sociologist nationally recognized for his study of conjugal violence, if I would allow a graduate student of his to ride along with me one Friday evening. At this time, Dr. Ford was just beginning his study of conjugal violence and was in the process of gathering information about it. He asked me to assist him because, since I was the first-line supervisor on the sector, I could go in on any dispatched run I wanted, and consequently I would have access to a larger number of family fight incidents than any of the district officers. Having known Dr. Ford for some time, I agreed, and Dr. Ford introduced me to his graduate student, Doris.

As we started out that night, Doris explained to me what Dr. Ford was trying to do, about his need to obtain statistics on the scope of the problem of conjugal abuse in Indianapolis, and then she showed me the forms she intended to fill out on each family fight we went to. She simply needed, she said, to sit down somewhere quiet and talk with the victim for a few minutes. Although a pleasant young lady, Doris, I found, seemed extremely naive about family violence, and didn't appear to realize the emotional chaos that often ensues in a family fight.

We had a number of family fight runs on the sector that night, but the first one was probably the worst I had seen so far (and since) as a police officer. The dispatcher sent two cars, and I notified her that I would also go. When we got to the address of the run, we found about a dozen people fighting, and several of them attempted to keep me and the other officers from getting into the apartment where the complaint was. We, of course, requested more officers, arrested the people who were attempting to stop us from getting into the apartment, broke up several fights on the way in, and once inside found a man on the floor of the living room, sitting astride a woman who turned out to be his wife, pummeling her with his fists. We still had to fight our way through a half-dozen other family members, who were fighting each other, before we could drag the man off of his wife, whose face was already puffy and covered with blood. It was like a redneck bar free-for-all.

Doris became so flustered by the scene of violence that it took several moments for her to compose herself and remember what she needed to ask the victim. Even then, however, she found that her forms had been lost during our fight getting into the apartment.

We recovered Doris's forms, and after everyone we had arrested had been taken to jail, and after a medical technician from the ambulance we called had cleaned up the wife's face (she refused to go to the hospital), Doris finally spoke with the victim. It turned out that the victim's husband had been beating her regularly for a long time, but the victim said she had never told anyone. Actually, no one would have known about the beating that night if the other family members hadn't started fighting (apparently some family members thought they ought to break up the husband and wife, while others thought they shouldn't). The victim showed us several scars she had from earlier beatings and held out a crooked left arm that she said her husband had broken once during a beating. After the beating, she told us, her husband wouldn't allow her to go to the hospital, and so the bone had healed crooked. She estimated that she had been beaten dozens of times. Yet no one knew about any of these.

❖ ❖ ❖ ❖ ❖

When a police officer is new, the first question he or she usually asks victims of intrafamilial physical abuse is why they didn't call us sooner. Why have they allowed the violence to go on for so long? We find that victims often haven't called us because they are frightened (with good cause) of the perpetrators, and because the perpetrators of the violence, particularly spousal or intimate partner violence, many times apologize profusely afterward and swear the violence will never happen again. The victims, romantically picturing what a normal marriage or intimate relationship should be, want to believe this, and far too often give the perpetrator of the violence one more chance, then another, then another.

Scientists who study family abuse find that, particularly in violence between spouses and intimate partners, the abuse follows a common cycle involving three phases: the tension-building phase, the actual violence, and then the honeymoon phase. During the tension-building phase anger is mounting inside the batterer. Often this anger is over seemingly small issues, but each one builds the anger more and more. This tension can come from minor arguments, perceived insults, or violated expectations, such as the house not being clean enough, supper not ready on time, etc. Spouses who have lived with a batterer learn to recognize this phase, and do everything they can to defuse the tension. But in many instances no amount of placating will ease the tension. People involved in long-term spousal violence report that often they can see that their spouses are seething with tension and anger, and just looking for any reason to begin the violence.

The second phase of the cycle is the actual battering or violence itself. Although this often happens when the perpetrator of the domestic violence is drunk, researchers have found that alcohol itself is not a cause of violence, but simply an excuse for it. A research project with college students found that those students who thought they were drinking alcohol (but actually weren't) acted more aggressively than those who thought they were being given a nonalcoholic drink.[6] Many batterers believe that being intoxicated is a "time out" from having to act responsibly, and that they cannot be held accountable for whatever they do while drunk. A number of spousal violence victims who don't want to admit that their marriage is a failure will also often blame alcohol for the violence, and insist that their violent mates would be ideal spouses if they just wouldn't drink.

The third part of the cycle of violence between spouses and intimate partners is the honeymoon phase. This comes after the physical battering and violence. The battering spouse or intimate partner apologizes, often profusely, and swears that the violence will never happen again. The battering spouse or intimate partner also often buys the victim little gifts and talks in endearing tones. This, of course, is the kind of person the victimized spouses or intimate partners fell in love with and want to have once more, and so they really want to believe that the violence will not happen again. One researcher found that 75 percent of the women in one shelter who returned to a man who had battered them did so because he was repentant and swore it would never happen again. Research shows that about 85 percent of physical batterers, at least at first, go through this three-phase cycle of violence. About 50 percent, though, begin skipping the honeymoon phase when the violence and battering become habitual.[7]

However, despite the battering spouse's or intimate partner's promise that the violence will never occur again, the possibility and memory of it are always there, and the couple's relationship after the violence can never go back to what it was before. And unfortunately, in most cases the battering spouse's or intimate partner's promise is hollow anyway, and soon the cycle moves again into the tension-building phase, as the following incident demonstrates.

❖ ❖ ❖ ❖ ❖

Sandy Henes, a widow with three children, lived in Ann Arbor, Michigan, when she met her future husband, John Abrahams. She found him very attractive, and he seemed taken with her, so after a few months of dating they decided to move in together. However, on the first night after moving in together John set a pattern for their future relationship: he beat her.

"I was shocked," she told *Dallas Morning News* reporter Pam Maples. "No one had ever hit me. He was very apologetic, said it would never happen again."[8]

Despite this episode, Sandy married John, and in the following years he beat, kicked, and injured her regularly, always apologizing afterward and insisting it would never happen again. More times than she can remember, though, Sandy had to go to the hospital emergency room.

Finally, after several years of regular beatings, Sandy had had enough and moved out, filing for divorce. John, however, like most physically abusive men, was emotionally dependent on Sandy, and wouldn't be gotten rid of that easily. He tracked her down, broke into where she was staying, and beat her.

Like the times in the past when he had beat her, John afterward became repentant, calling her on the telephone over and over, and begging her to take him back. After a year had gone by with no new violence, their divorce not yet finalized, Sandy took John back and they bought a house together. But almost as soon as they moved back in together the beatings began again.

During this time, John's brother, a high school coach, murdered his ex-wife with an ax, and John decided to try to get custody of his nephew. While he was doing this, John stopped beating Sandy because he didn't want to jeopardize his chances of getting the custody he was seeking. He was denied this custody, though, when Sandy spoke to the social worker handling the case about John's violence.

Sandy and John separated again shortly after this, and John moved to California. However, Sandy's respite was short-lived. John soon returned and once more began intimidating and threatening her. He would call her on the telephone continuously, one moment screaming threats, and the next begging her to forgive him.

Finally, one Friday morning, as Sandy walked from the bus stop to work, John came up behind her, brandished a .357 Magnum revolver, and forced her into a car. He kept her a prisoner for sixteen hours in both Ann Arbor and Detroit, sexually assaulting her twice.

Luckily, before they left Ann Arbor for Detroit, Sandy found a way to sneak a telephone call to a friend. The friend called the police, and the Detroit Police Department SWAT Team rescued Sandy several hours later. While John attempted at the scene to persuade the SWAT officers that Sandy had come along with him willingly, the many bruises and other injuries John had inflicted on her during the ordeal convinced them otherwise, and the police took John into custody.

❖ ❖ ❖ ❖ ❖

As shown in the case above, a particularly dangerous and vulnerable location for the victims of family abuse is the workplace. An abuse victim may flee the abuser and hide at motels or at friends' homes, but the abuser knows where the victim works, and, as in the case above, will often show up there. The Center for Women in Government at the State University of New York at Albany said that their research shows that women are at high risk for violent attacks in the workplace, and that much of this violence is perpetrated by family members or intimate partners. According to figures from the U.S. Justice Department, spouses and intimate partners commit more than 13,000 acts of violence against each other every year in the workplace.

When reading about spousal or intimate partner physical abuse, such as that which occurs in the home or in the workplace, the reader usually finds the male pronoun used for the abuser and the female pronoun for the victim. However, there are a number of intimate relationships in which the man is the victim of physical abuse and the woman is the perpetrator. An article in the *Journal of Family Violence* reported that in a study of 180 couples involved in domestic violence, both men and women were found to engage in similar aggressive acts. Additionally, researchers Jan E. Stets and Murray A. Straus found through their studies that women assault their partners at about the same rate as men assault their partners. Researchers Judith Sherven and James Sniechowski report that their studies reveal a large involvement of females in the initiation of violence between spouses and intimate partners. They tell about a study of violence in American families which showed that 54 percent of all violence termed as "severe" was committed by women. Yet, despite all of these studies, only about 10 percent of all family violence that is reported to the authorities is female-initiated violence against a man.[9]

The questions that immediately come to mind are why, if it is true that women are just as violent as men, are such a small percentage of the cases reported to the authorities, and why don't we hear more about the female abuse of males. There are a number of reasons for this. First of all, it is not considered manly in this country to admit that a woman beat you up. Men who are beat up by women are often looked upon with ridicule, and this is the reason, say researchers Sherven and Sniechowski, that women are nine times more likely to report violence by an intimate than men are. As an example of this ridicule of male victims and female-initiated violence, we can turn to Mr. Dithers, Dagwood Bumstead's boss in the comic strip *Blondie*. Daily readers of this comic strip know that Mr. Dithers is regularly assaulted and beat up by his wife, Cora, and that the comic strip author uses this violence in their relationship as humor. Many people see the idea of a woman beating up a man as funny. On a recent talk show a woman called in and told how she had chased her husband around their house with a claw hammer. The audience responded with laughter, a response that would have been looked upon with horror if the sexes had been reversed. Also, because of a man's physical size compared to a woman's, often even though the woman strikes first, the man retaliates with more force. When the police get there the woman appears to have been the assault victim, and, since many men feel it is unmanly to seek police protection against a woman, they often don't tell us who struck first, and the man gets the blame for all of the violence.

Along with all of the reasons above, very few men go to hospital emergency rooms, except in life-threatening situations, and tell the hospital employees that they have been beaten up by a woman. This causes the statistics collected about spouse and intimate partner violence to be skewed. Much of these statistics are gathered from victims who show up at hospital emergency rooms and also at women's shelters, where, of course, there are no male victims.

In response to the plight of battered men, an organization called the Domestic Rights Coalition has been formed in St. Paul, Minnesota. This organization's purpose is to fight for the rights of battered men. The members of the organization feel that, because there is a lack of information about female-initiated violence, the legal system is biased against male victims. Studies of women who batter male intimate partners, however, show that they share the same psychological problems as male batterers: extreme jealousy, immaturity, insecurity, depression, poor impulse control, and poor anger management. The Domestic Rights Coalition plans to open a shelter soon for battered men.

In the midst of all this discussion about spouse and intimate partner battering, the question naturally arises as to why spouses or intimate partners would want to assault each other. The answer is simple: it works. According to *Social Work With Groups*, as reported in the book *The Violent Couple*: "[A] fundamental truth about family violence: that it is often addictive behavior precisely because it is so immediately effective. Violence in the home 'wins arguments,' it stifles and cuts off dissent and opposition, and it gains (though perhaps grudging) support for 'proposed family choices.' "[10] What this is saying is that people do not continue with actions unless they are rewarding, and family violence is often immediately rewarding because through it the abuser gets his or her way. In addition, the abusers find that they can use violence and get away with it since very seldom are they reported to the authorities, and often even other family members don't know about the violence.

However, even when abusers are reported to the authorities, the criminal justice system many times falls down on its job of protecting the innocent. Domestic violence, at least on a minor level, is often inadvertently condoned by the authorities. When the police come to the scene of domestic disturbances, but don't do anything, even in those cases where someone has obviously been assaulted, this tells the abusers that their behavior is acceptable.

I saw this happen for many years as a patrol officer and sergeant on the street. We would go to the same houses over and over, literally dozens of times a year, and find the same story. A person came home angry for some reason, got into an argument, and then assaulted his or her spouse. The victim called the police. When we got there, however, all we usually did was send the abuser away or warn the couple about the need to quiet down for the rest of the night. In those days we had no mechanism available to truly remedy the situation, other than to make illegal arrests, and so nothing of a punitive nature ever happened to the abuser. And since there were no serious negative consequences because of the abuse, the perpetrator felt no compulsion to change the abusive behavior.

Fortunately, today almost all state legislatures have changed this, and have given police officers tools to work with in the form of allowing misdemeanor arrests to be made in domestic violence situations where the officer didn't witness the violence. However, this is not enough. After the arrest, if the abuser doesn't receive negative sanctions from the courts, if the only result of the abuse is dropped charges or a suspended sentence, the arrest then becomes merely an inconvenience, and certainly not negative enough to force a change of behavior. Without serious sanctions from the courts, the criminal justice system is still inadvertently approving abusive behavior.

However, it isn't only the criminal justice system that gives domestic violence approval. A large segment of society also approves of it. In a national survey on family violence, researcher Murray Straus found that 27.6 percent of the respondents, both male and female, thought that slapping a spouse could be necessary, normal, or good. This also must change. Abusers must know that society considers their behavior wrong and the person committing it a criminal.

Along with being rewarding, addicting, and having a certain level of approval, violence between spouses and intimate partners also tends to escalate in number and intensity over time. According to Dr. Kathleen H. Hofeller in her book *Battered Women, Shattered Lives*: "Apparently, the first incident has the effect of 'breaking the ice.' Many women have said that, in retrospect, once their husbands discovered they could get away with being violent, it seemed to lower their inhibitions against future and more severe abuse."[11] According to the Bureau of Justice Statistics's research paper *Violence between Intimates*, one in five females victimized by intimate partner violence said they had been the victim of at least three assaults in the last six months.[12]

Susan Hansen, a formerly battered wife, said in her statement to the United States House of Representatives hearing on domestic violence: "[T]he abuse took on a spiral effect. It started occasionally, every once in a while.... Near the end as the spiral grows smaller and smaller the abuse reoccurred [sic] on a daily basis."

Police officers also find that in families where there is violence between the spouses, particularly increasing violence, there is often violence directed toward children. This violence is many times masked behind the parents' rationalization that they are only disciplining their children. Police officers, however, often find that this discipline is closer to the description of felonious assault. Many times, when questioning parents about why they so viciously beat their children, parents will quote the Bible passage, "Spare the rod and spoil the child." (Ironically, the rod spoken about in the Bible is the shepherd's rod used to guide sheep, not beat them.) These parents clearly are maliciously assaulting their children, and breaking the law. Other abusers don't make this claim of discipline, but have other excuses for a child's injury. Doctors at hospital emergency rooms find many abusing parents will bring a child in claiming the child has hurt him- or herself "in a fall" or "while playing." However, there is often evidence of repeated violence in the child's medical record, healed broken bones, or extensive bruising in places other than where the child was injured "accidentally."

Interestingly, researchers find that mothers are more likely than fathers to physically abuse their children. Often, this is an outgrowth of violence between spouses. According to Lenore Walker in her book *The Battered Woman Syndrome*, women in abusive relationships are eight times more likely to physically discipline children.[13] Research by Dr. Murray Straus has also found that mothers are more likely than fathers to physically abuse children. He attributes this to the fact that women often have a larger share of the responsibility in child raising, and that for those who don't have outside jobs the constant contact with the children can build and add to the stress that leads to the abuse.[14]

Another finding about child abuse is that its occurrence and intensity often depend on the size of the family. The *Study of National Incidence and Prevalence of Child Abuse and Neglect: 1988* found that a family with four or more children was significantly more likely to have child abuse. The reason for this appears obvious: the more children, the more stress.[15]

While physical abuse against children can involve those of any age, a particularly cruel form of child abuse is violence against infants. Babies who "fall from their cribs," emergency room physicians often discover, are many times covered with old bruises, cigarette burns, or have partly healed broken bones. The police find that the parents and caretakers of infants often abuse them because they can't deal with the frustration and high stress that comes from having to care for a baby. Infants, as anyone who has cared for them knows, need constant care and attention, and occasionally all babies will cry and continue to cry no matter what a parent or caretaker does.

A particularly dangerous form of child abuse involving infants is what is called the "shaken baby syndrome." This occurs when someone violently shakes a baby, usually to stop it from crying. This violent shaking, which in effect smashes the baby's brain back and forth against the inside of the skull, can have severely damaging effects on the infant. According to *Juvenile Neurosurgery*: "The relatively large size of an infant's head, weakness of the neck musculature, softness of the skull, relatively large subarachnoid space, and high water content of the brain have been postulated to contribute to the susceptibility of shaking injuries in infants." An article in *The Washington Post* on shaken baby syndrome states that researchers estimate the force on a shaken baby's brain is thirty times the force of gravity. The article also states that fighter pilots black out at less than one-third of that force.[16] The outcome of this violent shaking can, besides possibly killing the child, also potentially cripple an infant, as the following incident demonstrates.

❖ ❖ ❖ ❖ ❖

Sharon Kelso and her infant daughter, Cara, had been living with Sharon's mother for the last few months, ever since Sharon's husband, Gerald, struck Cara so hard he broke the baby's collar-bone. But eventually Sharon decided to move back in with Gerald, who had taken parenting classes in an effort to learn how to properly respond to and treat a baby. Gerald, Sharon knew, had always had a bad temper, and in the past had quickly lost patience whenever the baby wouldn't stop crying. But still, she decided to give him one more chance.

One morning, about a week after moving back in with Gerald, Sharon saw him leaving the apartment. He told her he was going to see a friend, then quickly left. A half hour later, Sharon would tell the police, she looked in on the baby and found that Cara was having some sort of seizure. As she picked the baby up it stopped breathing. Sharon raced with Cara next door, and her neighbor called for an ambulance.

The ambulance arrived within minutes, and medical technicians began working feverishly on the infant. Gerald returned during this time, but didn't seem concerned about the rescue attempts, and instead went inside his own apartment.

When the baby arrived at the hospital, the doctors in the emergency room found that Cara had injuries comparable to those of being thrown around the inside of a car during a 35- to 40-mph-impact crash. The doctors discovered several bone fractures and that Cara had hemorrhaging behind both eyes. Although she survived, Cara suffered severe brain damage that will leave her mentally handicapped. The doctors at the hospital, unfortunately, had seen many cases like this, and correctly diagnosed it as shaken baby syndrome.

Hospital personnel referred the case to the police, and detectives found, upon interviewing Gerald and Sharon, that Gerald, upset because Cara wouldn't stop crying, had shaken her violently. The police also found that Sharon had actually discovered

Cara's severe injuries five hours before "racing" to her neighbor's house and asking her to call for an ambulance. Sharon had delayed reporting it, she said, because she was afraid of getting Gerald in trouble. The police arrested both Gerald and Sharon.

❖ ❖ ❖ ❖ ❖

Unfortunately, shaken baby syndrome is a very common form of infant child abuse in America, and one of the most damaging. An article in the *Indianapolis Star* called "Sunday's Child," a column which features children available for adoption locally, recently featured a child injured by shaken baby syndrome. The child, according to the article, will never be able to live independently, will probably never be toilet trained, is hyperactive and slightly autistic, must wear braces on her legs, has a short attention span, and suffers from seizures.[17]

Along with shaken baby syndrome, very young children also suffer another type of child abuse, Munchausen syndrome by proxy. In this unusual sounding abuse a parent, almost always the mother, takes a young child to the doctor and complains that the child has an illness for which there is no apparent cause. This often leads to the hospitalization of the child for testing and observation.

It is during this hospitalization time that the abuse begins. The parent will then do things to make the child appear gravely ill. Researchers have discovered that Munchausen syndrome by proxy abusers are often depressed, involved in unstable relationships, and have numerous personality needs. It is undoubtedly difficult for the average person to imagine what type of needs would drive a person to make her own child deathly ill just so she could become involved in a life-and-death situation. It is difficult to imagine that much of a need for attention. Police officers, however, see this need for attention expressed quite often. Regularly, people call the police wanting to confess to a crime they didn't commit, or will become involved in some spectacular crime, such as a hostage-taking incident, just to attract attention to themselves.

Here in Indianapolis we had a case where the police suspected Munchausen syndrome by proxy. Detectives installed a hidden camera in the child's hospital room. The police witnessed the mother inject fecal material into the child's feeding tube in order to make her daughter sick. Parents have also been known to smother their children while in the hospital, and then quickly call for resuscitation by hospital personnel. Police find that the perpetrators of Munchausen syndrome by proxy remain amazingly calm during the incident, at a time when most parents would be hysterical or at the very least highly distressed by the unknown malady striking their child. The abusing parent also appears to want to be intimately involved in the treatment of the child, and often is uncharacteristically well versed about the child's illness. As might be imagined, the mortality rate for this type of child abuse is very high, though its extent is not known because it is likely that many of the deaths from Munchausen syndrome by proxy are recorded as due to natural causes. Additionally, the police find that as the victims get older, or die because of the abuse, the perpetrators will then usually begin the abuse on other, younger siblings.

Another type of serious, and occasionally deadly, physical abuse of infants and small children is abuse by burning. This severe cruelty is extraordinarily common. So common, in fact, that child abuse detectives suspect abuse whenever a child is reported to have been burned, as the following incident demonstrates.

❖ ❖ ❖ ❖ ❖

Toni Crider, a nineteen-year-old mother of two, showed up at the hospital emergency room with her seven-month-old daughter, Melissa, who had severe burns on both sides of her face, and several lesser burns on her chest. Toni told hospital personnel that she had had two curling irons plugged in and sitting on a table in her bedroom. Apparently, she said, Melissa pulled them off of the table and burned herself.

Because of the severity and number of burns, though, hospital personnel suspected child abuse and notified the police. When the police questioned Toni she stuck to the story she had told hospital personnel, claiming that she often left the curling irons plugged in and hot all day. She told the police that when she heard her baby scream she ran into the room and found Melissa injured. Toni was unable to explain, however, why Melissa had such severe burns and so many of them, particularly since she said she had raced right into the room immediately upon hearing Melissa scream. Hospital personnel said that the burns on Melissa's face required contact with the curling irons for several seconds. When the police questioned Toni's husband, they found that Toni often appeared to be under tremendous stress because of having to care for both Melissa and her two-year-old brother.

The police arrested Toni, and a court eventually convicted her in the case. Unfortunately, cases such as Toni's are extremely common. Many times every year hospital emergency rooms receive young children suffering from severe burns caused when they "accidentally" spilled boiling water on themselves or "mysteriously" managed to climb into a bathtub full of scalding water.

❖ ❖ ❖ ❖ ❖

A truly sad finding in the research on child abuse is that disabled children are the target for violence and abuse more often than other children.   According to the authors of *Domestic Violence: No Longer Behind the Curtains*: "Children with disabilities can also incur the wrath of abusive parents because the child requires so much special care and attention, may be considered unattractive, and may not respond in a way that the parents can understand."[18] A recent study by the National Center on Child Abuse and Neglect found that disabled children suffer nearly twice the amount of abuse that other children do,   and that the cause of this abuse is usually their disability. Often, as the following incident demonstrates, disabled children are used as a target for other family members' anger.

❖ ❖ ❖ ❖ ❖

On 23 August 1994, the police in South Bend, Indiana, found 21-year-old, mildly retarded Dolly Hershberger dead on her family's living room floor. An autopsy discovered that she had a cracked sternum and ten broken ribs. The pathologist also discovered many old lacerations on her forehead, ears, and forearms that had been closed with home-made sutures. Pus seeped from all of the wounds.

After an investigation into Dolly's death, the police arrested Dolly's father, Frederick Search, and Dolly's stepmother, Martha Search. They also arrested Dolly's biological brother, twenty-three-year-old Frederick Search, Jr., known to everyone as "Freddie."

Freddie eventually confessed and pled guilty to Dolly's murder. In his confession, Freddie told the police how Dolly's home had become a torture chamber, in which he and his parents regularly beat and abused her.

As a young child, Dolly had been taken away from her biological parents because of physical abuse by her father and the fact that her mother was serving a prison sentence for arson. Dolly eventually ended up as a foster child in the home of Herman Hershberger, who, with his wife, has over the years taken care of over 400 foster children, and has adopted nearly two dozen of them. The Hershbergers eventually adopted Dolly.

However, just before Christmas 1992, Dolly told the Hershbergers that she wanted to go visit her biological family for the holidays. During the following months, she returned to visit the Search family several times. Finally, in September 1993, Dolly decided to move in permanently with her biological family.

According to Freddie's confession to the police, the beatings began soon after this. He said that his father and stepmother would use a broom handle to beat Dolly because she "would get into things" and "wouldn't listen to the other family members." Freddie said they would chain the refrigerator shut and lock up the cupboards so that Dolly couldn't get anything to eat. The family also cut off all contact between Dolly and the Hershbergers, and the few times that Dolly managed to run screaming from the house during one of the beatings the family dragged her back in, explaining to any inquisitive neighbors that Dolly was retarded.

While living with her biological family, Dolly was not allowed to watch television or to ever leave the house. Freddie told the police that sometimes he would beat his sister with a belt, and sometimes he would just kick her. His parents, he said, would often join in on the beatings, the stepmother usually using the broom handle (during their investigation the police recovered a broken broom handle covered with blood and human hair).

The Search family realized that they were breaking the law through their physical attacks on Dolly, and they feared that they would go to jail if the beatings were ever discovered. Therefore, several months before her death, they made a pact that they would stop the beatings long enough to allow Dolly to heal up so that they could send her back to her foster home. Because of this fear of going to jail, the family had never allowed Dolly to have medical attention for any of her injuries, but had tried to doctor her at home, including closing up her wounds with home-made sutures.

However, on the morning of 23 August 1994, the Search family broke their pact. When Dolly urinated on herself before she could get to the bathroom, Freddie told the police, he began hitting her, while his stepmother began beating her with the broomstick, and the father began pounding her with his fists. The beating went on several hours before Dolly died.[19]

Freddie Search is serving a thirty-year prison term for Dolly's murder. The parents, Frederick and Martha Search, also eventually pled guilty in Dolly's death.

❖ ❖ ❖ ❖ ❖

As the case above shows, the tragedy of child abuse is enormous, both in physical suffering and lives lost. It is also enormously expensive. A study by the National Committee to Prevent Child Abuse estimates that the annual cost of child maltreatment in the United States is $9 billion, which includes the cost of hospitalization, foster care, counseling, inpatient mental health care, and other services. This cost of counseling and inpatient mental health care, incidentally, can often be traced directly to child abuse. A study reported in the *Journal of the American Academy of Child and Adolescent Psychiatry* found that abused children suffer significantly more attention deficit hyperactivity disorder, oppositional disorder, and posttraumatic stress disorder, all of which can require extensive counseling and inpatient mental health care.

The prevalence of intrafamilial child abuse also negatively affects a community's safety and security by producing future citizens prone to criminal activity and arrest. A study reported in the National Institute of Justice's research paper *Victims of Childhood Sexual Abuse—Later Criminal Consequences* stated that: "People who experience *any* type of maltreatment during childhood—whether sexual abuse, physical abuse, or neglect—are more likely than people who were not maltreated to be arrested later in life." The study also found that the odds of arrest as an adult for a sex crime were four times as great for a physically abused child as a nonabused child. When researchers compared the medical records of 109 children labeled as delinquent to 109 nondelinquent children, they found that nine times as many of the delinquent children had been hospitalized for abuse-related injuries.[20]

A particularly disturbing finding reported in the journal *Child Abuse and Neglect* was that, in a study of mostly white, middleclass sibling incest offenders, 92 percent of the offenders had been physically abused, but only 8 percent had been sexually abused, which demonstrates the extraordinarily damaging effect physical abuse can have on a child.[21] Also disturbing is the finding reported by many researchers that boys in homes with spousal violence will likely become batterers themselves when they grow up, while girls who grow up in families with violence will likely become abuse victims as adults.

The infirm elderly are just as susceptible as children to violence in the home. Even minor physical abuse, because of the fragility of many of the elderly, can lead to serious health complications. The problem of elder abuse, however, like child abuse, while undoubtedly always with us, didn't really become a national concern until 1981 when Representative Claude Pepper held congressional hearings into the problem. A report released by his committee, *Elder Abuse: An Examination of a Hidden Problem*, sparked nationwide awareness and concern about the abuse of elderly people. The report stated that elder abuse was a problem so huge few people could even imagine its dimensions. Unfortunately, however, while the public may now be both aware and concerned about the problem, not much has improved since 1981. A March 1993 *Washington Post* article stated that statistics show elder abuse is on the increase, with a 20 percent rise in just 1991. The article also revealed that experts believe only one in every fourteen cases of elder abuse in the United States is reported.[22] There is a reason for this. The last census found that less than 10 percent of all the elderly people in the United States live in nursing homes; around 30 percent of the elderly live by themselves; and 60 percent, particularly those in need of care and help, live with their families. Unlike children, the infirm elderly are nearly invisible. They do not go to school or church or public places where others can see them. Infirm elderly under home care many times never leave the home, are often secluded in back bedrooms, and even those outsiders who visit the home many times feel uncomfortable around sick elderly people, and consequently avoid them. As a result, those elderly who are physically abused are seldom seen by anyone other than family members. To remedy this, as a part of its Physicians Campaign Against Family Violence, the American Medical Association exhorts its members to be on the alert for signs of elder abuse. Often, other than family members, a doctor is the only person to have contact with the infirm elderly.

The police often find when investigating those elderly abuse cases which are reported to us that we can seldom, except where the abuse is extreme, get much cooperation from the victims. Most victims feel extremely embarrassed that they have a family who would beat them, and many elderly people are terrified that if they do press charges they will be taken out of the home and put into a nursing home. Most elderly people would rather put up with the abuse because they see a nursing home as a way station to death, a lonely place to go and wait to die. In addition, family members who aren't the caretakers will often ignore the signs of physical abuse for a long time because they know that the likely outcome of them complaining will be that they, rather than the other family member, will have to take care of the elderly person, as the incident below illustrates.

❖ ❖ ❖ ❖ ❖

One afternoon while I operated a uniformed district car on the south side of Indianapolis, an area of mostly working-class, white residents, the dispatcher gave me a run she described as a domestic disturbance, a fight between a brother and sister. When I and another car arrived at the address of the run, we found a man and a woman, both in their late thirties to early forties, involved in a loud argument on the front porch of a house. After the other officer and I had separated the two, whose names we found were John and Martha, they told us that they were fighting over John's treatment of their mother, who lived with John.

"That son-of-a-bitch has been hitting her again!" Martha screamed and stepped forward as though she was about to attack John, but then stopped when the other officer blocked her path. "Just go inside and look for yourself!" She pointed toward the house. "You can see where he's been hitting her."

"I'm the one who takes care of her, not you!" John shouted back. "I'm the one who feeds her and cleans up after her, not you!"

After taking a few moments to calm them both down, I went with John into the house to check on his mother, while the other officer stayed on the porch with Martha. The instant I stepped into the house the odor of rotting food and human waste stopped me in midstep. After a second or two, I recovered and looked around. John's house was the kind of place in which I wouldn't want to let my feet stay still very long for fear something would crawl up my pants leg. Litter covered every square inch of the floors. The mother, a frail-looking woman wearing a filthy cotton nightgown, lay in the living room on a bed with a soiled, bare mattress. I could see bruises on the woman's emaciated arms and legs, and her lower lip had what looked like a partly healed cut.

"Look, Officer," John said as soon as we were out of earshot of Martha, "I'll admit I do occasionally lose my temper a bit with Mom, but she just won't do anything I tell her. She won't ever take her medicine like she's supposed to, and she's always messing in her bed. The bathroom's just down the hall, and I've got a bedpan for her, but she won't use them."

As we walked up to the bed and the elderly woman saw my uniform, her eyes jerked open as though she had seen an apparition and she drew back, pulling the cover up protectively. "Johnnie!" she screeched. "Please don't let them take me! Please, Johnnie, don't let them put me in a home! Please, Johnnie!"

I attempted to talk to the woman, but she wouldn't respond to me. She managed to grab onto John's arm and wouldn't let go, begging him over and over not to send her to a nursing home. Finally, after several more attempts to talk with her, but still getting no response, I told John to wait there. I walked back out onto the porch to talk with Martha.

"See, didn't I tell you!" Martha shouted the second I stepped out the door and into the fresh air, which felt like cool water to a parched throat. "Didn't I tell you he's been hitting her! Didn't I!"

Not really sure what we could do in this situation, but realizing she was right about her mother's abuse, I asked Martha, "Tell me, what do you want us to do?"

Martha started to say something, but then stopped and looked as though she hadn't really thought about it. Ten seconds or so went by before she finally answered, "Well, you've got to stop him from hitting her."

"Okay," I answered, "but since this is a misdemeanor and we didn't see it happen we're going to need you to go down to the Prosecutor's Office and file a complaint. But of course you know that if the prosecutor issues a warrant for John they're going to have to find some place for your mother. Wouldn't all of this be a lot easier if you just started taking care of your mother rather than John?"

The woman's face pulled into a horror-struck expression, and she took a half step backward. "I ... I can't take care of her," she stuttered. "I've got ... I've got a husband and children to worry about. I can't take care of mother too."

"Well then, ma'am," I said, "what do you want us to do?"

Several seconds passed as we stood on the porch and waited for her answer. "I'll tell you what," she said finally, "why don't you just warn Johnnie about hitting her. I'm sure that'll take care of it. Really, I think we've already made too big a deal of this."

I went back into the house, and did just that, warned John about the possibility of an arrest warrant being issued if he continued striking his mother. He seemed to take my warning well, promising that he wouldn't strike his mother again, and so I and the other officer left. I don't know what happened in the relationship between John and his mother, but I left the scene feeling very uncomfortable. Even though I notified the Health Department about the house, I felt as though I was simply leaving behind a serious problem that needed to be solved. I realized there was little doubt John had been striking his mother, and that being arrested and tried in court might stop further abuse. However, I strongly doubted the prosecutor would issue an arrest warrant (which would be needed since at that time we couldn't legally make an arrest on the scene). I couldn't see the prosecutor, even if it was medically possible, putting the mother on the witness stand and persuading her to testify against her son. She just wouldn't do it.

In addition to the mother's reluctance to prosecute, there was another problem. Prosecutors, while this action doesn't always serve the best interests of the community, want, for political purposes, to maintain a near-perfect conviction rate. Consequently, very few will try a case they have a good possibility of losing, which they do in many family abuse cases. This was true when I began as a police officer and is still true today. However, if we are ever to stop family abuse this must change. Prosecutors must stop thinking about their political futures, and instead think about protecting their constituents—the job they were elected to do. Abusers, such as John in the case above, must be made to realize that their actions are criminal and will be treated as such.

❖ ❖ ❖ ❖ ❖

As demonstrated in the incident above, and verified by a survey conducted in twenty-one states by the National Aging Resource Center on Elder Abuse, 32.5 percent of the abusers of the elderly are adult children of the elderly victims, followed next in numbers by spouses.[23] Often, the caretakers of elderly parents are part of what is known as the "sandwich generation." These are individuals who have children living at home (often nearing college age) and also have elderly parents who have moved in with them. Unfortunately, the elderly parents begin making large emotional, physical, and financial demands on the sandwich generation at the same time that their college-age children do. The stress from this can many times lead to abuse. But also quite often, the abuse of elderly family members is just a reversal of earlier violent roles.

"We see it all the time," said Amy Davis, an Adult Protective Services caseworker. "Mom or Dad beat up the kids when they were little, and now it's the kids' turn to do the same back to Mom or Dad."

There is an old English rhyme that goes:

> When I was a laddie,
> I lived with my granny,
> And many a hiding me granny gi'ed me.
> Now I am a man,
> And I live with my granny.
> And I do to my granny,
> What she did to me.

Often, when elderly mothers or fathers move in with their children, old problems that were never resolved, but just forgotten when the child moved out, begin to resurface. As the friction begins to build between the child and elderly parent, and the stress of almost constant care compounds, so does the possibility of physical abuse.

Many times, abuse problems develop because, even with the best of intentions, children promise their parents that they will never allow them to be put into a nursing home. The children don't realize the high level of stress involved in caring for an elderly parent, and this is particularly true for the extremely ill or frail elderly, those in need of professional care. A study reported in the *American Journal of Psychiatry* stated they found that the elderly with Alzheimer's disease or other dementia often put high psychological and physical demands on the family members taking care of them, which can many times lead to abuse. Anyone who has dealt with someone with this type of problem knows that the elderly person must be watched and cared for constantly, much like an infant, or they will wander away or do something that can endanger them. The stress, loss of privacy, financial costs, and necessity of constant attention, along with unrealistic expectations of what a person in this condition should be able to do, can many times lead to abuse. Support groups formed for those caring for the infirm elderly report that the caretakers often report feelings of both isolation and entrapment.

But not all elderly family members are physically abused because of the stress of constant care. Dr. Karl Pillemer in "The Dangers of Dependency: New Findings on Domestic Violence against the Elderly" reports that many of the abusers of the elderly are adult children living with the parents, adult children who are dependent on the parents for both housing and money for basic needs.[24] Dr. Pillemer believes the abuse comes about because the adult children want to equalize the unbalanced power ratio between them and the parent. The children feel weak because they still, even as adults, must depend on their parents for support. In addition, a large number of family abusers of the elderly have mental disorders or are substance abusers. This is often why they have to live with their elderly parents. Supporting this, an article in the June 1994 *Journal of Interpersonal Violence* said that, comparing adult children who abuse their parents with adult children who don't, the former are more likely to be alcohol abusers.

While all jurisdictions recognize a parent's right to discipline a child, none allow a child to be seriously assaulted or allow the assault of a spouse, intimate partner, or elderly family member. As talked about earlier in this chapter, physical abuse seldom stops or decreases in intensity on its own. Therefore, in order to stop physical abuse, action must be taken at the first instance of it, action which shows the perpetrator very clearly that physical abuse will not be tolerated. No matter what the reason for physical abuse, it should never be ignored.

Regardless, however, of why one family member wants to physically abuse another, be it a spouse, child, or the elderly, the problem is a tragically serious one in America. Every year millions of family members are physically assaulted and injured by other family members. Unfortunately, the victims are usually assaulted in the one place where they should feel secure: their own home. And while this may be a problem often invisible to those outside the home, it is a problem that has far-reaching and damaging effects on both the victims and society as a whole.

5

Financial Abuse

In our society money usually means power and security. However, because money means power, well-off family members many times become the target for abuse by family members without money, and, through this abuse, can be left powerless and destitute, as the following incident demonstrates.

❖ ❖ ❖ ❖ ❖

Regina and David Evans had been married for 41 years when David died suddenly of a heart attack. David had been a machinist and made a good living. At the time of his death, David and Regina had a sizable bank account and owned a large, two-story brick house. Although she had never taken care of the family finances, Regina found after David passed away that she was able to live comfortably on her husband's pension and the interest she received on their life's savings.

While David had always been a loving and supportive husband, he had told Regina many times, to her protestations otherwise, that their grown son, Ronald, was a "worthless piece of crap." Ronald had continually been after his parents to give him money or to buy him something. David, though, had been tough, and had always made Ronald work for whatever he got, even after Ronald had left home and gotten married. David had often chided Regina for being too soft and willing to give in to Ronald's demands.

Six months after David's death, Ronald began showing up at his mother's house at least once a month with a hard luck story about how one of his children was sick and he didn't have any money for a doctor or medicine, how his car payment was over-due and they were going to repossess it, or how he was having problems with his dentures but didn't have any money for a dentist. Regina began withdrawing more and more of her savings and giving it to Ronald. Finally, within a few years after David's death, she had no savings left, and Ronald began, instead of money, taking household items and selling them to pay for his "hard luck" bills.

Eventually, Regina had nothing of value left to sell, and so Ronald came up with an idea. He and his wife and kids would move into the upstairs of his mother's house and pay her rent. While Regina had begun believing that maybe David had been right after all about Ronald, the idea of him and his family moving in seemed to make sense to her, because the rent money would make up for what she had lost since she no longer collected any interest on her depleted savings. Before Ronald moved in, though, he presented his mother with a legal document, telling her it was a rental agreement so that there would be no confusion about the rent money he would owe. Regina didn't read the document and signed it.

The document, rather than a rental agreement, turned out to be a deed to her house. Soon after Regina signed it, Ronald sold the house for much less than its worth, collected the proceeds, and moved out.

❖ ❖ ❖ ❖ ❖

Financial abuse by family members is one of the most com-monly occurring types of family abuse. But, while common, it can also be difficult to detect right away. Until the victim notices the discrepancy in his or her bank or credit card statement, or until so much of an elderly family member's money or assets have been drained off that it raises someone's awareness, often no one knows that the abuse is occurring. If the abusing family member keeps the abuse small and only occasional, it can be months or years before it's discovered. And unfortunately, by the time the abuse is discovered, it is often too late to get any of the money or assets back, since many times they are already spent.

Although financial abuse can involve a victim of any age and family relationship, a large percentage of the financial abuse within families is committed against elderly family members. While it is well known among law enforcement officials that the elderly are often the target for professional con artists, who use every ruse imaginable to steal an elderly person's life savings, in actuality what these strangers con out of the elderly is quite small compared to what their own relatives steal from them.

According to *Growing Old in America*: "Criminal Justice professionals report that money and property are being stolen from today's elderly at alarming rates and that a large portion of the crimes are being committed not by professional criminals but by relatives."[1]

"Financial exploitation by family members is one of our fastest growing types of elder abuse," said Lori West, an Adult Protective Services investigator. But just how much of this financial abuse is there?

"The Forsyth County Aging Study," reported in *The Gerontologist*, found that 46 percent of the elderly people who told researchers they had been abused reported an exploitation of their resources.[2] The California State Department of Social Services in its study "Dependent Adult/Elder Abuse—Characteristic Survey" found that of all elder abuse reported, 42 percent was financial abuse. An article in *U.S. News and World Report* stated: "Most elder abuse laws, following the child abuse model, focus on physical, psychological, and sexual abuse, as well as neglect. But new research shows the elderly are more probably victims of financial exploitation ... although it is much harder to detect: A forged check is far harder to spot than a black eye."[3]

How are family members able to get this money and property away from other family members, both young and old? Some, like Ronald in the above incident, persuade the family members to withdraw the money from bank accounts for them. Some family members steal other family members' checks from the mail, some, like the incident below, forge checks against other family members' accounts.

❖ ❖ ❖ ❖ ❖

On 28 November 1995, Detective Ronald Meier received a radio call from the dispatcher that uniformed police officers were holding a forgery suspect at the People's Bank branch on North Lafayette Road in Indianapolis. When Detective Meier brought the forgery suspect to the Indianapolis Police Department West District Headquarters and questioned her, he found that at first she gave several false names and identifiers before finally admitting to him that she was Rebecca Kaufman, a woman who had a lengthy record of forgery. Once she had finally admitted who she was, Rebecca also confessed to Detective Meier that she had committed forgery at the same bank on North Lafayette Road at least four times that month. Rebecca told the detective she would enter the bank, request a blank counter check, and then fill it out with her sister's name and account number, usually making the check out to cash.

When Detective Meier talked to the bank security personnel, he discovered that Rebecca had actually forged her sister's name and account number seven times that month, twice for $60.00, once for $80.00, three times for $200.00, and once for $280.00. Upon speaking with Rebecca's sister, the detective confirmed that she had not given Rebecca permission to do this, and he also discovered that Rebecca had victimized her sister before. A few days after this, bank security personnel informed Detective Meier that Rebecca's mother had also filed a forgery affidavit with the bank. Continuing his investigation into Rebecca Kaufman's activities, the detective found that, along with stealing from her sister's bank account, Rebecca had also been making unauthorized withdrawals from her mother's account, once for $130.00 and once for $200.00.

❖ ❖ ❖ ❖ ❖

Along with forging checks, family members also fraudulently use other family members' credit cards. This can occasionally be expensive and troublesome to clean up, since the victim usually doesn't find out about the abuse until after he or she receives the monthly account statement and considerable debts have been incurred, as the case below illustrates.

❖ ❖ ❖ ❖ ❖

On 10 June 1995, a locksmithing company received a telephone call from a Mr. Jay Olson, asking them to send someone out to his home to unlock the door of his vehicle. Once the locksmith had unlocked the car and presented his bill, Mr. Olson said he would pay by credit card. However, he told the locksmith that he didn't have the card with him right then. His wife had it. But he did know the account number. He then gave the locksmith a credit card number and expiration date. The locksmith checked the credit card number and found that the account was active and in good standing. He filled out and presented Mr. Olson with a credit card slip, which Mr. Olson signed.

A few weeks after this, a Mrs. Betty Olson notified her credit card company that, upon receiving her monthly statement, she found there had been a number of very expensive unauthorized purchases made on her credit card. She suspected her son, Jay.

The police brought Jay in for questioning, and, after the locksmith positively identified him as the person who signed the credit card slip, Jay admitted everything. He told the police that he had found his mother's VISA card and PIN number hidden in her bedroom, and that he had purchased several thousand dollars' worth of merchandise on it, along with several ATM cash withdrawals.

❖ ❖ ❖ ❖ ❖

Some particularly greedy family members, and especially those who financially abuse elderly family members, go even further than forged checks and stolen credit cards, and use various ruses to convince elderly persons to give them power of attorney. A power of attorney is a legal document in which someone grants another person the right to act in his or her behalf. These are often used when the elderly are homebound and need someone to do their banking or to handle other financial transactions for them. Unfortunately, a power of attorney, while very useful for the homebound elderly, can also be greatly abused. Once a person has power of attorney, he or she usually has complete control over the elderly person's bank account and other assets, and can withdraw money from the account and dispose of any assets. According to an article in *The FBI Law Enforcement Bulletin*: "Powers of attorney may be the single most abused legal document in our judicial system. Most states do not require any form of accounting as it relates to the use of power of attorney to handle elderly individuals' finances."[4]

Power of attorney, as the article above points out, is an area where much more oversight is needed than now exists, both by the authorities and family members. Whenever a person obtains power of attorney over another family member, everyone else in the family should be alert to the possibility of financial abuse. If the person with the power of attorney suddenly begins buying things he or she could not afford before or begins paying off old bills, the other family members should become concerned and investigate. Also, state legislatures need to make it part of state law that anyone with power of attorney over another person must account for where the person's money or property goes. Monthly or bimonthly reports of where the money controlled under power of attorney was spent should be required by law.

Elderly people can protect themselves from financial abuse by first giving power of attorney only to a person they trust completely. Even then, however, the elderly person needs to ask another trusted family member to check on what the person with power of attorney does.

In addition to power of attorney abuse, many times family members will persuade the elderly to sign over property or bank accounts on the promise that they will be given lifetime care. Once the property or bank accounts change hands, however, the elderly person is usually powerless to do anything if the family members don't live up to their promise.

Studies have found, as might be expected, that the family members who financially exploit other family members are usually in desperate financial straits. It is very tempting for people who are in dire need of money, and who have control over another person's finances and assets, to appropriate some of the money for their personal use, particularly if the person over whom they have control has decreased mental capacities and likely won't understand what's happening. A study funded by the Massachusetts's Department of Elder Affairs and the Administration on Aging confirmed that the abusers of the elderly are usually indeed in desperate financial straits. Of these abusers, 64 percent, the study found, were dependent on the victim for financial support and 55 percent were dependent on the victim for housing. It should therefore be taken as a sign of alarm, or at the very least caution, when family members who have little or no income of their own, or who are in poor financial shape, want to move in with elderly family members with the idea of being caretakers.

Why is there so much financial abuse of elderly family members in particular? Some of this abuse can be blamed on advances in medical science. A hundred years ago, when a person got along in years and came down with a serious illness, he or she usually died soon afterward. But today, medical science has found many ways of keeping people alive for years, even with very serious illnesses. But doing this has a cost. Usually, by the time the person dies, he or she has spent nearly every cent saved over a lifetime on medical or other health care expenses. And even if the person doesn't come down with a serious illness, because medical science has made it possible to extend lifetimes to such an extent, often children must wait many more years for an inheritance. For these reasons, many children justify taking their elderly parents' assets with such logic as: "I know Dad would rather I had everything than the hospital"; "Mom always said I could have the house after she's gone, and if I wait I won't be able to get it"; or "I'll always take care of Mom and Dad, so what does it matter if they don't have anything?" This last bit of logic, though, soon loses its appeal when the children find out how much trouble, stress, and expense there is to taking care of the frail or sick elderly, especially after all of their money and property is gone.

Financial abuse of family members, clearly, doesn't have to involve just stealing from other family members. When one family member completely controls all of the money and assets of the family, thereby reducing the other family members to beggar status, and making them totally dependent on him or her, abuses in power will often arise. (I will discuss this type of abuse at length in Chapter 7 on "Emotional Abuse and Control.") Financial abuse, though, can be even more odious than this, as the following incident shows.

❖ ❖ ❖ ❖ ❖

One afternoon, when I worked as a uniformed district officer, I received a radio run to investigate a family who had requested help from the police department's Coffee Can Fund. This was a fund set up by the police department chaplain's office to give emergency assistance to people in desperate financial straits, usually in the form of groceries, but also occasionally with other items. Unfortunately, soon after the program began, the police department discovered that many undeserving individuals attempted to use the Coffee Can Fund to get free food or other benefits. Consequently, before any assistance could be given, the dispatcher would send a uniformed police officer to investigate the circumstances that led to the request for help. Several times, while investigating a request for help, I asked a young child what had happened to all of their food, and, in the honest response of a young child, he or she would tell me that mommy had hidden it all next door just before calling us.

When I arrived at the address of the run, an old, dilapidated house that had been converted into apartments, a young mother with three pre-school-age children clinging to her answered the door. Just from the look of desperation and bewilderment on her face I felt this was likely a legitimate call.

"Yesterday was payday," she told me after inviting me inside, "and I was waiting for my husband to get home with his paycheck so we could go to the grocery store. We always live from payday to payday, and I didn't have a bit of food in the house."

As it turned out, though, she told me, her husband didn't come home. Instead, he called her as he left work, told her he was tired of always being penniless, and that he had quit his job and was heading back home to Kentucky. He took his paycheck with him. The woman said that after buying dinner last night she had less than a dollar left. Looking around the apartment, I had no doubt the woman was telling me the truth. While not overly dirty, the apartment was sparsely furnished with obviously castoff furniture, and I didn't see any of the little knickknacks that people usually collect. Every cent, I figured, had likely been spent on bare necessities.

"I don't know what I'm going to do," the woman said, wringing her hands as the three little children clung to her. "Our rent's due in two weeks, and there's not a bit of food in the house."

Since, as I mentioned above, we had found that the police department received a large number of calls for help from people who really didn't need help, I was required to check into the woman's circumstances. I found that, indeed, her husband had left his place of employment (though I discovered he had been fired for drinking on the job rather than quitting) and that he did have family in Kentucky. According to several fellow employees, he said he was heading back home.

I used the Coffee Can Fund to purchase the woman and her three children a week's worth of groceries, and I also put her in contact with several social service agencies, since she and the three children would soon have to find a new place to live and would also have to find other income. As I was doing this, I tried to imagine the feeling of helplessness and desperation this woman must have experienced when she suddenly found herself left with three very young children, no job skills, and no money. It was a hollow, empty feeling. This was financial abuse at its worst.

❖ ❖ ❖ ❖ ❖

Financial abuse involving family members can also include financial manipulation of the children. Recently, for example, a court convicted a couple in Bend, Oregon, of racketeering and forgery. The couple had over the years, in addition to their own six children, adopted eighty-four additional children, most of them either from troubled homes or from Third World countries. The prosecution claimed that the couple kept adopting more and more children to make more and more money. The couple had won a number of awards for their adoption of these children, and apparently at one time had a steady stream of contributions coming in. However, these contributions eventually dried up, and during the trial the prosecution showed that the couple had siphoned off $10,000 of these contributions for their personal use. Fortunately, homes were found for most of the children.[5]

The obvious solution to much of the financial abuse within families is simply never to trust a family member in poor financial straits with the handling of someone else's finances. Also, a person must often guard his or her credit cards, bank accounts, and other assets as much from family members as from professional thieves.

While the financial abuse of a family member, be it a child, an elderly person, or a spouse, is perhaps not as dramatic and visible as the physical abuse of a family member, and maybe not as psychologically damaging as the sexual abuse of a family member, it can still have extraordinarily detrimental effects. Often, family members have worked their entire lives in order to accumulate a considerable amount of worldly goods, only to have another family member, someone the victim should feel he or she can trust, steal them. But even worse, occasionally once the victimized family members have nothing left, particularly elderly family members, they are discarded. They are left to fend for themselves, thrown onto welfare, or simply tossed out into the street penniless.

6

Neglect

"Charles-Nine, take a D.O.A. run, 4250 East Prospect Street."

I grimaced and felt my stomach clutching tight as I keyed the radio microphone and okayed the run. Even though I only had about five years' experience as a police officer at the time, I was already acquainted enough with D.O.A. (dead on arrival) runs to hate them. I knew that, by police department policy, a dispatcher gave a D.O.A. run to a uniformed officer rather than a detective whenever the information he or she had been given by the caller led the dispatcher to assume that the death was probably natural. But yet, even though presumed to be natural, policy required that a police officer check any death which didn't occur in a hospital or at a health care facility.

Police officers particularly dislike D.O.A. runs because there is very little they can do to help the family. The officers don't know the family or the deceased, and so they most often end up standing around while everyone is crying, and sometimes screaming, not knowing what to say or do.

Usually D.O.A. runs involved elderly members of a family, many of whom had been ill for some time. And even though the deaths don't come as a surprise or shock to the family, few people are really able to deal with them. In my five years as a police officer I had seen some almost unbelievably wild scenes of grief at homes where an elderly person had been suffering from cancer, or some other disease, for months or years.

In contrast, the absolute worst D.O.A. runs were SIDS (sudden infant death syndrome) deaths. In my five years I'd been dispatched to several of these and they had been horrible. What can you say to a mother or father who walks in and finds what he or she believed to be a healthy baby suddenly dead in its crib? Worst of all, if it appeared that the infant's death was a likely SIDS case, an officer had to call for a deputy coroner, which always took an hour or so. While waiting for the deputy coroner, the officer simply stood around with the crying, often hysterical, family, trying to be sympathetic, but understandably unable to help.

As I slipped my police car to the curb in front of 4250 East Prospect Street, I prayed I'd find a knife in the person's back, or maybe a bullet hole somewhere. A murder is much easier to handle emotionally. It's what a police officer is trained and equipped to handle. With a murder, a police officer is expected to be detached and unemotional as he or she investigates the circumstances.

A minute later, I began feeling almost relieved, my stomach loosening, when no one answered my knock. While I thought I could hear the sounds of a television set on inside the residence, I knew that the people in this neighborhood often kept their television sets or radios on when they left, hoping to fool any prospective burglars into thinking someone was home. Maybe, I hoped, it was just a crank call. But then, as my hopes were at the highest, I heard someone unlocking the door from the inside.

"Good afternoon, sir," I said to the balding, middle-aged man who answered the door. "Did you report a death here?"

"Yes, officer, my mother. Come on in."

The man, who I noticed held what looked like a white handkerchief in his hand, stepped back and waved for me to come in. I braced myself, preparing to deal with a grieving, weeping family. When I stepped into the house, though, I thought that perhaps the man had misunderstood me, or that maybe this was a joke or something. Two teenaged children sat on a couch eating a pizza and watching the television. They gave me a glance as I stepped inside, but then turned back to the television. From where I stood I could see through the living room and into the dining room, where at the table covered with food a woman sat eating. The chair at the head of the table sat empty, and I could see now that it wasn't a handkerchief the man carried, but a white paper napkin.

"Come on, I'll show you," the man said, waving for me to follow him.

He then led me through the dining room and down a short hallway. At the end of the hall, he opened a door which I noticed had a latch on it for a padlock. The man apparently saw me looking at the latch.

"Mother wasn't right in the head," the man said. "I had to keep her locked up or else she'd have been out wandering around the neighborhood."

Inside the room, which I judged to be about nine feet by nine feet, sat a single bed with a shriveled up little woman in it, obviously dead, but still clinging to the filthy sheet across her chest. The first thing I noticed about the room, though, because it hit me like a two-by-four across the forehead, was the almost unbelievable stench. It told me that the woman had been incontinent and that the bed linen hadn't been changed, nor the room cleaned, in months and months. Off the bedroom sat a tiny bathroom with just a sink and a toilet, but I didn't go near it. I was having a difficult enough time handling the stench in the bedroom. I had been in enough houses like this, though, to know to take only short, shallow breaths.

I reached over for the light switch since it was dim in the room, the only light coming in being what feeble amount managed to slip in around a shade pulled down over the single window. However, when I flipped the light switch several times nothing happened.

"Must be burned out," the man said.

"Had your mother been ill?" I asked the man as I walked over and tried to get the shade up. I could tell from its stiffness, though, that it had been down for a long time.

"I think she had heart problems."

I nodded as the shade finally went up, and then pulled out my notebook. "Did she have a family doctor?"

"Yeah, a Dr. Reynolds, I think, up on 10th Street."

Police department policy said that if a death appeared to be from natural causes, and the person had been seeing a doctor regularly for a serious illness, the officer could simply call the family doctor, and if he or she agreed to sign the death certificate, the officer could then release the body to the family for burial, and that would be all there was to it. However, as I looked around the room, I knew that what I saw wasn't normal or natural. What I saw was nothing.

There was nothing in the room except for the bed. There was no television, no radio, no telephone, no books, no magazines, no photos, no knickknacks, not even a chair for visitors. There were no pictures on the wall, no rug on the floor. There was absolutely nothing personal in the room, nothing to make the room look human. I had seen jail cells that looked more inviting.

"How long had your mother been living here?" I asked, finally forcing myself to walk over and look in the bathroom, all the while still taking only the shortest and shallowest of breaths, the stench though seeming to soak in through my skin. On the sink sat a bowl that appeared to contain some type of cereal with milk. The son had apparently been bringing his mother supper when he found her. But as I suspected, I saw no medicine.

"A little over five years," the man answered.

The woman, I noticed, looked so emaciated that it appeared she had actually died years before, and we were looking at her mummy. "Did she take any medicine for her heart problem?"

For the first time the man appeared flustered. "Uh, no, I don't think she did."

I took down all of the deceased woman's personal information, and then looked the body over as best I could while still respecting her dignity. There were no marks I could find, and from the many other cases I had seen it appeared that she had indeed died of a heart attack.

"Was your mother receiving Social Security?" I asked, not

really needing the information for my report, but suspecting something.

"No, but she got Dad's pension."

I wasn't surprised by the answer. I had suspected it. It didn't take much of a detective to figure out that after spending what little it took for them to keep her in this room, that left the family with most of her pension check every month. "May I use your telephone, please?"

"Sure," the man said, waving for me to follow him.

We passed again through the dining room, where the man's wife still sat eating her dinner as though nothing unusual at all had happened. The man pulled out the chair at the head of the table and sat down. I could smell pork chops and fried potatoes, and I thought about the woman's last meal: a bowl of cold cereal.

"It's right in there on the end table," the man said, pointing toward the living room.

Although I found his obviously uncaring behavior a bit puzzling, I was actually glad when he went back to eating because I wanted to speak to the family doctor without anyone listening in. The phone sat far enough away from the two teenagers that I doubted they could hear me over the television, and they didn't appear too interested in what I was doing anyway.

After obtaining the number through Information, I finally got through to Dr. Reynolds on the telephone, and he said, yes, he had been the woman's doctor but that he hadn't seen her in several years. When I asked if she had had any medicine she was supposed to be taking, he said that when he had been seeing her he had had her on a regimen of medicines for her heart and other health problems. As a matter of fact, the last time he saw her, the doctor said, she had been in such poor health, both physically and mentally, that he felt she needed to be moved into a constant care facility. But he also told me that since he hadn't seen her in several years he didn't feel comfortable about signing the death certificate.

I thanked him, then hung up the telephone and told the family that I would have to request a deputy coroner. Not really wanting to stay inside with the family, I waited instead in my police car. As I sat there and thought about what I had just witnessed, I felt a depressing sadness grip me. The situation just wasn't right. I was still a relatively new officer, and I felt that there should be something I could do about this woman's death. What had happened to her seemed very clear to me. Rather than going to a nursing home she had moved in with her son's family. I imagined that maybe at first they had treated her okay, but I also supposed that she had quickly become a burden to them, and so they simply locked her up in the room. I could only imagine the life the woman led with no stimulation, no activities, no one to talk to, and no one checking very often on her welfare. It was worse, I knew, than being a neglected child, because both family members and outsiders purposely avoid sick, elderly people.

Forty-five minutes later, a deputy coroner finally arrived, and I expressed my concern to him. He, however, only gave me a cynical laugh.

"You get used to seeing that in my job," he said. "I'll bet there ain't a week goes by that I don't see at least one case where I suspect the person was happy as hell to die and get away from their family."

In my naiveté, I said, "Wait until you see it. This is pretty bad. You might want to have the prosecutor take this to the grand jury."

The deputy coroner laughed again. It wasn't a laugh of humor, though, but of disgust. "You can't make one of these kinds of cases. Believe me, we've tried. The family always gets too much sympathy from the jury when they tell them about how hard it was taking care of mom or dad."

After his investigation, the deputy coroner had the woman's body taken to the county morgue, and I never heard anything more about the case. I suppose from this that the county coroner ruled it a natural death, though I have always felt that the family contributed to the woman's death, that the neglect the woman suffered by her isolation from both people and any of life's comforts dampened her will to live.

❖ ❖ ❖ ❖ ❖

Unfortunately, not much has changed in the more than

twenty years since I had this case. It is still very difficult to convict
families for neglect in cases where they gave a family member
only the barest of necessities. The problem is not one of an absence
of laws, but a lack of awareness by the general public (who make
up juries) of just how badly family members can treat each other.
In addition, while showing criminal intent in physical and sexual
abuse cases is usually easy, this isn't so in neglect cases. The
prosecutor in a neglect case will try to draw a dark picture of the
family, but the defense attorney will draw the opposite picture.
Most people, because of a lack of awareness, prefer to believe the
defense attorney's view that if neglect occurred it was out of
ignorance, not malice.

The answer to this problem, therefore, doesn't lie so much
with the criminal justice system, which often doesn't find out
about and become involved in neglect cases until too late, as it
does with the family and friends of neglect victims. Family members who know that a person is being neglected, like the woman in
the case above, must speak out and take action, even if it involves
assuming the care of the elderly person. To not do so means they
become a party to the neglect. Friends and neighbors also need to
check on the welfare of anyone possibly being neglected. An
occasional visit from someone concerned about them can greatly
increase the quality of life for the elderly.

The problems associated with neglect of the elderly, while still
very serious twenty years after the incident above, are, unfortunately, not likely to disappear in the near future. Instead, they will
probably become even larger and more chronic. According to the
Census Bureau, between 1990 and 2010 there will be a 26 percent
increase in the over-sixty-five population, while by the year 2040
over 25 percent of the population of the United States will be sixty-
five and over. Along with there being more elderly people in
America is the fact that as the over-sixty-five population continues
to grow so does the cost of institutional health care for the elderly,
meaning that more and more of them will be taken care of in the
home. And so, as health and medical advances keep allowing for a
longer life span, and more people reach their seventies, eighties,
and nineties, more of them will also need help with such life

functions as getting dressed, cooking, moving around, and attending to medical needs, and they will usually depend on family members for this help.

Interestingly, it is middle-class families who suffer most from the effects of this longer life span. The wealthy can afford expensive in-home nursing care or expensive institutional care, while the poor are eligible for public assistance in placing the elderly in nursing homes. Middle-class families, however, are often forced by financial constraints to take elderly parents into their home and care for them. And while the children may at first believe they can handle the extra work and stress, they soon find that taking care of the elderly, particularly the infirm elderly, is much more work and much more stressful than they imagined. This is when the neglect begins. Studies have shown that the average time the elderly must be cared for is 9.5 years, and many children discover that this is a long, long time, especially when an elderly parent needs complete and total care.

The police many times find that psychological and emotional neglect, which includes confinement, often comes about because the elderly will wander away, will do embarrassing things in public, or are incontinent. Besides locking them in rooms so that they cannot wander or embarrass the family, caretakers will also often withhold liquids from the elderly who are incontinent, or not move them because of their bladder problems, which leads to pressure sores (bedsores). We had a case here in Indianapolis in which a neglected elderly woman had not been moved for so long that, because of bed sores, her skin had grown into the sheet.

By comparison with elderly victims, neglected children are much easier to detect and recognize, yet still the problem of neglected children is huge in America. Many children receive little or no medical care, minimal amounts of food, and absolutely no emotional support from their family. Many children are also raised in squalid conditions, with no regard to their health or welfare. Far too often, babies are brought to hospital emergency rooms emaciated and with rampant diaper rash from never being fed or having their diapers changed. Unfortunately, like the neglected elderly, little is really done about the problem of child neglect, except in the most extreme cases. How extreme?

We had a case recently in the district where I now work in which the dispatcher sent an officer to check on the living conditions of a woman and her six children. Apparently, someone had reported the family to the Health Department. The officer's report read: "Upon arrival I found the house to be filthy. All of the rooms were packed with trash and rubbish, and the refrigerator had trash and mold in it. The water in the house was not running, and the residence was being heated by an open oven door and four burners on the stove. Several dogs lived in the house and apparently never went outside. All six children were filthy. The Health Department representative stated that the house was not fit for human habitation, and he gave the resident a forty-eight-hour clean up notice."

When victim assistance workers loaded up the six children to take them to the County Guardian's Home, one of the young children turned to another and said, "Boy, if they think this place is bad, they should have seen our house over on Pershing Street." The children, though obviously suffering from neglect, were eventually returned to the mother.

Child neglect can take many forms. There is, for example, physical neglect, which can include not supplying a child with the necessities of life, such as food, clothing, and necessary medical treatment. The police often find, though, that they must tread lightly with neglect of medical treatment. This can many times stem from the parent's religious beliefs, and if it is minor neglect it becomes a touchy area. This can include such things as the parents refusing to have a child examined by a physician, not allowing a child to be inoculated against childhood diseases, or insisting on home medical care over professional care. A number of court cases have ruled, however, that parents cannot allow religious beliefs to put a child's life in peril. Physical neglect can also include abandoning a child, throwing a child out of the house, and not providing a child with necessary supervision.

It is important to point out here, however, that occasionally the authorities find that neglect of children and elderly family members, particularly neglect of material items, comes not from willful mistreatment, but from poverty. Some families simply do not have or are unable to procure the items their children or elderly family members need because there is no money. Several studies have shown that family income and family size is directly related to the likelihood of neglect. Families making less than $15,000 a year have been found to be ten times as likely to neglect basic needs as families having more income. Neglect was also found to be more likely in families with four or more children. While this seems to make logical sense, not all neglect, even in poor families, comes from a lack of money. It is necessary to look at how money is spent to determine if the family is neglectful.

When I was a patrol officer working on the south side of Indianapolis, I patrolled some very poor areas. The police department chaplain's office had set up, as I mentioned earlier, a program called the Coffee Can Fund. I discovered that in many, many cases the people asking for assistance, though they claimed to have no money for food, and their homes looked poor and the children hungry, often had a stock of liquor, cigarettes, and coffee in the house—items certainly not necessary for basic survival and whose cost could have easily paid for the needed groceries.

In addition to all of the types of neglect already mentioned, there is also educational neglect. This includes not signing a child up for school, allowing a child to be a constant truant, or neglecting a child's special educational needs. This type of neglect, of course, ties in directly with our country's literacy problem. Without proper education children grow up to be less than fully functioning adults. At best they are able to hold only the most menial, low-paying jobs.

For both children and the elderly, neglect can also include emotional neglect: when family members do not provide any emotional support or nurturing. While damaging to anyone, a lack of family love particularly harms children and the infirm elderly. In many families children and the elderly are looked upon as burdens, are ignored whenever possible, and are provided with only just enough basic human needs in order to keep away the authorities and charges of neglect. While these victims may bear no visible physical scars, emotional neglect can still injure by taking away a person's self-confidence, self-esteem, and often, for the elderly, the will to live.

With all of its types, neglect is the most common type of family abuse there is. A study done by the American Humane Society found that over 60 percent of all cases of reported child maltreatment were reports of neglect. This same study found that, in 1986, 68 out of every 1000 children in this country were neglected. The U.S. House of Representatives Select Committee on Aging, in its report *Elder Abuse: An Examination of a Hidden Problem*, came to the conclusion that neglect rates for people at both ends of the age spectrum, children and the elderly, were very similar. According to the National Aging Resource Center on Elder Abuse, neglect is the largest single form of elder abuse.

"It's the cycle of life," said Adult Protective Services investigator Amy Davis. "You start out dependent on others as a baby, and then you end up being dependent on others when you're elderly." Unfortunately, the family members that the people at both ends of this cycle depend on don't always provide them with life's necessities.

Julie Williams, a child abuse detective for the Indianapolis Police Department, recently investigated a neglect case that had her fuming. The case that upset her involved a "failure-to-thrive" incident. This condition involves an infant or young child who isn't growing and thriving as it should. Doctors consider an infant to be a failure-to-thrive case when the baby is 20 percent below the ideal weight for its age. Of course, doctors always first check the infant's family history before reporting a case of failure to thrive. There are some families in which the members are just naturally lean.

Unfortunately, seldom is this the situation with failure-to-thrive cases. Instead it signals neglect or abuse: usually, for various reasons, the parents are not feeding an infant enough, or at other times not at all. In the case Detective Williams investigated, doctors found an infant to be extremely thin and undernourished, but found no tendency for this in the family, and felt that the baby had probably been receiving practically no nourishment at all. Detective Williams called the mother and asked her to come down to the Family Advocacy Center. The woman arrived and brought along her husband. When Detective Williams went out to the waiting room to talk to them, she found the couple munching on potato chips and Twinkies, and washing it down with Pepsi. Detective Williams discovered that the couple had brought along a grocery bag full of snacks for themselves, yet hadn't been feeding their baby. The reason for this? They told the detective that they just didn't have any milk. Also, Detective Williams found, if the baby cried during the night, both refused to get up and feed it.

In another recent case, public school officials reported to Child Protective Services that two young brothers who attended public school appeared abnormally thin. When county health authorities checked them, they found that the brothers were indeed much too thin for their age group. After the county health authorities talked with the mother they found that the problem stemmed from her unusual personality problems. The mother was obsessed with her weight, likely suffered from anorexia, and hardly ever ate. Unfortunately, she allowed this obsession with her own weight to carry over into neglect in the care of her children.

The two preceding cases raise particular problems for the courts. While the parents in both cases were obviously guilty of neglect, the reason for the neglect was more likely ignorance of how to care for children than intentional harm. In these type of cases, under the threat of reinstating a suspended sentence, judges can order the parents to attend parenting classes. Child abuse workers find that this is occasionally successful, but also find that often the parents' problems are so severe that the only answer is to put the children in foster care.

Along with not providing the necessary material items for their children, a large number of mothers are also charged with neglect because they know that their husbands or intimate partners are abusing their children, but they either do nothing about it or attempt to help the abuser escape any legal consequences for the abuse. In February 1996, the police charged an Indianapolis man with the murder of his girlfriend's two-year-old son. An autopsy showed that the infant had suffered systematic beatings and torture over a long period of time. The infant had old fractures, bite marks, genital cuts, needle punctures, and many bruises, scrapes, and scars. The police charged the mother with neglect because, even though she didn't inflict the abuse herself, she knew that her boyfriend was doing it but did nothing to stop it.

In a case handled by my wife, Melanie, a child abuse detective for the Indianapolis Police Department, a thirteen-year-old girl complained to the police that her mother's fifty-two-year-old boyfriend had been fondling her. Upon investigation of the young girl's complaint, Melanie arrested the boyfriend. The mother immediately began pressuring her daughter to recant and tell the police that she had lied. The young girl courageously resisted the pressure. Eventually, however, the pressure became intense and started coming from both her mother and the boyfriend, whom the mother had bailed out of jail. Finally, the mother and boyfriend forced the young victim to sit down and write a letter to the court that they dictated to her. My wife, upon discovering this, arrested the mother for neglect.

In cases such as the one above courts often order mothers not to allow the arrested boyfriends to have any further contact with the victims. However, mothers many times ignore this order. Under these circumstances, if the police find that the mother has violated the order she can be arrested for neglect. It is important, therefore, that when family, friends, or neighbors become aware that an arrested molester is back with the family that they notify the police.

Occasionally, when the stress of caretaking becomes too great, neglect can also take the form of abandonment, when a parent or guardian actually dumps a child or elderly person somewhere and never returns. I had a case of this once that still leaves me sad.

❖ ❖ ❖ ❖ ❖

One day when I worked as a uniformed district sergeant on Edward sector I heard a radio run come out on an abandoned child at a day care center just a block or two from where I was. Since I had dealt with day care centers with my own children, I figured this wasn't an abandonment but just a case of a parent being a little late picking up a child. I had found from my own experience that the workers at day care centers often began making these types of calls almost exactly at closing time. I really wanted to give them a piece of my mind about not allowing the parents even a few minutes leeway, and so I told the dispatcher to disregard the officer and that I would take the run.

When I arrived at the day care center, though, I found that it was actually almost two hours past their closing time. In the office of the center sat a frustrated-looking young woman and a cute little girl of about three years, who appeared terrified, both of her situation and apparently of the police.

"I've been trying for over an hour," the day care worker said when I asked if she had tried contacting the little girl's parents. "The phone company says that her mother's number has been disconnected, and when I called where she works, they said she hasn't been working there for a couple of weeks."

The standard procedure in this type of case would be to take the child to the County Guardian's Home, and then let the mother pick her up there. However, the little girl looked so frightened I decided to try something else first. The mother's apartment was only about a half-mile away, and so I told the day care worker that I would run over there and see if I could find out what had delayed the mother. The mother's telephone being disconnected didn't really worry me because I knew that the people on Edward sector, most being poor, were always having their telephones disconnected for nonpayment.

I had been to the apartment building before, and knew that it was one of our sector's seediest, occupied mostly by drunks and drug users. I walked up four flights of stairs that smelled of urine and vomit (I knew better than to trust the elevator in this type of building) and knocked on the mother's door. After a minute or so of knocking, a woman came out of an apartment down the hallway and stared at me for a second.

"If you're looking for her you're too late," the woman told me. "She moved out this morning."

Only then did I begin to suspect what I really had, an actual child abandonment and not just a mother late in picking up her child. "Do you know where she moved to?"

The woman gave me a look that said I should have known better than to ask a question like that, and then walked on down the hall. I thanked her and then began looking for the building superintendent, finally locating him in an apartment in the basement. He told me that the woman had been fired from her job, was two months behind in the rent, claimed she had no money, and swore to him that she would send the rent just as soon as she got back home to Houston.

Whether or not the mother and daughter were ever reunited I don't know. The little girl cried the entire trip out to the County Guardian's Home.

❖ ❖ ❖ ❖ ❖

Although child abandonment is much more common than most would suspect, children are not the only ones abandoned. There is also a new phenomenon in this country called "granny dumping." These are cases in which the caretakers of an elderly person, usually the children, not wanting to care for the person any longer, simply dump the elderly family member somewhere.

"It happens here probably once a month," said University of Chicago emergency-room physician Cai Glushak in an article in *Time*. "Before you can turn around, the person who registered the patient has gone. They've left no phone number, no address."[1]

"Not a day goes by when a hospital emergency room somewhere in America doesn't have a case where some elderly person has been abandoned, usually by the children," said John Meyers, a spokesperson for the American Association of Retired Persons.[2]

"It's shocking and terrible," said University of Chicago geriatrician Dr. Christine Cassell, talking about the dumping of the elderly, "but it doesn't surprise me at all. The families of Alzheimer's patients sometimes just give up in despair."[3]

The case, though, that undoubtedly brought the problem of "granny dumping" suddenly and dramatically to the public's attention was that of John Kingery, who made national headlines in 1992 after he was dumped by his daughter. Found sitting in a wheelchair next to the restrooms at the Coeur d'Alene Greyhound Park in Post Falls, Idaho, Mr. Kingery had been left with no identification, other than two typewritten notes attached to the side of his wheelchair that identified him as "John King." His daughter had cut the labels from his clothing, and had removed the identification marks from the wheelchair. When taken to a local hospital, Mr. Kingery, who suffers from Alzheimer's, talked to the physician about being a farmer, but could not remember his name.

Eventually, the personnel at a Portland, Oregon, nursing home recognized Mr. Kingery from pictures the police had released to the media. The authorities later discovered that Mr. Kingery's daughter had removed him from his nursing home in Portland when personnel at the nursing home began questioning her about irregularities in her father's finances. She checked him into another Portland nursing home for a short time, and then checked him out of that home and drove 320 miles to the racetrack in Idaho to dump him in an attempt to make him "disappear" and to escape any further questioning about the misuse of his money. A court eventually convicted the daughter of kidnapping and theft. She was reported to have stolen almost $10,000 of her father's pension money.

This case shows how family abuse can involve several types of abuse with the same victim. While the Kingery incident originally involved only financial abuse, once the daughter took Mr. Kingery out of the nursing home and drove him to Idaho to dump him, it also became neglect. Although the court convicted the daughter only of kidnapping and theft, this doesn't mean she also wasn't guilty of neglect. She was, but just not in the legal sense. As it turned out, dumping her father as she did, unbelievably, was not against the law at that time in Idaho. The kidnapping charge arose from the daughter's actions in Oregon.

"To me, it's a sin and a crime," said Post Falls police detective Harlan Fritzsche, "but I'm left in a quandary." There is no law in Idaho against abandoning the elderly.[4]

Neglect of a child or an elderly person, however, can end much worse than Mr. Kingery's case did. In June 1995, in McMinnville, Tennessee, a woman drove to a local motel, left her two children, age one and two, strapped in the car, and then partied in one of the motel rooms with her boyfriend and three other men. The mother apparently drank too much, passed out, and left the young children in the car for eight to ten hours, during which time the temperature inside the car reached an estimated 120 degrees.

Autopsies showed that both children died of hyperthermia, or overheating. Tragically, the father of the children had recently filed for divorce and requested custody of the children, saying he believed that his wife drank too much. A court convicted the mother of two counts of aggravated child abuse, each of which, in Tennessee, carries a penalty of fifteen to twenty-five years in prison.

In a case in Indianapolis, the police charged a woman with neglect of a dependent after she confessed to dumping her four-year-old son's body along Interstate 65 in northern Indiana. She admitted that she had left her four-year-old home alone for at least a week, and found him dead when she finally returned to check on him. Just as bad, in circumstances that didn't kill the victim, another mother recently received six months in jail for locking her seven-month-old baby in a closet and then leaving Indianapolis to visit friends in Louisville, Kentucky. The infant's grandmother, fortunately, rescued the baby twenty-four hours later when she heard noises coming from the closet.

The preceding case and the one from McMinnville, Tennessee, demonstrate how laws and penalties vary widely from state to state. While the mother in Tennessee received a fairly severe sentence, the woman who locked her baby in the closet, and who showed the same lack of concern as the woman in Tennessee did, received a very minor sentence. It would take a large book to list and compare all of the abuse laws from the different states. What a person can be arrested for in one state may not even be illegal in the next state. Because of this, readers would do well to contact their state attorney general's office or a local abuse prevention agency to find out what the laws in their state are in relation to family abuse.

As several of the cases above demonstrate, neglect kills many victims each year in this country. Between 1992 and 1994, according to *Current Trends in Child Abuse Reporting and Fatalities: Results of the 1994 Annual Fifty State Survey*, 42 percent of all the children who died in this country from maltreatment died from neglect. Also, according to the above study, neglect is nationally three times more prevalent than physical abuse, and six times as prevalent as sexual abuse. All of these figures point to the tragic fact that neglect of family members is a problem of unbelievable proportions.[5] And while authorities have a fair estimate of how many children die each year from neglect, sadly, no one really knows how many elderly people die each year from neglect, because their passing, since they were elderly and often ill, is many times attributed to "natural causes."

"The problem is that no one really cares about the elderly," said Monty Combs, an investigator for Adult Protective Services in Indiana. "They are a lost generation."

While the outcomes of neglect I've discussed so far are extreme, though still much too common in our country, there are other outcomes of neglect that are not quite as shocking, but just as disturbing. A study reported in the National Institute of Justice's research paper *The Cycle of Violence* found that childhood victims of neglect were significantly more likely than nonneglected children to be arrested as adults. This held true for both males and females. The Office of Juvenile Justice and Delinquency Prevention's booklet *Child Abuse: Prelude to Delinquency* states that a number of studies of institutions for delinquents around the country show that the majority of the children confined to these institutions have been neglected.[6] A study reported in the *American*

Journal of Education said that: "Deficits are evident for maltreated children in areas of school outcomes, test scores, and grades."[7]

"Neglect is the biggest common denominator among the children that we see," said Margaret Nickish of St. Gabriel's School, a Philadelphia facility for delinquent boys.[8]

Attorney General Janet Reno, appearing on *Bill Moyers' Journal*, said that neglect was the cause of much of our country's youth crime and violence. "And it's not just a matter of children in poverty," she said. "There are some middle-class children who are not supervised in the afternoon and in the evening. It's a problem throughout America."[9]

A final type of neglect I need to talk about is probably considered passive neglect, yet it can do as much, or even more, damage than the other types of neglect. This is the neglect that occurs when pregnant women take illegal drugs. An unbelievable number of babies enter the world every year underweight, sickly, or already addicted because of illegal drugs the mother took while pregnant. How big of a problem is this? An article in *The Los Angeles Times* reports that in Los Angeles in 1991, 2551 babies were born addicted to drugs, an increase of 39 percent in just four years. And that is just in one community.[10] A *Chicago Tribune* article estimates that the number of babies exposed to illegal drugs in the womb is annually from 100,000 to 350,000 nationwide.

Even after the child is born, drug abuse can still figure into its neglect. When parents become involved in drugs, drugs are all they care about, and children with parents on drugs are often neglected. How bad can this neglect be? In Detroit the police recently discovered that a woman, in order to pay off a $1000 crack debt, gave her son to the drug dealer, who then used the boy as a drug runner.

Neglect, unlike some types of family abuse, is not that difficult to detect, but it can only be detected, and consequently corrected, by people who care enough to make it their business to check on the welfare of children and the elderly who may be at risk. Helping a child or elderly person who is suffering from neglect is everyone's responsibility.

As should be obvious from all of the information I have given in this chapter, neglect of family members is a very common, very damaging, and often fatal type of abuse in our country. In many ways it can be the most damaging type of family abuse, because while physical and sexual abuse are episodic, neglect is chronic.

7

Emotional Abuse and Control

In the spring of 1975, Hedda Nussbaum met attorney Joel Steinberg at a party given in East Hampton, Long Island. She found herself immediately attracted to him. "He had these bright, sparkly eyes and was very outgoing," Hedda told *People* magazine. "He was very intelligent, and I loved listening to him talk."[1] Hedda, a beautiful, well-educated, and quickly rising children's book editor at Random House, could not suspect that twelve years later her body and mind would be in ruins from a decade of almost unbelievable physical and emotional abuse. Nor could she suspect that twelve years later she would become Joel's alleged accomplice in the murder of their illegally adopted daughter, Lisa.

In 1976, Hedda moved into Joel's Greenwich Village apartment on West 10th Street. Immediately, Joel became Hedda's counselor and mentor. "I was so flattered," she said. "Here was this handsome, successful, intelligent lawyer taking such an interest in me."[2] With his help, she obtained several promotions and raises at Random House, and became known as a rising star. But then, two years into their relationship, the dark side of Joel began to emerge.

It began in March 1978 with a blow to the face. "Joel gave me a karate chop in the left eye," Hedda said. "But then he took me in his arms and hugged me, and it made me feel good that he was sorry."[3]

The blow, Hedda said, stunned her both physically and emotionally, but afterward, because Joel was so affectionate, she felt certain it would never happen again. But of course it did. A decade later, at Joel and Hedda's trial for Lisa's death, the prosecutor, in order to show Joel's propensity for violence, compiled a list of thirty-one incidents in which Joel had inflicted injuries on Hedda. These injuries included black eyes, broken ribs, a broken nose, a ruptured spleen, a cauliflower ear, a broken knee, damaged vocal cords, burns from a blow torch (to improve her coordination, Joel told her), lost and chipped teeth, severely damaged lips, hair ripped out, and a permanently damaged tear duct. A doctor who examined Hedda after her arrest said, "She was a wasted woman, like an old person who had cancer."[4]

As part of his physical abuse of Hedda, Joel also instituted certain "disciplines." These included not allowing Hedda to eat, making her beg for food, or forcing her to consume large quantities of water. He also often forced her to sleep on the floor or in the bathtub with no blanket, and to take ice-cold baths.

Like many victims, Hedda kept believing that the beatings and abuse would end. "I always thought each one was the last," she said. "I loved Joel so much I felt there was much more good between us than not."[5]

Just as damaging, though, as the physical abuse, and perhaps even more so, was Joel's emotional abuse of Hedda. Although in the first few years of their relationship he had built Hedda up and gave her confidence, he soon began criticizing her and tearing her down, telling her again and again that she wasn't meeting his standards. He started finding fault in everything she said and did, and would embarrass her in front of her friends. By this intense fault finding, Joel began systematically destroying Hedda's self-esteem, and, through this, making her more and more dependent on him. And even though extraordinarily harsh in his criticism of her, Joel was still able to persuade Hedda that what he was doing was for her own good, that it was part of his attempt to help her.

During their relationship, in addition to the physical and

emotional abuse, Joel and Hedda also began taking drugs, finally reaching the point where Joel freebased cocaine almost every night. It is the heavy use of cocaine that probably fed and intensified his paranoia. Joel convinced Hedda that there was an evil hypnotic cult out to get them, and that all of her family and friends belonged to this cult. Evil members lurked everywhere, he told her, and anything bad that happened to them was because of this cult. Joel warned Hedda that members of this cult could hypnotize a person instantly with just a look. Because of both her fear of Joel (from the many beatings) and her love and admiration of him (she would tell people that she believed Joel was God and could heal people with his touch), Hedda began breaking contact with, and then finally avoiding, her family and friends.

Eventually, Joel became completely obsessed with this hypnotic cult, who he truly believed could hypnotize simply by looking at a person. He became extremely sensitive to people staring at him, and he would often poke Hedda in the eye for this offense (which eventually led to the permanent damage to one of her tear ducts). Joel also forced Hedda to admit to the many sexual encounters he imagined she had had with the members of this cult, and to tell him in detail about the pornographic videos he claimed she had made with its members. Because of her cocaine-induced psychosis, Hedda went along with Joel's delusions, and eventually began sharing them.

"Cocaine causes people to be hypervigilant," said Dr. Michael Allen, assistant professor of medicine at New York University's School of Medicine. "With the amount Hedda and Joel were ingesting ... it's enough to say that their fantasies were complementary."[6]

What Dr. Allen is saying is the cocaine Joel took made him so paranoid that he constantly watched for anything people did which would fit into his paranoid fantasy, such as staring at him. In addition, since Hedda also used large amounts of cocaine, and was extremely subservient to Joel, she began sharing his paranoid fantasies.

Once the violence in their relationship began Hedda did everything she could to please Joel, yet still the beatings and

emotional abuse continued and grew worse. Hedda began missing more and more work because she didn't want anyone there to
see her injuries. Eventually, Random House fired her because of all
her absences. With no outside work, Hedda became more and
more dependent on Joel, and finally his prisoner. He forbade her
to leave the apartment without his permission, and she could only
talk on the telephone when he was listening in on the line. Joel told
her that the evil cult members could hypnotize her just by saying
the phrase "Teapot Hedda."

Although involved in a violent and abusive relationship, Joel
and Hedda tried for some time to conceive a child, but without
success. When a nineteen-year-old unwed mother contacted Joel
for legal aid in finding a home for her daughter, Joel decided he
had found a way to start a family. He charged the woman $500 and
then took the infant, named Lisa, home, but never legally adopted
her. On the night of 1 November 1987, Joel, deeply into the drug-
induced paranoia, struck Lisa so severely it caused a brain hemor-
rhage, from which she would eventually die. Joel did it, he said,
because she was staring at him. At Joel's trial for murder, a neuro-
pathologist said Lisa's injuries were similar to going through the
windshield in a car crash or falling from a three-story building.

What incensed so many people who followed the trial, however, was that, after knocking her unconscious, Joel left Lisa lying
on the bathroom floor and then went out to dinner with a friend,
leaving Hedda there with the injured girl. Although one might
expect that Hedda would have called for medical assistance for
Lisa during the three hours she was in the apartment while Joel
was at dinner, she didn't. By this time in their relationship, Hedda
was so much under Joel's control that she patiently waited for him
to return. "I didn't want to show disloyalty to Joel," she said,
explaining why she didn't call for medical help. "I thought Joel
would be able to restore her because I trusted he would do it when
he came back."[7]

When Joel did come back, however, he didn't restore Lisa.
Instead, he freebased cocaine and talked to Hedda until 6:30 the
next morning, and only then, after letting Lisa lie unconscious for
twelve hours on the bathroom floor, did he finally allow Hedda to

call 911. When medical personnel examined Lisa, and saw the extent of her injuries, they notified the police, who arrested both Joel and Hedda for Lisa's murder.

The charges against Hedda—whose once beautiful face now looked like that of an often-losing prize fighter, with a flattened nose and cauliflower ear—were eventually dropped. The prosecutor said he believed she had suffered so much physical and emotional abuse that she had been rendered incapable of murder or of acting to save Lisa. Hedda then became the prosecution's main witness against Joel, even though afterward the jurors would say that they gave no weight at all to her testimony since most believed she bore some of the responsibility for the crime.

The jury convicted Joel of first-degree manslaughter. He was disbarred and in March 1989 a judge sentenced him to 8⅓ to 25 years in prison. In January 1996, after spending nearly seven years in prison, Joel appeared for the first time before the New York State Parole Board. The board refused his request for parole.

Hedda, after the trial, underwent three plastic surgery operations in order to correct the years of physical abuse, and also became a patient at the Four Winds Psychiatric Center in Katonah, New York. Eventually, Hedda filed a civil suit against Joel, demanding $3.6 million for what she called twelve years of physical and emotional devastation.

❖ ❖ ❖ ❖ ❖

I used the Joel Steinberg/Hedda Nussbaum case in this chapter for several reasons. First, it shows the classic pattern of how physical abuse begins and then builds in a marriage or intimate relationship. In most cases, the battering starts out small and then increases over time to often grotesque levels, hardly believable to someone not familiar with this crime. Also, as in this case, the batterer is many times affectionate and apologetic afterward, making the victim believe that the violence was just an aberration and will never happen again, keeping the relationship together in spite of the violence. But more important, this case shows what almost all types of family abuse are about: power and control. Family abusers use violence, threats, intimidation, and other forms of abuse for one reason and one reason only: to control other family members. A former wife batterer recently wrote to the advice columnist Ann Landers. In his letter he said: "Control is the center of a wife batterer's existence. When the control of my spouse became threatened, I developed an inner rage that was overwhelming."[8]

A former abuse victim I spoke with told me: "Our life was 100 percent control. He had to know where I went, how long I was gone, who I had seen, and who I had spoken with. I wasn't allowed to answer the phone when he was gone, and sometimes he would call to see if I would answer it."

The Joel Steinberg/Hedda Nussbaum case also shows the classic pattern for how emotional abuse begins and then grows in a marriage or intimate relationship. This type of abuse also has only one objective: total control. The perpetrators begin the emotional abuse by criticizing the victims about everything imaginable, making the victims feel that they are worthless, and extremely lucky to have someone like the perpetrators to take care of them. The perpetrators also begin attempting to isolate the victims from family and friends so that they will have no outside support system, no one outside the relationship who can help bring clarity to what is actually happening. Usually, the perpetrators isolate the victims by constantly criticizing the victims' family and friends, or by convincing the victims that their family and friends are out to harm them or the relationship. The victims, both afraid of and under the control of the abuser, often then begin breaking contact with their family and friends. If this doesn't work, perpetrators also many times try to isolate the victims by making their family or friends feel uncomfortable or unwelcome, and, through this, make them not want to come back or have contact with the victim. Whichever way it is done, once isolation is in place, the victims are totally alone and dependent on their abusers—the perpetrators have complete control over the lives and actions of those they victimize. Then, when the abuse continues and grows, the people being victimized feel they are so low and worthless that they deserve it. And, being isolated, there is no longer anyone to turn to for help.

Interestingly, while abusers may appear to be powerful and almost omnipotent to those they victimize, in actuality perpetrators of family abuse often feel weak and insecure. They use and need the power they are able to exert over others to shore up these feelings of weakness and to give them a sense of being someone powerful.

According to researcher David Finkelhor: "Many abusers give a sense of being pathetic and ineffectual, not always people who would be described in objective terms as socially powerful. This is another commonality among the different kinds of abuse: Although they are acts of the strong against the weak, they seem to be acts carried out by abusers to compensate for their perceived lack or loss of power."[9]

This feeling of weakness and insecurity is why the police see a large number of abuse cases among families where the resources are scarce and the jobs held by providers menial and lacking in power. In the article "Force and Violence in the Family," researcher W. J. Goode states: "[M]arital violence emerges as a power tactic utilized by an individual who has relatively few resources in other realms."[10] Of course, this does not imply that poverty leads inevitably to abuse. Nor does it mean that family abuse doesn't also occur in marriages or intimate relationships where the participants are successful in their careers and in control of considerable resources. The case of Joel Steinberg and Hedda Nussbaum proves otherwise.

The case of Hedda Nussbaum and Joel Steinberg also struck a raw nerve with many people in the United States because most of them refused to believe that anyone, particularly an educated, upper-middle-class woman like Hedda, could be so completely under the control of someone like Joel. Few people could believe that a woman of Hedda's background could be so cowed that she would leave a young girl lying critically injured on the bathroom floor for twelve hours and not call for help, especially when Joel had left her alone with the injured girl for several hours while he went out to dinner. No one, most people believed, could have that kind of power over another person. But even more, people wondered why Hedda didn't just leave the relationship altogether.

Why would an educated, successful woman stay in such a violent relationship?

Actually, what Hedda did is not that unusual. She truly wasn't crazy. There is an explanation for it. An article in the June 1994 *Journal of Interpersonal Violence* by Christopher R. Goddard and Janet R. Stanley proposed that abuse victims react and respond similarly to hostages.[11] This started me thinking about an explanation for the behavior displayed by Hedda Nussbaum.

Police officers see this type of behavior millions of times in the millions of family abuse cases they are called to. The victims, like Hedda, have many times suffered horrendous physical and emotional abuse for years, yet refuse to leave the relationship, even though urged and given the opportunity to do so by the police. I believe that their behavior can be explained by a phenomenon often encountered by police SWAT teams during hostage incidents that have gone on for a long time, a phenomenon called the Stockholm syndrome. This syndrome causes people involved in violent situations—both perpetrators and victims—to develop positive, caring relationships for each other, despite abusive treatment.

This syndrome, named after a hostage incident that took place in 1973 at the Sveriges Kreditbank in Stockholm, Sweden, can develop whenever hostages and hostage takers spend long hours together under danger and stress. Ironically, even though the hostages are taken prisoner by force, often treated roughly at first, and many times threatened with death, hostages will often begin developing affectionate and long-term feelings for their captors, and vice versa. But in order for the Stockholm syndrome to develop there must be positive contact between the hostages and hostage takers, as Hedda said there often was between her and Joel in the intervals between the beatings, and as many times occurs in even the worst cases of family abuse. Often abusers will use force against the people they victimize, hold them in the relationship against their will, and even threaten to kill them if they try to leave. Yet still, even the most horribly abusing family members will many times be tender and loving between the episodes of abuse.

At the beginning of the incident in Stockholm (which lasted ten days) the hostage takers treated the hostages roughly, refused them food and bathroom privileges, held them at gunpoint, and often threatened to kill them. After a few days, though, the hostage takers started treating the hostages better, gave them considerable freedom to move around, and finally began treating them more as friends than as hostages. This type of positive treatment, research shows, is what causes the Stockholm syndrome to develop. When the incident at the Sveriges Kreditbank in Stockholm finally ended and the hostages were freed, both hostages and captors had developed close personal relationships with each other. One of the hostages even later became engaged to one of the hostage takers.

Due to the Stockholm syndrome, hostages begin seeing the hostage takers as the good guys and the people who are trying to rescue them as the bad guys. In the case in Stockholm, for example, one of the hostages, in a telephone call to the Swedish Prime Minister, claimed that their abductors were not holding them hostage, but rather were protecting them from the police. The police see this same attitude very often in family abuse incidents. Even though the police come only to help, they are often met by hostile and uncooperative victims, who see the police as the bad guys.

How strong is this bond that can develop? Probably the most famous case of the Stockholm syndrome was Patty Hearst. This young heiress, who was kidnapped and held hostage by a group of terrorists, eventually joined the group and took part in a bank robbery with them. In Indianapolis, we had a case that demonstrated very graphically the enormous strength of the Stockholm syndrome. The police SWAT team had responded to a hostage-taking incident in a high-rise office building, and during it, unknown to the hostage or hostage taker, the police positioned a surveillance team with high-power binoculars in a building across the street. When the incident, after many hours, finally began coming to an end, the hostage taker, in a telephone call to the authorities, told them to give him a few minutes and he'd come out and surrender. The SWAT officers then watched in disbelief as the hostage and hostage taker both suddenly stripped naked, fell to the floor, and made love. Victims involved in long-term family abuse situations often have bonds just this strong, and will remain fanatically attached to their abusers, even though they have experienced tremendous violence and abuse at their hands.

The Stockholm syndrome, it has been found, is a long-term condition that is believed by many experts, like a knee-jerk reaction, to be beyond the control of the victim. Many people who have been held hostage for a long time tell afterward of finding themselves cooperating with the hostage takers much more than they would ever have thought possible. Hostages have afterward even set up defense funds for the hostage takers, and have visited the hostage takers in prison. A paper prepared for the FBI Training Academy tells of a study in which a question was asked of a number of former hostages. They were asked what they would do if an easily identifiable police officer, who had stormed the hostage site, ordered them to get down, but the hostage taker ordered them to stand. The overwhelming majority said that they would obey the hostage taker. Long-term victims of family abuse also find that they cannot explain or understand the attachment they have for the abuser. It is just there.

Because of the strong effects of the Stockholm syndrome, training officers warn police SWAT team members to question any information given by released hostages, as the hostages will sometimes lie in order to help the hostage takers. Of course, this is an action also seen many times in family abuse cases. The victims often claim that they have run into doors or have accidentally fallen, rather than tell how they really got the bruise, the black eye, or the broken nose, and possibly get the abusers in trouble.

Training officers also warn police SWAT team members that, because of the effects of the Stockholm syndrome, when storming a hostage site they must anticipate bizarre actions by the hostages, such as jumping between the police and the hostage takers, or grabbing a police officer's gun. Bizarre behavior is also common in family abuse incidents. Practically every police officer with any experience at all can tell tales of being attacked by a family abuse victim when the officer tried to arrest the abuser, even though a moment before the victim may have been demanding the abuser's arrest. I have had this happen to me and it is very disconcerting and confusing. This type of behavior is what leads many police officers to mistakenly believe that some family abuse victims must like and desire the abuse. Few officers realize that the behavior is actually the result of a very complex relationship.

As for the question of why Hedda Nussbaum didn't just leave, again police SWAT teams see this behavior many times in long-term hostage incidents. Often, once the Stockholm syndrome has developed, the hostages, because they have developed a positive relationship with the hostage takers, are given much more freedom to move around. Yet still many don't escape, even when they have good opportunity to do so. In the case of Patty Hearst, for example, she had many chances in the latter part of her relationship with her captors to escape, but didn't.

Finally, the Stockholm syndrome knows no social class. Anyone can be affected by it, regardless of class, financial status, or educational level. Even those who know about and have observed the Stockholm syndrome are many times not immune from its effects. One of the jobs of a police SWAT team secondary hostage negotiator is to watch over the primary hostage negotiator. The primary hostage negotiator often spends hours and hours talking with a hostage taker, and, because of this, even though a highly trained professional, he or she can easily fall under the influence of the Stockholm syndrome.

While the Stockholm syndrome probably doesn't apply to every case of long-term family abuse, I believe it does to the majority of them, and recognizing this makes the actions of family abuse victims less "crazy" and more understandable. It makes sense of some of the bizarre behaviors displayed by family abuse victims. Although few abusers are probably aware of the syndrome, or have even heard of it, they nevertheless use its effects to control other family members. Control is what the abusers crave.

In order to gain this control, victimizers often use emotional abuse, as shown in the Joel Steinberg/Hedda Nussbaum incident above, in tandem with physical abuse. One is used to support and enhance the effects of the other. Occasionally, however, emotional abuse becomes the only controlling force.

"The distinction between physical and emotional abuse may be more artificial than real," says Gayla Margolin of the University of Southern California. "Even when physical abuse ceases, emotional abuse may play a significant role in sustaining terror in the victim."[12]

As stated above, occasionally physical abuse is no longer possible, and emotional abuse then becomes the only weapon available to family abusers. The police find, however, that seldom do abusers give up using physical violence out of any feelings of remorse. More often, this comes about because the abusers have been arrested and sentenced by the court to probation or to a treatment program, with the added threat that any more physical violence will result in jail time. When the perpetrators realize that they can no longer physically abuse their victims without endangering their own freedom, they find other methods to maintain total control over those they victimize. They turn to using emotional abuse with a new, horrible intensity.

Former physical abusers, under the threat of jail, will use emotional abuse to sustain fear in their victims because even though emotional abuse in certain forms, such as sending threats through the mail, is clearly against the law, many types of emotional abuse are not illegal. A spouse who makes threatening gestures or gives threatening looks is usually not breaking any law. And often any verbal threats made by an abuser take place only when the abuser and victim are alone, reducing proof of the abuse to one person's word against another's. Emotional abuse can be a powerful weapon for a perpetrator who wants to maintain control, but doesn't want to leave any proof of the abuse.

This emotional abuse can include threatening to kill or take away the children, threatening suicide, threatening or actually destroying property, threatening to move out and take all of the money, or threatening the victim's family. An article in *Ebony* tells of an abused woman named Sandra Majors, who is now on the board of the Washington, D.C. Coalition Against Domestic Violence. Ms. Majors's husband's method of emotional abuse included abusing her cat, threatening to blow up her parents' home, and making her sign "weight contracts" in which she promised to lose a certain number of pounds.[13] In a Pulitzer Prize-winning series of articles about domestic violence in Kentucky, which appeared in the *Lexington Herald-Leader*, one report tells of an emotional abuser who would very conspicuously and ceremoniously clean firearms in front of his family in order to intimidate them.[14]

While physical abuse can cause pain and suffering, often the effects of emotional abuse can be far worse. An article in the *Journal of Marriage and the Family* tells of a study in which researchers interviewed 130 abused women. Of the women who suffered both physical and verbal abuse, 77 percent said that the verbal abuse was more difficult to deal with. One woman in the study wrote: "Bruises, cuts, etc. heal within a short time. When you listen to someone tell you how rotten you are and how nobody wants you day after day, you begin to believe it. Verbal abuse takes years to heal, but before that happens, it can ruin every part of your life."[15]

Yet, even though perpetrators will use any type and any level of abuse in order to control their victims, few will take responsibility for their actions or admit the real reason for it. When confronted about their actions, many family abusers will tell the police and other authorities that the victims drove them to it, that the victims put them under such stress they simply couldn't help themselves. This excuse is particularly absurd. These same abusers don't verbally or physically assault their bosses when they put them under stress. They don't assault the police officers who put them under stress by confronting them about the abuse. Perpetrators use physical and emotional abuse for one reason: to gain control over people they know *they can get away with using it on*. An article in *Corrections Today* tells of an abuse prevention program used in the Dauphin County, Pennsylvania, prison system. In this program a female facilitator confronts abusive men, shouts at them, and acts intimidating. Afterward, the men are asked why they didn't verbally assault or hit the woman as they did their wives when the female facilitator did exactly the same thing the men claimed their wives had done to instigate the abuse they were incarcerated for. The almost universal answer by the abusive men is that they knew they couldn't get away with it, and that it wouldn't have given them control over the situation.[16]

How much control over their victims do abusers want? Victims often report that abusers will regularly go through their wallets or purses, make them account for every second of the day, every cent they have spent, and every person they have spoken to. Jealousy, it turns out, is a large part of the reason the abusers are attempting to intimidate and control their victims. Abusers, while perhaps appearing strong and powerful to their victims, actually often feel weak and insecure, and are convinced that their spouses or intimate partners are going to leave them for someone else. Because of this, the abusers many times imagine that their victims are involved in all sort of sexual liaisons with everyone imaginable, as Joel Steinberg did with Hedda Nussbaum. Abusers have been known to beat their victims until they admit to some imaginary affair, which, of course, then only feeds the abusers' jealousy. Amazingly, abusers also see any time that their victims spend with friends, family members, and even their own children as a threat to them. At first, in the early stages of a relationship, many victims feel flattered by this jealousy. It makes them feel really cared for. But soon this caring becomes a dark obsession. The victims of emotional abuse find that no matter what they say or do they can never convince their abusers that they are faithful.

"My husband was convinced I was seeing the sixteen-year-old boy across the street," a former abuse victim told me. "I did everything I could to convince my husband I was faithful. I even cut off my hair and stopped wearing makeup. It didn't help."

Emotional abuse, however, can go far beyond just intense jealousy and demeaning words. It can also include actions intended to intimidate. Stalking, which has just in the last decade become a common term in American society, can be used as a potent means to supplement and intensify emotional abuse and control. Stalking, according to the laws in many states, is defined as: "A knowing or intentional course of conduct involving repeated or continuing harassment of another person. This conduct, to be criminal, must be such as would cause a reasonable person to feel terrorized, intimidated, or threatened."

Stalking can be a potent weapon in the hands of an emotional abuser. Even if the abusers don't actually physically harm the victims, constantly showing up wherever the victims go and making intimidating gestures or statements can be enough to cause great fear and emotional harm, as the following incident demonstrates.

❖ ❖ ❖ ❖ ❖

Ten years or so before the term *stalking* became common in America's vocabulary, I had a case that demonstrated to me just how far stalkers will go in the attempt to terrorize their victims. One afternoon, when I worked as a uniformed district officer, I and another unit received a run described by the dispatcher as "an ex-husband threatening his ex-wife." The dispatcher then added the warning: "The victim said that her ex-husband is walking around the outside of her house right now carrying a scythe."

When I and the other unit arrived at the address of the run we found a rather thin but determined-looking man standing in the front yard of a house shouting and waving a scythe (we later discovered that he worked as a weed cutter for a construction company). Since just a few weeks before we had had an officer in Indianapolis killed during a domestic disturbance, most of us went to these runs with electricity in our veins. With our hands on our guns, we ordered him to put the scythe down, which he did immediately. We then placed him in the backseat of my police car, and, while the other officer watched him, I went into the house to talk with the man's ex-wife.

The couple had been divorced, I found, for almost five years. Yet still, she told me, her ex-husband had been showing up at her house and threatening her almost weekly. She also told me that, because of her ex-husband, she had moved four times during the last five years. Somehow, she said, he always seemed to be able to find out where she lived, and would show up continually.

In those days we had no law against stalking, and the

stalker's ex-wife really didn't want to prosecute him anyway. All she wanted was just for her ex-husband to leave her alone. She told me that during their marriage he had often physically abused her and that he had had several extramarital affairs. But still, she said, she felt sorry for him. While she didn't want him to go to jail, she said she feared that some day he would hurt her. Legally, there wasn't much I could do. He hadn't physically harmed her. And so, I went back out to my car to talk with the man, who I found was now crying and pleading with the other officer not to take him to jail.

When he discovered that he wasn't going to jail, the man quickly regained his composure and told me that he still loved his ex-wife, and that he would never give up threatening her until she took him back. I found that the stalker lived almost ten miles away, had no money at all, and had walked over to his ex-wife's home. The best solution to the problem, I felt (though temporary at best), was to drive him back home. At least that would put some miles between him and his ex-wife, who said she was going to spend the night with some friends.

On the ride to the man's home we talked about his relationship with his ex-wife. Yes, he admitted, he had beaten his wife while they were married, but he insisted that the Bible said it was okay for a man to beat his wife. Having been raised by a very religious mother who saw to it that her children attended church regularly, and never having heard such claims before, I asked him for specific verses. He couldn't name them, but very self-confidently assured me that they were there, because he told me that his father had often quoted them when he beat his wife. As to having extramarital affairs, he grinned and said that this too was a male privilege condoned by the Bible, but again, I found, he couldn't quote me a specific passage or verse.

I tried to talk rationally with the man about giving up his quest for his ex-wife, since she obviously didn't want him back, and about the wisdom of his tactic of trying to threaten her into reconciling with him, hoping to be able to point out the obvious problems with this approach. However, I found that this man, as with most stalkers I have encountered since, seemed totally fixated on his victim, completely obsessed with the idea of getting his ex-wife back. She had married him, he said, and so she was his forever. He told me that he would never, as long as he lived, give his ex-wife a moment's peace until she took him back.

By the time I dropped him off at his residence I had had a truly frightening look into the mind of an obsessed and likely dangerous man. His quest to regain his wife totally dominated his thoughts. It was as if he felt he wouldn't be a real man again until he got her back. But most disturbing, he truly felt that what he was doing was not only morally and religiously correct, but his absolute right.

I don't know what became of their relationship, but at the time I felt that the stalking would end only if the victim moved far enough away so that he couldn't find her, or there occurred a tragic face-off that left the man arrested or dead. At that time, with no stalking laws, I didn't see any other outcome.

❖ ❖ ❖ ❖ ❖

Fortunately, since the time of the incident above, most states have passed laws that would make this man's actions illegal. Yet, as anyone who follows the news knows, stalking has still become very popular in the last decade or so. This is true not just for big stars like Madonna or David Letterman, but also for ordinary people involved in relationships with unstable individuals. From my years of experience I would advise anyone who is stalked to call the police as soon as they become aware of it. Studies have shown that stalking usually goes through stages, building from minor incidents to major crimes. To ensure your safety, stop stalking early. Call the police immediately.

Unfortunately for the victims of stalking, the perpetrators, besides harassing them habitually at their homes, also often stalk them at their places of employment. Actually, in the cases of severe, prolonged stalking, where there is the greatest potential for harm, stalkers most often find their victims at the workplace. The victims, fearing for their lives, many times live with friends, at a hotel, or at some other place where the stalkers aren't able to find them. The stalkers, though, know that the victims must show up for work, and will often be there waiting for them.

"A stalker knows if they can't catch you at home, they can catch you at work," said Yvette Miller in a *Los Angeles Times* article. Ms. Miller had been stalked continuously at her place of employment by an ex-boyfriend.[17] Along with visiting and threatening their victims in the workplace, emotional abusers can also cause problems by telephoning their victims continuously at work, or by sending them embarrassing faxes that they know will be seen by others.

According to the Bureau of Justice Statistics's research paper *Female Victims of Crime*, 74 percent of employed female abuse victims are harassed by abusive husbands and intimate partners at work, either in person or on the telephone, often causing them to lose their jobs.[18] This loss of employment becomes particularly damaging because many of these women have left their abusive husbands or intimate partners and are working in an attempt to support themselves without the abusers. The stalkers know that the women will be much more willing to take them back if they are out of work and in need of money.

For the victims of emotional abuse who aren't employed, abusers often extend their dominance over them by controlling every aspect of the family finances. Doing this totally binds the victims to the abusers. Victims cannot escape without money or assets without extreme difficulty and hardship. Victims with children especially know that they cannot provide for the children without money. They are forced to choose between staying in the relationship or leaving the children behind with the abuser, something most are unwilling to do. This type of emotional abuse and control becomes even more effective after the abusers have cut the victims off socially from family and friends, because the victims then have absolutely no one to help them. Once the victims have been sufficiently isolated both socially and economically by the abusers, they are helpless. They have no job, no money, no credit of their own, no close friends, and no family members who will help them. The victims have almost no choice but to stay with their abusers.

Along with giving abusers total dominance over their intimate partners, the control gained through emotional abuse can
also be used as an avenue to incest. A study reported in *Child
Abuse and Neglect* stated that in interviews with forty men involved in incestuous relationships with their daughters or step-
daughters the men said that at the time of the incest their thoughts
were not just of sexual gratification but also of control, power, and
anger at everyone, as the following incident shows.[19]

❖ ❖ ❖ ❖ ❖

Thirteen-year-old Melissa Ellison, after attending a talk about
sexual molestation, told her middle school social worker that
she needed to speak with her. What Melissa said to the social
worker was so alarming she contacted the police, who then had a
child abuse detective meet with Melissa. Melissa told the detective
that her stepfather, Jeffrey Hazlett, had said that he wanted to
teach her about sex, and so he had been sitting daily in the parents'
bedroom with Melissa and her mother, Shirley Hazlett, and talking about sex. Soon after this started, Melissa said, her stepfather
also began wanting them to take off their clothes while they
talked.

"At first I didn't take everything off, just my shirt and pants,"
she told the child abuse detective. "I left my underwear on. But
then he began looking at me like he was mad, so I got scared and
took my underwear off. But I didn't want to."

"Does he have a temper?" the detective asked.

"Yeah, a real bad temper."

"So, you're afraid of him?"

"Uh huh."

"What does your mother think about all of this?"

"I don't think my mom wanted to go along with it either, but
I think she's scared of him too. He gets real mad sometimes."

The detective knew that incidents like this usually had a
tendency to increase in severity over time, and so she encouraged
Melissa to continue with her story.

"Well, one day while we're sitting there naked he pulled my
hand over and made me touch him."

"Where did he make you touch him?" the detective asked, knowing that specifics would be needed if a warrant was to be obtained.

Melissa couldn't answer for a few moments, but fiddled with her blouse and looked at the floor. Finally, she said, "You know, on his penis. But I moved my hand away real fast when he let go. Really, I did."

"Did anything else happen?"

"Well, he made me wear some of my mom's things."

"What kind of things?"

Squeezing her lips together for a moment and still fiddling with her blouse, Melissa finally told the detective, "You know, little see-through nighties and all." Tears began forming in Melissa's eyes. "He made me. I didn't want to."

"Where did you wear them?

"Just in the bedroom. He was afraid that if the other kids saw me they would know what was happening."

"Did he ever say what would happen if someone found out?"

Melissa nodded. "He told me that I wasn't ever supposed to tell anyone about this because he didn't want to get into trouble."

"Did you do all of these things because you were afraid of him?"

She gave a quick, hard nod of her head. "Yeah, he gets real mad sometimes. He get real mad and he throws and breaks stuff if you don't do what he says."

The detective then had Melissa's mother, Shirley Hazlett, in for questioning, and, after advising her of her rights against self-incrimination, asked her about the incidents Melissa had described. Shirley reluctantly admitted that it was all true.

"Why don't you just tell me what happened then," the detective said.

"Well, one day Jeffrey came to me and he said he wanted to teach Melissa about sex. He said that maybe me and him would do it in front of her, that she wouldn't have to do anything, just watch."

"What was your response to this idea?"

"Well, in some ways, you know, I wasn't so sure it was a good idea, but he just kept pushing. He's a real strong type of guy and he just won't let up if he wants you to do something. Sometimes I just can't say no to him."

"So the three of you just sat around there naked talking about sex?" the detective asked.

Shirley winced and looked down, but then nodded. "Yeah, at first."

"Okay, what happened then?"

"Jeffrey, he's a real pushy type of guy, and he told me he wanted me to jack him off in front of Melissa to show her what would happen."

"And what did you do?"

Again Shirley winced and continued to look down. "Well, I didn't want to do it, but Jeffrey just kept at me and wouldn't let up, so I finally did it."

The detective realized that Melissa had probably been too embarrassed to tell the total story of what had happened. "What else did Jeffrey have you do."

Suddenly, Shirley tried but couldn't seem to look at the detective, and instead kicked at the floor with her foot. "He wanted me to, you know, lick him in front of Melissa."

"Oral sex?"

Shirley nodded and continued kicking at the floor.

"And did you?'

"Yeah, I think I did," she mumbled.

"Did Jeffrey ever touch Melissa?"

"He made her touch his penis."

"Did he ever do anything else? Did he ever have intercourse with her?"

"No, I think he wanted to, but he was scared. You know, I knew from the start that we shouldn't have done any of this because it was wrong."

"Well then tell me, Mrs. Hazlett, if you knew it was wrong, why did you go along with it?"

"It's just that Jeffrey is, you know, so strong. You can't say no to him."

The detective discovered that Jeffrey totally controlled every aspect of his wife's life. She couldn't leave the house when he wasn't there and she couldn't talk on the telephone. Shirley said that she couldn't even go down to the store for laundry powder unless Jeffrey was with her. Through several years of emotional abuse, Jeffrey had gained complete control and dominance over his wife.

The prosecutor approved arrest warrants for both Jeffrey and Shirley Hazlett. In order to get probation and to keep from going to jail, Shirley pleaded guilty to child neglect and testified against Jeffrey. A court convicted Jeffrey of two counts of child molesting and sentenced him to four years in prison, a sentence fairly typical in Indiana for this type of offense. Sentences for child molesting, however, can vary widely from state to state.

❖ ❖ ❖ ❖ ❖

Spouses, intimate partners, and children aren't the only victims of emotional abuse. Abusers also often inflict emotional abuse on elderly family members. The abusers, in order to control the elderly, can use the same emotional abuse methods as with spouses and intimate partners, in which they physically threaten and then belittle and berate the victims, or they can use tactics and threats specifically designed to intimidate the elderly. These include such things as refusing to give elderly family members their glasses, hearing aids, or dentures. Abusers also often withhold food, water, and medicine from elderly family members in order to control them. But the most potent weapon an emotional abuser has to control elderly family members with is the threat that if they don't do as they're told they will be sent to a nursing home. This probably frightens elderly people more than any other threat, and is often used as a method of emotional abuse and control.

Emotional abuse is one of the most difficult types of abuse to deal with. A black eye or a busted lip is tangible evidence of abuse. Verbal and emotional abuse, on the other hand, while just as damaging, don't leave visible marks like this. Yet still, they also must be stopped. In order to do this, spouses, intimate partners, and other family members must insist that they always be treated with dignity and respect, and refuse to accept anything less.

As I've shown in this chapter, not only emotional abuse, but almost all types of family abuse have but one underlying reason: control. Perpetrators, because they often lack power elsewhere, use various types of family abuse to gain and then maintain total control and dominance over those they live with. Control is at the heart of almost every serious case of family abuse.

8

Murder

By Friday morning, Donna Montgomery, a bank loan officer, had been in hiding for almost a week from her husband, Robert. On Thursday, Robert had been served with divorce papers, and Donna well knew his explosive temper and cruel tendency toward violence. Physically and emotionally abusive throughout their thirteen-year marriage, Robert had once tied Donna up, put a gun in her mouth, and threatened to kill her. Also pathologically jealous, Robert always picked out Donna's clothing for her, would fly into a rage whenever she came home even minutes late from work, and refused to allow her to mingle with the other bank employees, even demanding that she pack her lunch every day rather than go out with them. When Donna called Robert on the telephone after leaving him, he told her that he had burned all of her clothing. He also told her that he was going to kill her and himself because marriage meant " 'til death do us part." Donna had been in hiding now for almost a week because she knew he meant it.

Other people who knew or had dealings with Robert Montgomery also feared him. A woman involved in a lawsuit against Robert had finally been forced to obtain a restraining order against him because he had harassed her in person and on the telephone. A former employer said of Robert, "He was the kind of guy who gives the automobile business its sometimes bad reputation."[1] To protect herself, besides hiding out with friends, Donna had also obtained a restraining order against Robert.

Even though in hiding, Donna had to work to support herself, and Robert knew this. Donna, however, apparently felt relatively safe at her job in the bank, assuming that Robert would not do anything violent in front of the people there. Also, all of Donna's fellow employees knew about Robert and his temper, and they had developed a set of signals and plans for what to do if he should show up. This feeling of safety, however, turned out to be a bad assumption.

On Friday morning, Donna returned to her job at the bank. At 9:30 A.M., Robert sped his black pickup truck into the bank parking lot, slammed on the brakes, and then raced into the bank in such a hurry that he left the engine running. Yanking out a .357 Magnum revolver as he stormed into Donna's private office, Robert ordered a male customer out. When the man quickly left, Robert shut the door and then shot Donna twice with the revolver, once in the stomach and once in the right temple. A few seconds later, standing in front of the desk where Donna now lay dead, Robert killed himself with a gunshot to the left temple.

"Her worst nightmare actually came true," said Donna's divorce attorney.[2]

Reportedly, Donna, in an attempt to escape Robert, had inquired about staying at several local women's shelters, but found they were all filled. In Donna's memory, her employer donated $25,000 to a local shelter for abused women.

❖ ❖ ❖ ❖ ❖

Every year in the United States, hundreds of spouses or intimates kill their partners. In the book *It Could Happen to Anyone*, authors Ola Barnett and Alyce LaViolette tell about a study of homicides followed by suicides, such as the one in the incident above involving Robert and Donna Montgomery. Of the cases studied, 85 percent involved family members.[3]

While Donna Montgomery had certainly done just about everything she felt she could to be safe, still she was murdered. Actually, it would have taken a concerted effort by both Donna and the police to have prevented this tragedy. Robert appeared to be on a mission of death, and was willing to give up his own life in order to accomplish it. Whenever potential murderers have decided they don't want to live any longer, but first want to kill the family members responsible for this feeling, it becomes very difficult, though not impossible, to stop them.

In 1994, statistics gathered by the FBI showed that family members or intimate partners committed over 15 percent of all the murders in the United States. During the same time, more than 28 percent of all the women murdered in the United States were killed by husbands or boyfriends.[4] But these spousal and intimate partner murders usually don't come about without some warning to those knowledgeable about abusive relationships. Most spousal or intimate partner murders occur, research shows, when one partner either states the intention of breaking up an abusive relationship or actually takes some action to sever it.

According to an article that appeared in *Time*: "Women are most in danger when they seek to put a firm end to an abusive relationship. Experts warn that the two actions most likely to trigger a deadly assault are moving out of a shared residence, and beginning a relationship with another man." The same article said researchers have distinguished two types of men who are most likely to kill their wives: the "loose cannon" with impulse control problems, as in the incident at the beginning of this chapter, and those who are calculated and focused, whose heart rate drops as they prepare to do violence to their partners.[5] The police in Madison County, Indiana, recently had a case that apparently involved just such an individual. They arrested a man and charged him with attempting to kill his estranged wife, with whom he was involved in a bitter divorce and custody battle. According to the police, the man allegedly built and then placed a pipe bomb under his wife's car. Luckily, the man's wife heard the bomb dragging as she backed her car up. When she got out and saw the device, she called the police. Bomb experts removed the device and safely detonated it.

While severing an abusive relationship is a dangerous time, spouses and live-in intimate partners still often move out and then back in several times before finally severing the tie for good. "It takes about five to seven times before the woman leaves the relationship for good, but every time a woman leaves, she is moving closer to the final exit," said Anna Kosof in her book *Battered Women: Living with the Enemy*.[6] Unfortunately, by the time a woman decides the relationship is over the battering has often reached horrendous levels, and leaving often results in a murder.

Explaining this drive toward murder, the author of *Next Time, She'll Be Dead*, Ann Jones, says: "Absolutely dependent on her submission for his own sense of power and control, he cannot bear to lose her. In many cases, this false sense of power is the only identity a man has; to lose 'his woman' is to lose himself. Thus, he is far more likely to kill her (and perhaps himself as well) as she tries to leave or *after she has left*, than if she stays with him."[7] Supporting this idea, the Bureau of Justice Statistics's research paper *Violence Against Women* states that 75 percent of the women who are killed by spouses in the United States lose their lives after a separation. In addition, a 1982 study of men who had killed spouses or intimate partners found that the most common reasons given for the murders were that the men felt rejected or they felt they were unable to control what the women did. According to the National Woman Abuse Prevention Project: "Murder is … the ultimate expression of the batterer's need to control a woman's behavior."

What do the victims of family abuse need to know so that when they do leave an abusive relationship it won't end tragically, as Donna Montgomery's relationship did in the incident at the beginning of this chapter? Donna made two wrong assumptions. First she thought a restraining order would protect her. These orders (which also include no-contact orders, protection orders, and peace bonds) are just pieces of paper, not some invisible armor. They will only stop people who have respect for the law, who have a clear mind, and who feel threatened by the consequences of violating them. This often isn't the case for jealous and enraged spouses and intimate partners, who instead many times see these orders as a challenge to the legitimacy of their claim on the other person.

"A restraining order is a way of getting killed faster," said Dr. Park Dietz, a forensic psychiatrist. "Someone who is truly dangerous will see this as an extreme denial of what he's entitled to, his God-given right."[8] In other words, a restraining order tells abusers they no longer have the control they crave so dearly. Since many abusers truly believe that spouses or intimate partners are theirs to do with as they wish, and a restraining order takes this power away, many no longer see any point in living and will do desperate things, as Robert Montgomery did.

And yet, while a restraining order will not protect anyone against a person with murderous intent, obtaining one is still important. It can serve as the basis for police intervention in the event they catch the abuser violating it before he or she has attempted any violence. Still, these orders should *never* be thought of as any kind of real protection against violence.

The second wrong assumption Donna Montgomery made was believing she would be safe at her place of work. She couldn't have been more wrong. Homicide, according to the Bureau of Labor Statistics, was the second leading cause of workplace fatalities in 1994. For women it was the number one cause.

Just as dangerous as the workplace, though, and probably even more so, is the victim's home. According to the Bureau of Justice Statistics's research paper *Violence between Intimates*, 86 percent of all spousal murders occurred in the home. Actually, no place where an abuser with murderous intent can find the victim should ever be considered safe, as the following incidents demonstrate.

❖ ❖ ❖ ❖ ❖

Shirley Lowery had recently fled from her live-in companion, Benjamin Franklin, and had gone into hiding. Requesting a temporary restraining order against the man, she said in her complaint: "He raped me and threatened my life. He has raped me before and threatened me with a gun. He follows me twenty-four hours every day and threatens my life." Friends and family of Shirley said that her former live-in companion had stalked her, and followed her wherever she went. He also threatened to kill Shirley and her entire family if she left him.

On 9 March 1992, Shirley walked into a Milwaukee, Wisconsin courthouse, a building full of uniformed police officers, where she was scheduled to appear before a Family Court Commissioner concerning her request for a permanent injunction against Mr. Franklin. She didn't make it to court. Just a few feet away from the courtroom, her former live-in companion attacked her, stabbing her nineteen times with a butcher knife and killing her.

"My mother had so much confidence in the courthouse," Shirley's daughter, Vanessa Davis, said. "But if you can't go to the courthouse, what kind of hope do these women have?"[9]

A similar case occurred only weeks later in a suburban St. Louis courtroom. Ken Baumruk was attending his divorce hearing, when suddenly, as his estranged wife's attorney began speaking, Ken pulled two pistols from a briefcase he carried, shot and killed his estranged wife, Mary, and then shot both his and his estranged wife's attorney. Racing out of the courtroom, Ken next shot a bailiff and a security guard. Moments later, several police officers shot and critically wounded Ken.

❖ ❖ ❖ ❖ ❖

Clearly, spousal and intimate partner murderers are dangerous not just to the intended victims. Often, when spouses or intimates intend to kill a partner, they don't care who's there or what kind of danger they put others in, even close family members, as the following incident shows.

In June 1994, Joselina Quezada went to the 34th Precinct police station in the Washington Heights section of Manhattan and reported that her husband, Thomas Rodriquez, had punched her, pulled her hair, and taken her purse. Three weeks earlier, Thomas, an unemployed furniture mover, had moved out of the apartment he shared with his wife and two small children. The police attempted to find Thomas, but couldn't locate him.

Obviously concerned for her and her children's safety, Joselina moved out of their apartment and in with her mother. However, Thomas knew where Joselina's mother lived. Crouching in the stairwell of his mother-in-law's apartment building, Thomas waited for Joselina to come out. When she eventually walked out of the apartment, carrying her infant son, her three-year-old son walking at her side, Thomas leaped out of the stairwell and shot Joselina four times as she held their infant son in her arms. She dropped the baby as she fell to the hallway floor, dead from the gunshot wounds. Thomas then put the .38 caliber revolver up to his own head and killed himself.

When a neighbor peeked out after hearing the shots, he saw the three-year-old holding the revolver. The little boy told the neighbor, "Papi shot Mami."[10]

❖ ❖ ❖ ❖ ❖

Even more dangerous than incidents such as the one above, where other family members are put in danger by happening to be close by, spouses and intimates with murderous intent often decide not only to kill their intimate partners, but also other family members as well. In September 1995, for example, a man estranged from his wife took her and their three children to a shopping mall in Essex, Maryland, on the pretext of buying the children school clothing. Instead, in the shopping center parking lot, he blew up their car, killing all five of them.

In Anaheim, California, a man argued with his wife about her desire to get a job. He felt that he made enough money without having her work. She insisted, however, that she wanted to get a job and have a life outside of the home. The man took his four small children into a bedroom, spread a flammable fluid around the room, and then burned all of them to death.

In Long Beach, California, in February 1995, the police charged Donna J. Fleming with the death of her one-year-old son. In a little over a year's time the police had been called six times to Donna's home because of domestic fights. Allegedly despondent over the violent relationship she shared with her husband, Donna tossed her two sons, aged three and one, into the Los Angeles river from the Ocean Boulevard bridge, and then jumped in after them. Rescuers saved her and her three-year-old son.

❖ ❖ ❖ ❖ ❖

As the three cases above demonstrate, children are often the victims of deadly family abuse. Unfortunately, the murder of a child by a parent is very common in the United States. While practically everyone in America has heard of the Susan Smith case in South Carolina, in which the young mother pushed her car, with her two little boys still strapped inside, into a lake, this wasn't by any means a unique or isolated case. In August 1995, Dayton, Ohio, police arrested Therressa Ritchie and a neighbor for the killing of Therressa's daughter, Samantha. For four days the police had knocked on doors, searched the nearby woods, and handed out leaflets containing Samantha's picture. Therressa, like Susan Smith, had gone on television and gave several sobbing interviews about her daughter's disappearance. The police, however, said that, upon questioning, Therressa and the neighbor confessed to killing Samantha, and led them to the body.

In West Palm Beach, Florida, Pauline Zile went on television tearfully pleading for the return of her seven-year-old daughter, Christina, who she said had been abducted from the restroom of a flea market in Ft. Lauderdale. Eventually, however, John Zile, Pauline's husband and Christina's stepfather, led the police to the little girl's body, which had been buried in a field about ten miles from where John and Pauline lived. The little girl had reportedly been beaten to death by the stepfather for soiling her pants.

❖ ❖ ❖ ❖ ❖

Often, rather than deliberate murder, as in the above incidents, child victims die as a result of long-term abuse and neglect. According to the U.S. Attorney General's Task Force on Family Violence: "During infancy and the early preschool years, when child abuse is of lesser visibility, the life-threatening quality of physical abuse is much greater. A substantial majority of all known child abuse fatalities occur before the age of five, and the rate of such fatalities per thousand children is far higher in the early years."[11]

The report *Current Trends in Child Abuse Reporting and Fatal-*

ities: The Results of the 1993 Annual Fifty State Survey states that in 1992 the various child protective services in the United States confirmed 1299 child abuse and neglect-related fatalities nationwide. Fifty-one percent of these deaths were by abuse, 43 percent by neglect, and 6 percent by a combination of the two. According to the U.S. Advisory Board on Child Abuse and Neglect, however, at least 2000 children, most of them four or younger, die each year from parental abuse and neglect, with the fathers more often killing through abuse and the mothers through neglect. The report said: "Abuse and neglect has become one of the biggest threats to the lives of infants and small children in America."[12]

A study reported in the journal *Child Abuse and Neglect* recently substantiated the preceding statement. This research matched 11,085 abused children against a control group of nonabused children. Researchers found that the abused children had three times the risk of death as the nonabused children.[13]

These deaths from abuse and neglect, researchers find, are often connected both to the economy and to drug abuse. "There seems to be a connection between child homicides and the economy," said Deanne Tilton, executive director of the Inter-Agency Council on Child Abuse and Neglect. "As many families slip into poverty and the stresses on these families increase, so does the risk that children in these families will be exposed to drugs, abuse, and other forms of violence."[14] As to the effect of drug usage on the rate of child abuse and neglect, an article in the *Washington Post* states: "Increasingly, drug abuse plays a part in many child abuse deaths, figures show, as many parents are too whacked out to know or care how they are treating their children."[15]

Quite often, though, family members kill infants, not so much through neglect, as through not knowing or respecting how fragile a baby is. Infants are particularly susceptible to injury from shaking and other rough treatment. Roughly shaking a baby causes the infant's head, which is not as well supported as an adult's, to violently jerk back and forth. Doing this smashes the brain against the inside of the skull and tears tissue and blood vessels. Shaken baby syndrome, as discussed earlier, is an extraordinarily common crime in the United States. It often occurs when someone shakes a baby out of rage and frustration when the baby is crying. In Easton, Pennsylvania, James Alan Austin, a bank analyst and bachelor who apparently wanted a family, paid the Infertility Center of America $30,000 to inseminate a woman with his sperm. James then took a boy born from this insemination home to raise. A little over a month later, the child died at the Children's Hospital of Philadelphia from a fractured skull and internal head injuries. The infant apparently had an ear infection and cried constantly. James admitted he beat the child and hit him with a plastic coat hanger to stop his crying. An autopsy concluded the infant died of shaken baby syndrome.

Some parents can react even more drastically and horribly to a crying baby. A mother in Chicago, apparently under tremendous personal pressure, took her sixteen-month-old son, who wouldn't stop crying, into the bedroom of an eighth-floor apartment where she was visiting with friends. The residents of the apartment heard breaking glass, and when they rushed into the bedroom they found that the woman had thrown her baby out through the window. The infant, wearing only a diaper, was found dead on the muddy ground below.

Occasionally, a parent, often an unwed mother, will murder an infant to hide the fact the child was born at all. In New York City, the police charged Violeta Castellanos with the murder of her infant daughter. Her family, not knowing she was even pregnant, was at home but unaware she had given birth to a full-term baby girl. Police allege she put her hand over the baby's mouth and nose until it died.

In Boynton Beach, Florida, the police charged a father with killing a child he had conceived during an incestuous relationship with his daughter. The twelve-year-old daughter delivered the baby on the bathroom floor, and the father first tried unsuccessfully to drown the infant, and then buried it alive in the backyard. Police dug up the baby's remains.

While parents more often kill their children, children also do kill their parents. In November 1992, John Lahtinen, age 44, and his father, Ray Lahtinen, age 82, got into an argument in their four-story, brick co-op in Brooklyn. During the argument, the son apparently beat his father so badly that (after waiting five days) he took his father to Maimonides Medical Center. The elder Mr. Lahtinen eventually succumbed to the injuries he sustained in the fight. Several neighbors of the father and son said that it was not unusual for them to become involved in loud arguments.

Arguments aren't the only reason that children kill their parents. Sometimes it's money. In Fort Wayne, Indiana, nineteen-year-old David W. Liechty pleaded guilty to killing his father by shooting him twice in the head with a shotgun, and then setting a fire to cover up the crime. The son allegedly killed his father in order to inherit $200,000.

Along with spouses and intimate partners killing each other, and parents and children killing each other, siblings also often strike out fatally at each other. In Washington State, a teenager's behavior reportedly became so violent that his mother, in constant fear of him, slept with a baseball bat under her bed. It didn't save her. The police charged the sixteen-year-old youth with killing his mother and drowning his five-year-old brother.

Twin sisters Dorothea and Mary Margaret Beck, 68 years old, had never married, worked at the same hospital, and had always lived in the same home in Alton, Illinois. The sisters, though twins, were very much different. A neighbor said of them, "The little one, who died, she seemed like the humble one. The big one would raise hell all the time. Some days she would fuss and cuss and carry on all day."

In November 1995, Dorothea called the police, who, upon arriving, found Mary Margaret's body in the home. An autopsy showed that Mary Margaret had died from a beating, the result (police found later) of her refusal to eat. The autopsy also showed signs of previous beatings. The police charged Dorothea with first-degree murder.[16]

Family murders don't occur just between close blood relatives like parents, children, and siblings. Less closely related relatives are also at risk. In November 1995, fourteen-year-old Rachel Doss pleaded guilty to killing her three-year-old nephew, Rueben Traylor. Rachel reportedly took her sister's three-year-old son along when she ran away from home.

Rachel and a sixteen-year-old girlfriend, Carolyn Langston, spent the first week after running away from home partying with several traveling salesmen at the USA Inn on the east side of Indianapolis. The girls, however, while enjoying the partying, eventually tired of taking care of three-year-old Rueben, who reportedly wouldn't stop crying.

"We were in the motel room and he was crying," Rachel told the court during Carolyn's trial. "Then she [Carolyn] told me to hold my hand over his mouth."[17]

Carolyn, according to Rachel's testimony, had already put her hands over Rueben's nose and mouth. The two girls told police it took almost twenty minutes to finally kill the kicking, struggling child, and that afterward they dumped his body into a trash barrel and then went to have some breakfast.

In May 1992, the state of Virginia executed Roger Keith Coleman by electrocution. He had been convicted over ten years before of raping and murdering his sister-in-law, nineteen-year-old Wanda McCoy. Although Roger steadfastly maintained his innocence, the evidence presented at the trial, along with his previous convictions of indecent exposure and sexual assault, convinced the jury otherwise, and they convicted him of the rape and murder.

Murder within families has recently been the subject of several research projects reported on by the Bureau of Justice Statistics. In one of the research papers, *Murder in Families*, it is reported that, in the murder of children, women account for 55 percent of the killings. When a mother killed a child, it was more likely to be a son (64 percent) than a daughter (36 percent). For fathers, it was about evenly divided between sons and daughters. When a son killed a parent, it was just as likely to be his father as his mother, while for daughters it was much more likely to be the father (in 81 percent of the cases). Sons more often than daughters were defendants in the murder of parents (82 percent of the time). Whenever a sister murdered a sibling, 55 percent of the time it was a brother. When a brother killed a sibling, 74 percent of the time it was a brother.

When the murder victim is under twelve, the research said, a family member is the best suspect. Family members were responsible for 63 percent of all murders of children under the age of twelve, while parents were responsible for 57 percent of these murders. According to the research findings, the murder of a child under twelve is also often preceded by physical abuse. For a murder victim over 60 years of age, 11 percent were killed by a son or daughter, and 27 percent were killed by a family member.[18]

Another Bureau of Justice Statistics' research paper, *Spouse Murder Defendants in Large Urban Counties*, reported that in spousal murders in the United States husbands are defendants in 60 percent of the cases. Of those arrested for a spousal murder, 80 percent were convicted, and 89 percent of these were sentenced to a state prison.[19]

As stated earlier, many of these spousal murders occur when the abused spouse indicates the intention of ending the marriage. These murders, however, seldom come about without some warning. In most cases, the signs of potential murder are present long before the actual crime. The best advice therefore is never to allow a relationship to deteriorate to the point where these signs appear, but if they do, take action immediately and get out.

Obtaining some type of restraining order against the abusive spouse is an excellent idea during this time, since it gives police the right to intervene any time the abuser comes near the victim, regardless of the abuser's intentions. There are many types of restraining orders, those that allow no contact at all between the abuser and victim, those that only allow the abuser to come within a certain number of feet of the victim, and those that do allow contact between the abuser and victim, and only forbid violent contact. What type of order a victim can obtain depends on the jurisdiction the victim applies in and the circumstances of the case. Obviously, victims want to obtain a restraining order that provides the most protection. Once obtained, protection orders should be carried when away from home, and copies of the order should be kept at home, at work, and at any place the abuser is likely to turn up. But most important, abuse victims should *never* depend on a restraining order to stop a spouse with murderous intentions. In some cases, in order to prevent a murder, a potential victim may have to leave a long-time job or home. And while the potential victim may think this is totally unfair, the alternative is even more unfair.

Before reading this chapter, many readers may have believed that being with their family was the safest place to be. However, as I've shown, far too many times each year this isn't the case. For several thousand people every year being with family members proves to be fatal. Within families, murder often becomes the final, ultimate instrument of control.

9

Spread and Perpetuation of Family Abuse

On 3 May 1992, police officers patrolling the north side of Indianapolis responded to a run in the 3800 block of Emerson Avenue described by the dispatcher as: "A woman calling for help." When they arrived at the address, the officers found Janice Foley standing in the middle of Emerson Avenue, grimacing and holding her side. Able to talk with the officers only in small gasps, Janice told them she believed several of her ribs were broken. She said that her husband, Ronald Foley, had gone crazy and begun beating and kicking her. Mrs. Foley also told the officers that she was twenty-one weeks pregnant.

Ronald, the police learned, had fled in an old, rusty, gray Mustang when Janice ran from the house screaming. These same officers had been to the Foley residence many times before on similar calls, and the last time there they had arrested Mr. Foley. The officers figured he had left in a hurry in order to avoid that happening again, particularly since Mrs. Foley had gone to court after the last incident and obtained a no-contact order against him. A no-contact order means just that, the person the order is against can have no contact with the person protected by the order. However, the officers would later find that, despite getting the order against her husband, Mrs. Foley had allowed him to live in the home.

The officers took Mrs. Foley back into her house while they waited for the emergency medical personnel to arrive. The home, the officers found, appeared to be in shambles, with a mirror smashed on the wall, several chairs overturned, and a lamp broken. Within a few minutes, the emergency medical personnel arrived and began attending to Mrs. Foley. During this time, Mr. Foley called on the telephone twice, threatening to come back and kill Mrs. Foley.

The emergency medical personnel said they believed Mrs. Foley's ribs were only bruised, and against their advice she declined to go to the hospital. After the emergency medical personnel left, the two officers who had been dispatched on the run parked their police cars, with the lights out, a block north and south of the home. Within five minutes, a rusty, gray Mustang, with its lights out, turned the corner and cruised very slowly up to the Foley house. The two officers sped in from both directions and pinned Mr. Foley's car in. The officers arrested Mr. Foley, who was extremely intoxicated, for battery, invasion of privacy (for violating the no-contact order), and operating a motor vehicle under the influence of liquor. As a result of these arrests, he served a total of four days in jail.

On 14 September 1994, police officers patrolling the north side of Indianapolis responded to a domestic disturbance call at the Foley residence. When they arrived at the address, they found Mrs. Foley hiding between two parked cars in the driveway of her house. Blood streamed from a gash on her forehead, and she told the officers that her husband had gone crazy and begun beating her. When the officers went inside the home they discovered several chairs overturned, the coffee table broken, and spots of fresh blood on the living room carpet. The police arrested Mr. Foley, who was too drunk to flee this time, for battery. The prosecutor, however, because Mrs. Foley changed her mind and refused to cooperate, eventually dropped the charges.

On 26 January 1995, police officers patrolling the north side of Indianapolis responded to a call from the Foley residence. The dispatcher said that a woman had called 911 from there, screamed, "Send the police!" and then hung up. Expecting to find that Mr. and Mrs. Foley had been in another fight, the officers found instead that there was a new victim of Mr. Foley's violence, an occurrence which is very, very common in cases of domestic violence. The new target of Mr. Foley's violence was his ten-year-old stepdaughter, Megan. Because a child was involved, the officers called for a detective from the Family Advocacy Center.

"I wasn't here but Megan told me that she and her brother were fighting," Mrs. Foley said to the detective. "You know how kids do. Well, all of a sudden, I guess, my husband just jumped up out of the chair and grabbed Megan by the hair and began beating her."

"Did you talk to your husband about it?" the detective asked her.

Mrs. Foley nodded. "He just said that she deserved it. And that she couldn't live here no more."

"Where was he wanting her to go?"

"I guess just out of here," Mrs. Foley said with a shrug. "Just out of the house period. He doesn't like her because she isn't his real daughter, just his stepdaughter. But she's a good kid. Really, she is."

The detective, who had seen hundreds of cases like the Foleys, asked, "Had your husband been drinking today?"

Mrs. Foley gave another nod. "Yeah, all day today and all day yesterday."

"Is he usually violent when he drinks?"

This time Mrs. Foley shook her head. "Nah, he's mean whether he's been drinking or not. They say most people only want to fight when they get to drinking. Not Ronald. He always wants to fight."

"Has he ever struck any of the children before?"

"No, but he threatens them all the time."

"What kind of threats?"

"Oh, sometimes he says stuff like he's going to kill everyone in the house. And then sometimes he'll start on Megan about her cat. She's got a little black kitten, and he says that it's bad luck.

Anyway, he's always telling her that he's going to break the cat's neck. So whenever the cat's not around he always tells Megan not to bother looking for it because he's broke its neck. Then, of course, that gets her to bawling."

The detective arrested Mr. Foley for battery. The next day, Mrs. Foley went back to court and obtained a new no-contact order against Mr. Foley.

On 29 January 1995, three days after the last incident above, police officers patrolling the north side of Indianapolis once more returned to the Foley household. They found Mrs. Foley with a black eye and a chipped tooth and Megan with welts on her side from a belt. The day before, the officers learned, Mrs. Foley had bailed Mr. Foley out of jail. Also, the officers found, despite having obtained a no-contact order against him, Mrs. Foley allowed Mr. Foley to move back into the home. She said he had watched the Super Bowl that day, got intoxicated, and then began arguing with her about his arrest for beating his stepdaughter. The argument soon became physical.

The police arrested Mr. Foley for battery and invasion of privacy. He never went to trial, though, as the prosecutor dropped the charges because of a lack of cooperation from Mrs. Foley.

❖ ❖ ❖ ❖ ❖

Anyone who has worked with family abuse cases knows that, as in the incident above, seldom is the violence ever a one-time event, and just as seldom does the violence ever stay at one level or stay directed against just one person. Instead, in most cases, the violence is repeated over and over, grows in severity over time, and often spreads to other members of the household.

Researcher Murray Straus, in a national survey of over 2000 households, found that men who frequently and severely assault their wives were significantly more likely than nonviolent husbands to assault their children. Also, the research discovered, the more violent a husband was toward his wife, the more violent she was toward the children. The survey found that even women who suffered only minor violence from their husbands were significantly more likely to assault their children. "One of the clearest findings to emerge from the two National Family Violence Surveys," said Dr. Straus, "is that violence in one family relationship is related to violence in other family relationships."[1]

A study reported by the National Woman Abuse Prevention Project found that battered women were eight times as likely as nonbattered women to abuse their children. Other studies have shown, however, that children are at most risk for physical abuse in families in which both parents assault each other. Also, in the first of the two national surveys referred to by Dr. Straus above, 100 percent of the children from families surveyed in which both spouse and child abuse were present had severely assaulted a brother or sister during the previous year.

Perhaps even more damaging than the physical abuse suffered by children in families where the abuse spreads from the parents to the children are the lessons that violence teaches children. Children model themselves after their parents, and pick up both good and bad traits. Witnessing violence in the home can be a learning experience that shapes a child's life forever. It also tends to affect boys and girls differently. Boys who witness their fathers batter their mothers often see domestic violence as a workable strategy for getting their way. They see it as a way to end fights and settle arguments in their favor. Unfortunately, because of this, young boys who witness violence between their parents often grow up to become wife batterers themselves. Studies have found that as many as eighty percent of spouse batterers have lived in homes filled with violence. Researcher Murray Straus, in the book *Behind Closed Doors: Violence in the American Family*, states that boys who witness their fathers being violent are ten times as likely to become spouse abusers as those from nonviolent homes.[2]

In the book *The Violent Couple*, authors Hazlewood, Shupe, and Stacey state. "The most established principle concerning aggression in social psychology is that violence in the family begets violence.... The likelihood of inter-generational transfer of violent tendencies—from adults to their children—is an empirically validated one."[3] In an editorial in *The New York Times*, writer Brent Staples tells of a young man he knew who had recently been arrested for pistol whipping his wife. A sad and telling part of the story was that Mr. Staples also knew the man's family history and knew that the man's father and grandfather had also both been wife batterers.[4]

Young girls who witness domestic violence also suffer significant damage, but in a different way: witnessing such violence often has the effect of creating more victims. An article in *Parents Magazine*, "How Domestic Violence Hurts Kids," states: "Girls who see their mothers abused are far more likely to be abused as adults. As many as eighty percent of battered women who have fled to shelters remember seeing their own mother being assaulted by their father when they were growing up."

"As part of their identification with their mother, when girls see their mothers abused, they tend to assume that this is an aspect of the female role and take it for granted," said Dr. David Zinn, a child psychiatrist at Northwestern University Medical School. "What it teaches boys is that this is the way you deal with frustration. If you're upset and tense, you discharge your frustration by hitting someone—and it's okay to hit women."[5]

While I have witnessed hundreds of such cases in my twenty-eight years as a police officer, this tendency to learn violent behavior by witnessing it as a child actually became apparent to me when I was in college. As part of my undergraduate work, I enrolled in a child psychology course, a segment of which involved lab work with children.

The child psychology lab we used appeared to the children to be simply a large playroom with very high ceilings. However, the top six feet of the walls were actually two-way mirrors through which we could observe from the overhead gallery what the children were doing in the playroom. The professors had filled the room with various toys, including a large number of stuffed animals. As a part of a demonstration, the professor placed a four-year-old boy in the room and let him play for a few minutes, then had one of the teaching assistants go into the room and talk with the child. While the teaching assistant was talking with the boy, she stroked one of the stuffed animals lovingly and kept saying how cute it was. When the teaching assistant left the room, we all watched the child, who we found also began stroking and talking to the stuffed animal.

A few minutes after this, the professor entered the room, talked with the child for a few moments, and then suddenly picked up one of the stuffed animals (a lion) and began slamming it down on a table, yelling that it was a bad cat. She then left the room. We all watched, and within a few seconds the young boy picked up the lion and began slamming it on the table, telling it how bad it was. I think I learned more about the behavioral shaping of a child from watching this one demonstration than I learned in all of my other psychology courses. But what concerned me most was that this learning experience had come from simply witnessing one incident by a stranger. What would be the learning impact on the child, I wondered, if he saw violence like this every day from his parents?

This learned violent behavior, wherever it comes from, doesn't affect just future spouses and children. It can also backfire on the parents and negatively affect them by causing their children to abuse them when they become elderly. Dr. Suzanne K. Steinmetz, director of Resources for Older Americans at the University of Delaware, found that only one out of 400 children raised in a nonviolent home physically abused his or her parents later in life, while one out of two children raised in a violent home did so.

"We find parent beatings when the parents set the example of solving problems through brutality when the children are growing up," said Chicago psychiatrist Mitchell Messer. "The response is simply following the example the parents set."[6]

"We see this all the time," said Lori West, an Adult Protective Services investigator. "They tell us that Mom did it to me when I was growing up. Now it's her turn."

Witnessing and experiencing violence in the home can do serious damage to a child's psychological and emotional development in other ways too. Richard Gelles, a professor at the University of Rhode Island, says studies have shown that half of the children who witness a parent being beaten are also abused, *but that watching is worse than actually suffering the beating.* It is worse because the children feel powerless and helpless. "The learning experience is stronger," said Dr. Gelles. "There are more suicide attempts, more dysfunction in school, more likelihood of violence later in life, more withdrawal."[7] One can only wonder what witnessing *extreme* marital violence must do to a child's personality development. Dr. Gelles states that, in 1993, 1421 women were killed by husbands or intimate partners, and that in three-fourths of these cases a child was watching.[8]

Witnessing and experiencing abuse as a child can also affect a child's likelihood toward future criminality. According to the National Institute of Justice's research paper *Victims of Childhood Sexual Abuse—Later Criminal Consequences*: "People who were sexually victimized during childhood are at higher risk of arrest for committing crimes as adults, including sex crimes, than are people who did not suffer sexual or physical abuse or neglect during childhood."[9] The following incident demonstrates this.

❖ ❖ ❖ ❖ ❖

On 31 May 1993, a thirteen-year-old boy, after attending a program about sexual abuse, reported to his school counselor that he and his six-year-old brother had been sexually abused by their grandfather, Charles Reis, for as long as he could remember. When a child abuse detective questioned the boy and his brother, she found that the sexual molestation would occur whenever the two boys visited their grandfather. The grandfather, the boys told the detective, would always pretend to want to wrestle with them, but once he had them pinned down he would tell them, "I'm going to grab that thing!" and would then reach into their pants.

Upon further investigation, the detective also discovered that the grandfather had molested the ten-year-old sister of the two boys. She told the detective that her grandfather would stick his hand down her blouse, and make her stick her hand down his pants.

The detective arrested Charles Reis for child molesting. A court later convicted and sentenced him to twelve years' imprisonment.

On 8 November 1994, the same detective from the above incident went to a home to investigate a complaint of child molestation. The mother in this home told the detective that her twelve-year-old daughter had revealed to her just that morning that her father had been molesting her and two of her friends for a long time. The father turned out to be William Reis, the son of Charles Reis (the grandfather in the incident above). When taken in for questioning, William Reis tearfully admitted molesting his daughter and the other two girls. He also told the detective that his father, Charles Reis, had molested him and his brothers and sisters for as long as they lived with him. Further investigation also showed that a sister of William Reis had been involved in the molesting of a niece. The niece told the detective that her aunt had made her suck on her breasts and watch her as she used a vibrator.

❖ ❖ ❖ ❖ ❖

Is the above just an isolated case of one degenerate family? Unfortunately, it is not. Child abuse investigators often find that parents who sexually molest their children are actually teaching these children to become molesters, and that these young victims will then many times prey on younger brothers and sisters, other children, or their own children when they grow up. For this reason, it is important to take action at the first sign that any kind of abuse is being perpetrated against children, physical or sexual, before the learning experience can take hold.

The major point I hope I've been able to make in this chapter is that there are no isolated, single victims of family abuse. Far too often, adult victims of family abuse will stay in a relationship "for the sake of the children," mistakenly believing that they are the only one being harmed. They couldn't be more wrong. Family abuse affects every member of the family.

10

Backgrounds of Family Abusers

On 26 February 1985, John Fedders, the chief enforcement officer of the Securities and Exchange Commission, resigned from his $72,300 a year job. The reason?

Along with being embroiled at the time as a "subject" in a bribery and conspiracy inquiry, John Fedders also found himself in the midst of bitter divorce proceedings instituted by his estranged wife, Charlotte. During the proceedings, Charlotte alleged a series of beatings that she said began practically at the start of their marriage. She also testified at their divorce trial that John assaulted her when she was pregnant with their first child. "John attacked me with his fists and hands," she said in court. "I remember he was yelling he didn't care if he killed me or killed the baby."[1]

John's real troubles, though, began when Charlotte heard President Reagan's 1984 State of the Union message, in which he outlined a crusade planned against spouse abuse. Inspired, she wrote the president a letter, which eventually ended up in the hands of White House counsel Fred Fielding. In her letter, Charlotte told of the many beatings she had suffered at John's hands, of a blow to the head that ruptured an eardrum, and of being pulled over a bannister by her hair. She also told about the psychological abuse she suffered, of John's isolation of her, and of his tearing down of her self-esteem.

White House counsel Fred Fielding called John Fedders in for a meeting about the letter. Later, though a spokesman for the White House denied there was any pressure to force John Fedder's resignation, he nevertheless resigned.

❖ ❖ ❖ ❖ ❖

The example of John Fedders, unquestionably a person high in the ranks of government service, offers clear evidence against the myth that family abuse is a problem confined exclusively to the unemployed or those of the lower socioeconomic classes. It is a problem present in every level of our society.

Going even higher than Mr. Fedders in the ranks of government service, members of Congress and their families are also not immune to the problems of family abuse. Dr. Saul Edelstein, head of Emergency Services at George Washington University, when testifying at a public hearing, said: "[W]ives of congressmen will admit it [being beaten] to nurses, but they don't want it on their charts.... Battered wives in Washington refuse to report their husbands because the publicity could ruin their spouses' careers, cutting back on their own source of income..."[2]

Republican Congressman Dan Burton (Indiana), in an article in *Parade Magazine*, recalls how his father would drive the family out into the woods so that no one could hear his mother scream as he beat her. Sometimes, the young Burton would be awakened in his bed by the crash of breaking furniture and the sound of his mother screaming.[3]

Family abuse can reach even higher, into the very highest government office in the land: the Oval Office. President Bill Clinton's stepfather, Roger Clinton, an abusive alcoholic, made the young president-to-be's life, and the life of his mother and brother, a living terror. When Bill Clinton was five, his stepfather tried to kill the young Clinton's mother by shooting at her, but missed and hit the wall next to her. When Bill Clinton got older, he often managed to intercede in the violence by calling the police or helping his mother and brother get out of the house and harm's way. Finally, the future president grew large enough to be able to exert his own intimidation and stop some of his stepfather's abuse of his mother and brother, but he realized it only worked when he was there to protect them. Bill Clinton's mother finally divorced Roger in 1962.

While the above few examples should make it clear that politicians and their families are certainly not immune to the problems of family abuse, what about those specializing in medicine and other "helping" professions? Does family abuse also touch their lives?

In November 1995, the police arrested Dr. Deborah Green, an oncologist married to a doctor specializing in cardiology, for first-degree murder and aggravated arson. On 24 October 1995, a fire destroyed the couple's six-bedroom, $400,000 home in a suburb of Kansas City, killing two of Deborah Green's children. The police believe that Dr. Green purposely set the fire.

The police also charged Dr. Green with two counts of attempted murder, one count having to do with the fire and the other with a poisoning attempt. Her husband had been hospitalized three times for an unexplained illness just a few weeks prior to the fire. When asked about a motive for the fire and murders, District Attorney Paul Morrison said: "It's a domestic (family) situation, and that's where I'm going to leave it."[4]

In Indianapolis, a court recently convicted a physician specializing in childhood cancer, Dr. Deborah Provisor, of child molesting after she admitted to having sex with a thirteen-year-old relative. Dr. Provisor was also reportedly having marital problems. On 30 September 1995, the police arrested Dr. Deborah Provisor's husband, Dr. Arthur Provisor, a pediatrician, for violating a restraining order which forbid him from coming within fifty feet of his estranged wife's house. They also charged him with resisting arrest when he allegedly struggled with deputies who attempted to remove him from the house. This was the second time deputies had been called to Dr. Deborah Provisor's house about a violation of the restraining order.[5]

According to a study reported in the *Journal of the American Medical Association*, physicians, though in a "helping" profession and highly educated, are not exempt at all from the problems of family abuse. When asked about abuse in their own lives, the researchers found that 14 percent of the male doctors and 31 percent of the female doctors reported a history of either child abuse or physical abuse with a partner.[6]

Other examples of family abuse among highly educated people abound. In the book *Healing Your Life: Recovery from Domestic Abuse*, author Candace A. Hennekens tells of her life with an abusive husband. She said: "He had punched me, threatened me with a knife, dragged me down the hall by my hair when I was pregnant, kicked me in the stomach, twisted my arm behind my back, hit my ear so hard it swelled up like a boxer's, and thrown things at me.... He had called me 'crazy,' a 'bitch,' and other foul names. He had blamed me for every problem he ever had."

But then she also went on to say: "My husband was a college professor.... We owned a lovely home in a nice neighborhood. We travelled, collected antiques, and were involved in the community."[7] The police see these two faces of family abusers often. When we arrive at the scene of a family disturbance, many times the abuser appears very affable and friendly. The injuries to the victim, however, tell of another personality.

In December 1994, the police arrested a high school principal in Lebanon, Ohio, and charged him with seventeen felony counts of sexually molesting his stepson. Just a month earlier, the police had charged this same principal and his former wife with attempting to hire the same hit man to kill each other. The ex-wife pled guilty in the case.

An article in *The New York Times* tells of a survey done of another highly educated group of people in a "helping" profession: psychotherapists. The results of this survey showed that 21 percent of the female and 6 percent of the male psychotherapists reported sexual abuse by a relative, while 10 percent of the females and 13 percent of the males reported physical abuse. Overall, 40 percent of the female psychotherapists and 25 percent of the male psychotherapists reported some type of childhood abuse.[8]

If not education, what about money? Does being wealthy mean a person won't experience family abuse?

At 3:50 A.M. on 1 January 1994, firefighters had to assist police officers in the exclusive Westchester County (New York) village of Bronxville forcing their way into the home of Scripps newspaper heiress Anne Scripps Douglas. Once inside, they found the forty-seven-year-old woman in an upstairs bedroom badly beaten and unconscious. She would die six days later. Mrs. Douglas, the authorities learned, had earlier obtained a protective order against her husband, Scott Douglas, whom the police charged with the bludgeoning. Neighbors of the Douglases said they were often surprised to see police cars answering domestic disturbance calls at the home in the exclusive neighborhood. On the night of the attack, the police found Scott Douglas's car parked on the Tappan Zee Bridge over the Hudson River, a bloody hammer inside. His body washed ashore along the Hudson River the next March, an apparent suicide.

In August 1995, Massachusetts police arrested Richard Rosenthal, a senior financial officer for the John Hancock Mutual Life Insurance Company in Boston, after finding a bag full of bloody clothing in the backseat of his car. Police followed a trail of blood from his stately home in a Boston suburb to some nearby woods, where they found the body of his wife. She had been disemboweled with a butcher knife, and her organs impaled on a stake. Her face had been smashed so badly with a rock as to be unrecognizable. Mr. Rosenthal told officers that he and his wife had fought about him burning some ziti.[9]

An article in *The New York Times* about family abuse in East Hampton, Long Island said: "Though wife beating seems improbable amid the beachfront mansions of the scions and stars who live here, it is serious enough that East Hampton has taken the highly unusual step of financing a private shelter for battered women, one of only three shelters for all of Long Island."[10] Another article, also in *The New York Times*, this one about family abuse in Connecticut, said: "There is a myth that it does not happen here, in an affluent, suburban town.... Society does not want to believe that an educated, professional man could do this, or that an educated, professional woman would put up with it."[11]

For a number of years I worked as a district sergeant and lieutenant on the north side of Indianapolis. There, amid neighborhoods of rundown homes and people living in abject poverty, sit pockets of beautiful, stately mansions, built long before economic blight struck the surrounding neighborhood. These homes, of course, are owned by very affluent people. Yet still, the police receive family abuse runs to these homes.

I would occasionally go along with my officers when they received a family abuse run to one of these homes, and always found the attitudes of the residents amusing. I could see that it took all of the perpetrators' willpower to keep their mouths shut as I or one of my officers lectured or scolded them about family abuse. It took all of their willpower because the perpetrators, being wealthy, obviously felt they were much higher class than a police officer. These people, who regularly blackened eyes or split lips, who daily used terrorism to rule and control their families, and who regularly acted like thugs, felt they were just too high class to be lectured by the police.

Of course, some readers might question why the police would want to lecture rather than arrest these abusers. Police officers may know that a person has committed abuse, but there is often no evidence at the scene to justify an arrest (wealthy abusers are often very careful about this). The officers, however, know that if they leave the scene without doing anything then they are just reinforcing the abuser's behavior. Since an arrest isn't possible, many officers feel they must do something to show abusers that their behavior is unacceptable, and often this is a lecture. In some cases, the effect of a stern lecture by a police officer is negative enough that an abuser doesn't want to go through it again and will stop, or at least decrease, the abuse.

As demonstrated by the above incidents, though it appears otherwise, family abuse definitely exists in wealthy families. Many of the studies conducted on family abuse obtain their statistics from government social programs and from government or public institutions that cater to poorer people. Middle- and upper-class victims of family abuse, rather than visiting community health centers or hospital emergency wards, often go to private physicians. Private physicians, particularly if they are the family physician, seldom report this abuse to the authorities.

If not the wealthy, what about our religious leaders? Would their lives be so different that they would not experience family abuse?

In an article in the 19 July 1993 issue of *Christianity Today*, author Linda Midgett tells about the plight of a woman, Lonnie Collins Pratt, married to a pastor/evangelist. "If they stayed in one place for too long," the article said, "people began to notice her black eyes and the bruises on her arms and legs.... Pratt suffered regular beatings from her husband throughout their marriage. The same man who preached from the pulpit slowly isolated her from her friends and convinced her that she was worthless."

In August 1992, the police arrested a formerly prominent Dallas minister, who had become church administrator at the Immanuel Presbyterian Church in Los Angeles. They charged him with an attempted murder in Dallas. The police accused forty-five-year-old Walker Railey of strangling his wife five years earlier and leaving her for dead. During the attack, she lapsed into a coma and never came out of it. Although Reverend Railey told the police at the time that he had come home and found his wife unconscious on the garage floor, he later attempted suicide and refused to answer questions of a grand jury, citing his Fifth Amendment protection against self-incrimination. The police also learned that, at the time of the attack, Reverend Railey was romantically involved with another woman.[12]

If not religious leaders, then what about movie stars and other celebrities? Would the glamour that surrounds their lives insulate them from family abuse?

The movie *What's Love Got To Do With It?* vividly documented Tina Turner's abuse at the hands of her husband, Ike. Television personality Oprah Winfrey went public with her own history of sexual abuse as a child. The police recently arrested television star Sasha Mitchell, who plays Cody on *Step by Step*, for allegedly beating his pregnant wife, Jeanette.[13] Joan Crawford's daughter, in the book *Mommie Dearest*, told of the movie star's physical and psychological abuse of her as a child. Former Miss America, Marilyn Van Derbur, now tours the country telling about her recovery from incest. In April 1993, the police responded to the call of a domestic fight at the Manhattan apartment of LaToya Jackson. They arrested her husband Jack Gordon for assaulting her.[14]

Of all celebrities, however, probably the worst when it comes to family abuse are sports stars. A 1994 study by *The Washington Post* found that, since 1989, fifty-six current and former professional football players have been reported to the police for violent behavior toward women.[15] And this is just one of many professional sports. A few of the many famous sports figures accused of some type of family abuse include boxers Sugar Ray Leonard and Mike Tyson, golfer John Daly, baseball star Jose Canseco, and basketball players Moses Malone and Robert Parrish.[16] The list of all victims and perpetrators of family abuse among sports stars, however, is much, much longer, and would go on for pages.

Another group of individuals, police officers, work regularly with the problem of family abuse and almost daily see its widespread damage. One might suppose that witnessing hundreds of cases of family abuse every year would make police officers want to avoid this type of behavior.

Actually, the opposite is true. As a group, police officers and their families become embroiled in an unusually large amount of family abuse. In 1991, researchers conducted a study at the National Fraternal Order of Police 50th Biennial Conference. Surveys were completed by 891 married, divorced, or cohabiting male police officers, thirty-two female police officers, and 199 Women's Auxiliary members (wives of police officers). Almost half of the police officers surveyed were the rank of sergeant or above. This means that the survey sample consisted of the more experienced and professional officers, and consequently that the amount of family abuse found would likely be less than for police officers overall.

The results were startling. At least one episode of physical violence was found in 24 percent of the male officers' relationships, 22 percent of the female officers' relationships, and 28 percent of the Women's Auxiliary members' relationships. These rates were double what studies have found the prevalence of family abuse to be in the general population.[17]

I troubled over and pondered these results for some time, wondering why, before finally coming to the conclusion that they made sense. Police officers, in their jobs, are trained to demand compliance when they issue orders or demands. If they do not receive this compliance, police officers are trained to use force, and to increase the level of this force, until they do obtain compliance. This is the exact recipe for family abuse, though certainly not any type of excuse for it.

In addition to this training, however, personality problems also likely cause some of the police family abuse. When I was in charge of the Indianapolis Police Department's personnel branch, I found that every year a number of people applied to become police officers not because of a desire for public service, but because they suffered from personality inadequacies. These people felt weak and insecure and hoped that if they became police officers then people would see them as powerful and consequently treat them with respect. This type of person, besides making a poor police officer, also fits the mold for a family abuser. He or she would be the type to demand respect from family members, and become violent when this respect wasn't forthcoming. Unfortunately, a number of these people get by the screening process every year and become police officers.

The high stress levels police officers experience, some people believe, could also explain the high level of family abuse. This to me seems to be only an excuse because many occupations have high stress, and many police officers who experience high stress don't abuse their families. My wife has one of the most stressful jobs a police officer can have: child abuse detective. Everyday she sees examples of how horribly people treat their children. Yet, there is no one who loves her family more.

Finally, some have said that because police officers are around family abuse so much in their jobs they pick up abuse as a learned behavior. This also strikes me as only an excuse. Otherwise, many police officers would be robbers, burglars, and rapists.

When I researched the literature on family abuse, not surprisingly, I found a large number of incidents involving family abuse and law enforcement officers. For example, in Beaumont, Texas, the former wife of a sheriff's deputy was on her way to a county courthouse to complain that he was harassing her. She didn't make it. Confronted by her ex-husband, who was in uniform, she died after being shot six times. In New York City, a police officer quarreled with his girlfriend outside Police Headquarters, where a large number of people were arriving to attend a ceremony honoring police officers killed in the line of duty the preceding year. This officer had previously been on "modified assignment" (meaning he carried no badge or gun) for a year and a half because he had threatened another woman. The officer shot his girlfriend four times, killing her, and then turned the gun on himself and committed suicide.

Recently, in Alexandria, Virginia, the police answered the call of a domestic disturbance at the home of an FBI agent, where they found that the agent had broken his wife's nose. The wife tipped off the police that her husband had been stealing property from the FBI. The officers found 200,000 rounds of ammunition, grenades, night vision gear, and other equipment stored in the house. The agent had previously been a firearms instructor at the FBI Academy.

Summing up everything I have stated in this chapter, Murray Straus, director of the Family Research Laboratory at the University of New Hampshire, said: "[F]or the ordinary violence in family life, the pushing, slapping, shoving ... there's not much difference by socio-economic status or race."[18] A survey of 1040 African-American college students reported in the *American Journal of Orthopsychiatry* found that the rates for child sexual abuse were similar in this group to those of all college students.[19] According to the book *Family Violence*: "There are no significant differences in rates of sibling violence for children from blue or while collar families." The authors of this book, when talking about elder abuse, say: "Poverty alone does not lead to elder abuse; one of the few studies of the relationship between social classes and elder abuse reports that a majority of the cases were from the middle class."[20] The Attorney General's Task Force on Family Violence concluded: "Family violence permeates all levels of our society. It is not unique to any particular social or economic group nor is it restricted to any one sex or age group."

As the cases in this chapter clearly show, the myth that family abuse is confined only to the poor or uneducated is just that: a myth. Family abuse knows no social boundaries. It may be better hidden in some classes of people, but it is still there.

11

Family Abuse Investigation

"Edward 23, Edward 24, domestic disturbance, 2322 North Central Avenue."

At last! I felt a wave of cool relief wash over me as I grabbed the radio microphone off the dashboard clip. "Edward 15 to Control," I said. "I'm just a few blocks from that run on Central. Disregard one of those cars and I'll take it."

I had been on duty now as Edward sector sergeant for three hours, and absolutely nothing of consequence had happened so far. While this usually wouldn't bother me much, it did this night because I had a friend from the Air Force riding along with me. Since our discharge in 1968 my friend and I had exchanged letters every few months, and I had always told him how exciting and exhilarating police work was. I hadn't expected such a quiet evening, which was unusual for a hot Friday night in July 1976.

As we pulled onto Central Avenue, I could tell that this was going to be a loud and angry family fight by the large crowd of people gathered on the sidewalk in front of the address. In inner-city neighborhoods, any kind of loud disturbance always drew the people off their porches, where they usually sat in the evenings to escape the heat inside their houses. The other police car pulled up to the address at about the same time we did, and so the officer and I pushed through the crowd of hot, sweaty spectators, and up to the house, my friend following close behind.

As we stepped up onto the porch, I could hear a man shouting inside the house and a woman screaming for him to quit hitting her. We knocked several times on the screen door, but the people inside, continuing to shout and scream, apparently didn't hear us. Since I knew someone was obviously in peril, I pulled open the screen door and went inside. The shouting, we found, came from upstairs, and so, with nightsticks out, we hurried up the steps and into the room where the noise was coming from.

Inside, we found a man on a double bed sitting astride a woman and pummelling her with his fists. When he saw us run into the room with our nightsticks out, he immediately stopped hitting her and got off the bed, seeming to try to appear as though nothing was amiss. The woman, her face already red and swelling, continued to lay on the bed crying. Telling the other officer to check her and see if she needed an ambulance, I then took the man into another of the upstairs rooms.

"Look, officer," the man told me, after I asked his name, which was Johnnie Jenkins, "I really don't need any trouble right now. I'm on probation. Why don't I just leave for awhile. What'd you say?"

It immediately became obvious to me that Mr. Jenkins had been through this before. Since he realized we had witnessed the assault and could arrest him, he knew what he needed to say and do in order to keep from going to jail.

"Who's the woman you were beating up?" I asked.

"Uh, she's my wife," he said. "Well, that is, she used to be my wife. We're divorced, but we still live together."

"What were you two fighting about?"

"Shit, officer, you know how these bitches are. I mean, I worked hard today, and the minute I come home, I mean the second I walked in the door, she wants to know where I've been. Then she tells me not to bother lying because she already knows where I've been. She says I've been out drinking."

I looked at him with a questioning expression, the odor of whiskey coming off of him in huge, thundering waves.

"But I wasn't out drinking," he said, then stopped when I raised an eyebrow. "Well okay, I was out drinking, but not really out drinking. What I mean is one of the guys where I work just had a baby, and so we were celebrating. That's not really out drinking."

"What are you on probation for?" I asked him.

"Drunk driving."

I nodded and told Mr. Jenkins to stay put. After slipping my nightstick back into my belt loop, I leaned around the corner and asked the other officer to come in and wait with Mr. Jenkins, while I walked back to the other bedroom. My friend from the Air Force and the woman were talking, and she now seemed calm, and almost matter-of-fact, about her ex-husband's violence.

"That's why we got divorced," she told my friend. "He used to come home drunk every Friday night and beat on me."

"Then why'd you move back in with him?" I asked.

She shrugged. "He got into some trouble driving after he had been drinking. I guess he hit a couple of cars and hurt some people. Anyway, the judge told him that if he got arrested again for drunk drinking he'd send him to the state farm for a year. So Johnnie told me he needed me to go down with him to the probation office and tell them that I would drive him everywhere since they took away his license."

She winced as she touched the puffiness on the side of her face, then let out a long breath. "I also came back because I really need the extra money. I don't make that much. I made Johnnie promise me though that he wouldn't hit me any more if I helped him. But he lied. He started hitting me again just as soon as we moved back in. And now he's started beating on the kids too. Genny's been black and blue for the last month. Hell, the other night he chased her around the house with a butcher knife, telling her he was going to kill her."

The victim refused my offer to send her to the hospital, and didn't even want to have an ambulance come by and look at her. She also insisted she didn't want Mr. Jenkins arrested, just out of the house. So, not being able to do much more since in those days we didn't arrest in misdemeanor domestic battery cases (even if we had witnessed it) unless the victim wanted to prosecute and cooperate, I sent Mr. Jenkins on his way, with the warning that if he came back that night and the police had to return he would go to jail. The officer and I then left and marked back into service.

❖ ❖ ❖ ❖ ❖

The above case is typical of the hundreds and hundreds of family abuse runs I have responded to over the years. The resolution of the situation was also typical for the 1970s. There was no report made, and no follow-up investigation to check on the welfare of the victim or her children. It was, at the very best, a Band-Aid put on a major wound. But in the 1970s this was the way the police handled family fight runs.

Today, the case would have been handled differently. An arrest would have been made. The emphasis in law enforcement today in America is to arrest in cases of domestic battery, even if we didn't witness it. While I doubt that even in the 1990s much would happen legally to Mr. Jenkins if his ex-wife didn't want to cooperate, still he wouldn't have been allowed to just leave.

In the 1970s, though, unless someone had been shot, seriously stabbed or cut, or had some other type of deadly force used against them, which then made the assault a felony, the police did not intercede. What constitutes a felony, then and now, varies from state to state. Generally, though, felonies are considered more serious crimes, usually punishable by a term in prison rather than the local jail.

In those days, some cities (though not Indianapolis) even had an informal "stitch rule." This rule stated that an injury in a family abuse case had to require a certain number of stitches before an arrest would be made. This demeaning rule said that punches, shoves, and slaps between spouses were okay. The abusing spouse, to escape arrest, simply had to keep the violence below the stitch rule level.

While all of these policies and informal rules likely strike the reader as unsympathetic and unfeeling, they weren't just measures used locally, but nationwide. A training manual published by the International Association of Chiefs of Police in 1967 stated: "In dealing with family disputes, the power of arrest should be exercised as a last resort." The *Standards for the Urban Police Function*, published by the American Bar Association in 1973, stated that the police should: "engage in the resolution of conflict such as that which occurs between husband and wife ... in the highly populated sections of the large city, without reliance upon criminal assault or disorderly conduct statutes." The reasoning behind these two national standards was that family abuse, in those days, was considered a private family matter to be resolved within the family. The criminal justice system only intervened when the violence reached life-threatening levels.

Of course, that was the 1970s. Today, there are laws on the books of most states that either mandate or encourage the arrest of batterers when there is evidence of any physical violence, misdemeanor or felony, in a family abuse incident. Of course, these incidents must first come to the attention of the police. The Second National Family Violence Survey found that only 6.7 percent of all husband-to-wife assaults were reported to police. Still, family disturbance police runs numbered an estimated 1.37 million in 1991, which should mean there would be a large number of arrests. But this is not necessarily so, even in communities which mandate arrests. Far too often arrests in family violence situations are not made. In some ways not much has changed since the 1970s.

The reason for this lack of arrests in family violence situations, even when mandated, was explained by the former chief of police of Minneapolis, Anthony Bouza, when he once commented that in any police department the greatest amount of power lies at the lowest levels. What Chief Bouza meant was that while police chiefs and other administrators can develop and implement any number of new programs to combat crimes like family abuse, the decision of whether or not these programs will work rests with the lowest rank: the street patrol officer.

The reason for all of this power being situated at the lowest end of a police department is that police work usually consists of individual officers acting as independent units, each of whom resolves the situations he or she is called to with a very minimum of supervision. Many times, because sergeants and lieutenants

have large numbers of officers to supervise and many other du-
ties, days or weeks will go by before an officer sees a sergeant or
lieutenant on a radio run. The officer, therefore, has complete
authority at most of the runs he or she is sent on. And so, while a
local community may have laws on the books mandating or en-
couraging arrests in family abuse situations, unless the officers
agree with the law and want to implement it, they can simply
choose to ignore it, and often do.

In most communities, rather than being mandated, family
violence arrests are at the police officers' discretion, even though
the officers are often given additional ability to make these arrests
if they wish. For example, while in the past officers had to witness
a misdemeanor assault before they could arrest for it, a majority of
the states now allow for misdemeanor arrests to be made in family
violence situations even if the officers did not witness the offense.
The officers only have to have probable cause (reasonable belief)
that the violence took place, such as a victim having a black eye or
bruises, torn clothing, etc. The officers then, at their discretion, can
make an arrest.

This police discretion in whether or not to make arrests applies not just to family violence cases, but to most crimes. In a
study done of 176 incidents in which both the victim of a crime and
the suspect were present, as was sufficient evidence for making an
arrest, arrests for *all* types of crimes (not simply those involving
family violence) were made in only 58 percent of the felonies and
44 percent of the misdemeanors. Police discretion, the study
found, was widely used in deciding whether or not to make
arrests, regardless of the amount of evidence available.[1] Unfortunately, many times this police discretion enables family abuse
perpetrators to get away with their crimes.

Some of this police reluctance to make arrests in family abuse
situations can be explained by a study conducted by Dr. David A.
Ford of Indiana University at Indianapolis. Police officers were
asked for their responses on a number of key questions concerning their attitudes on family violence. Nineteen percent of the
officers questioned agreed with the statement: "A man does not
deserve to be arrested for slapping his wife," while 38 percent of

the officers felt that acts such as shoving or slapping should not be considered crimes at all.[2] As might be imagined, arrests by one of these officers, particularly in minor family abuse cases, are highly unlikely.

An article in the *Affilia Journal of Women and Social Work* tells of a study of fifty-one battered women in Florida. The police in this study made arrests in only twelve of these cases, even though thirty-six of the women had requested an arrest, and the law allowed for such an arrest to be made.[3] A 1995 poll of 1000 people by the Scripps Howard News Service found that only sixteen percent of those surveyed felt the police did a good job of protecting domestic violence victims.[4] In two other studies of abused spouses the police were rated as the least helpful source of assistance to the victims.

On the other side, police officers can cite a number of reasons why they don't like making arrests in family violence situations. Rarely, but often enough that every police officer with over ten years of experience has likely seen such a case, the victim in a family violence situation, after insisting that the police arrest the batterer, physically attacks the police when they try to do so. While these are rare occurrences, still they leave deep impressions on police officers, and are the type of events that are remembered and often become part of police lore. Also, in addition to this possibility of violence from the victims, there is also a likelihood of violence from the abuser. Family abuse situations are both dangerous and completely unpredictable, and as such officers like to get in and out of them as quickly as possible, seldom taking the time to look for a permanent, or even long-term, solution to the problem. In addition, police officers are often frustrated by the outcome of those family abuse cases they do try to solve. Even when the officers assist the victims in getting out of the abusive environment, or assist the victims with filing criminal charges against the abusers, the victims more often than not change their mind before anything substantial can be done, and many times move back in with the abusers. The cycle of abuse begins all over again.

According to domestic violence researcher Lawrence Sherman in the National Institute of Justice's research paper *Domestic*

Violence: "In explaining why arrests in domestic violence cases are not more common, police also cite the frequent change of heart victims have the day after the assault and their refusal to cooperate with a criminal prosecution--both reasons for dropping the charges. Police argue that it is pointless to make an arrest if there will be no court-imposed punishment to produce a deterrent effect, and there often cannot be court-imposed punishment unless the victim cooperates."[5] A study done in the Marion County, Indiana (Indianapolis), courts found that 70 percent of the men arrested for domestic violence had the charges against them dropped because the victim didn't show up for court or because the victim did appear in court and asked that the charges against the man be dropped.[6] A study in Washington, D.C. found the rate to be 80 percent, and in Detroit it was an unbelievable 90 percent.[7] Almost all police officers believe that victims, if they want the abuse to stop, must follow through on prosecution, and, more importantly, must be committed to changing their situation. Giving the abuser one more chance will often only perpetuate the abuse, as the following incident shows.

❖ ❖ ❖ ❖ ❖

When I was a fairly new police officer running a beat on the south side of Indianapolis I had a number of abusive families whom I responded to so regularly I knew them on a first-name basis. One family in particular was so regular that I could almost depend upon being called to their home at about eleven o'clock every Friday night. As inevitably happens in abuse cases like this, the violence soon began increasing in intensity. At first it was only shouting and shoving. Eventually it became slapping and slugging. When the violence finally reached the level where the victim started showing injuries such as bruises, black eyes, or chipped teeth, I began advising her to go down to the Prosecutor's Office and swear out a warrant. It was the only way, I told her, that the violence would ever stop. While she would always promise me that she would, and several times I went down and waited at the Prosecutor's Office on my time off to assist her, she never showed up. Eventually, the violence reached life-threatening levels.

One Friday evening when I responded to the call of a domestic disturbance at her house the victim told me that her husband had recently purchased a revolver and had threatened her with it. She said she was frightened that he might actually shoot her. But still, she wouldn't go down to the Prosecutor's Office to do anything about it. Finally, a month or so later, he actually did take a shot at her, but luckily missed. This time, finally frightened enough, she went to the Prosecutor's Office and swore out a complaint.

Since I was the reporting officer and had encouraged the victim for so long to take this action, I of course showed up for the trial. However, when I didn't see her in the courtroom I checked with the court personnel and found that the case had been taken off the docket. After a little more checking I found that the victim had asked the prosecutor to drop the charges.

The violence in the relationship began again almost immediately, but with a new intensity. It was as if the abuser knew he had little to fear. The threats with the revolver also began again. As before, every Friday night I would be called to the house, and each time the victim would swear to me that she would be down at the Prosecutor's Office Monday morning. She actually did file charges against her husband two other times, once when he beat her with an aluminum baseball bat, and once when he cut her, but she also dropped these, and so the abuse continued unabated.

When I left the beat on the south side and moved on to another assignment, he was still assaulting her on a regular basis. I don't know what happened in their relationship, but I suspect it only got worse.

❖ ❖ ❖ ❖ ❖

These kinds of incidents naturally discourage police officers from wanting to become involved in family violence situations beyond doing the minimum amount needed to quiet the situation for that night. Most police officers see family violence incidents as no-win situations in which no one involved really wants to cooperate with the police to solve the problem. Dr. Lawrence Sherman, in his book *Policing Domestic Violence*, said: "The fundamental police attitude about domestic violence is not one of sympathy for the male, but rather a frustration at feeling unable to do anything about the kinds of people chronically involved in such incidents."[8]

As Dr. Sherman suggested above, the victims of family abuse often complain that police officers inevitably take the abuser's side and are insensitive to the needs of family abuse victims. While it is not true that police officers automatically take the abuser's side in a family abuse situation, it is true that the officers seldom empathize with the victims. This happens because after taking a few hundred family abuse runs the officers soon become desensitized. The police are often exasperated because they have to keep coming back to the same house, and it seems that nothing they do can correct the situation. The officers are also exasperated because it seems to them (though perhaps wrongly) that the victims really don't want a long-term solution. Yet still, calling the police is often a family abuse victim's only way of stopping the violence, even though only temporarily.

In a study done by Dr. David A. Ford, he found that: "Surprisingly, few women who went to the Prosecutor's Office really wanted a man imprisoned or even fined. Most would have been content to have the man arrested, jailed, and immediately released. They were not likely to support further efforts to prosecute."[9] Most police officers suspect that family abuse victims don't even want this much. They suspect that all the victims really want is for the police to punch the abuser in the nose for them, and then leave. I had a case once that demonstrates this.

❖ ❖ ❖ ❖ ❖

When I was a patrol officer on the south side of Indianapolis during the mid-1970s I had a man in my district who beat and terrorized his wife and children constantly. The wife was so intimidated that she would never call the police, and the only time we went to their house was when one of the neighbors heard her or one of the children screaming. When I would get to the house the woman and children were always so cowed and frightened by the man that they wouldn't speak to me or say anything about what had happened. I learned from the neighbors, though, that he beat all of them nearly daily and that he treated them like slaves, once even chaining his wife to the doghouse in the backyard.

One afternoon, I and another unit received a run to this family's house on the complaint from a neighbor that he had heard a woman screaming. As usual, the man answered the door, told us we weren't needed there, and that we could leave. This time, however, I decided I wasn't going to leave. He had gotten away with the abuse for too long. I pushed past him and stepped inside. The woman and two little children were, as usual, cowering in a corner.

"Hey, you can't just come barging in here!" the man told me.

I could smell the alcohol on his breath as he walked up to me. "Be quiet for a second," I told him. "I just want to make sure that everybody's all right." The police do have the authority to make a forced entry if they believe someone might be in danger.

"It ain't none of your damn business what's going on in here. You don't see anyone complaining, do you? This is my house!"

The man now stood right up in my face, breathing cheap liquor fumes onto me. The expression on his wife's face as she huddled in a corner with her children seemed to say she wanted help desperately, but was terrified to speak. I gave the man my most threatening stare as he continued violating my space. "Look, if you don't be quiet and get out of my face," I told him, "I'm going to lock you up."

I didn't realize it, but by threatening him I was undoing his years of work at convincing his family that he was omnipotent. Although the police had been called to his house many times, because his family would not complain or even say anything to the police, he had never been arrested. I later found out that he had convinced his family the police were frightened of him. And while the man had never been this confrontational in the past, I suspected that the liquor and the fact that the police had never arrested him before was giving him the courage to go a little further.

I suppose if I had left that day without doing anything, as officers had apparently done many times in the past, this would have only been more confirmation to his family of what he had been telling them. But I wasn't about to leave without doing something.

For several moments the man appeared uncertain what to do as he looked at me and then at his family. Finally, the liquor seemed to kick in and his courage returned. He sneered at me.

"Oh yeah, you cops are real tough with your big guns and all," he said. "You take that gun off and I'll kick your ass!"

That was it. I'd had enough of this man and his brutality toward his family. Although today I would severely discipline any of my officers I caught doing this, since it is totally unprofessional, I unhooked my gunbelt and handed it to the other officer. "All right now, hotshot," I said, "let's see how tough you are."

The man's eyes bulged when he saw me take off my gunbelt, and he began looking around, licking his lips over and over. He took several steps backward as I punched him in the chest with my finger, until finally he had backed himself up against a wall.

"Come on, you're big enough to beat up your wife and kids," I said. "Let's see how tough you really are." I had my fist cocked and ready, waiting for the man to take a swing at me. I have found in my career that even people who really don't want to fight will fight if they are pressured enough and see that they are about to lose face. With his back up against the wall and nowhere to go, he appeared both confused and terrified. I'm sure, based on his previous experiences, this was the last thing he expected to happen.

However, rather than taking a swing at me, even though I finally grabbed him by the shirt and lifted him up on the wall, he instead did something I didn't expect. He began crying. Now I didn't know what to do. The man actually began bawling, slumping down on the floor when I let go of him and crying like a little child. The other officer rolled his eyes at me and then gathered up the woman and two children and offered to drive them to a relative's house. I simply put my gunbelt back on, left the man crying on the living room floor, and walked back to my police car, feeling both ashamed and confused. I didn't understand what had just happened.

What I had done, I knew, was totally unprofessional. Police work is not a macho contest of who's the toughest. It's a profession whose job is to protect innocent people, not challenge someone to a fight. Today, of course, this confrontation likely wouldn't have happened. An officer today could have arrested the man for misdemeanor battery. We had no such option in the 1970s.

Six months or so later, I received a radio run on a robbery at a fast food restaurant. The man's wife, I found, worked as a waitress at the restaurant and had been a witness to the robbery. I didn't remember her, but she remembered me. While she didn't really come out and thank me, she told me that my confrontation with her now ex-husband had shown her a side of him she had never seen. She said after that day she had never gone back to him, and he had not protested when she filed for divorce, even though for the previous ten years he had told her over and over that he would kill her if she ever tried to divorce him.

❖ ❖ ❖ ❖ ❖

While adult victims of family abuse, including elderly victims, often don't or won't talk with the police out of fear, victims of child abuse many times don't know they even have the right to complain. Often, the police don't find out about child abuse in a family, particularly child sexual abuse, until the children have attended a sex abuse prevention program and learned that what is happening to them is wrong and not their fault. Even then, verifying and proving child sexual abuse is not easy. Studies report that 80 to 85 percent of sexually abused children show no medical signs since the abuse often involves touching or oral sex. Therefore, in child sexual abuse cases where there is little or no physical evidence and no other witnesses, only the child's statement is evidence that the abuse occurred.

In order to prosecute, therefore, the police must question the children. With very young children this questioning is often fraught with difficulty. When asked open-ended questions, questions that require more than a yes or no answer, young children many times say nothing or don't understand what the interviewer is asking. In a study reported in *Children Today*, researchers Gail Goodman and Karen Saywitz tell of an experiment using thirty-six five- and seven-year-old girls. Half of the girls received total medical examinations, including a genital exam. The other half received the same examination, but without the genital examination. When asked broad, open-ended questions about what the doctor did, very few of the girls mentioned the genital exam. However, the majority told about it when asked specific questions using an anatomically correct doll.[10]

Still, even when using direct, specific questions, investigators must be very careful when interrogating children so as not to be so leading as to help them invent a story which the children then confuse with reality, essentially creating a "memory" of something that may not have actually happened. This is very possible with young children. To be a good interviewer of children requires years of training and practice. The interviewer must know how to build rapport with children, and must be able to speak with them on their level. A good interrogator must know how to question children and get them to tell about abuse without leading them.

"Questioning young children can be really tough," said child abuse detective Michael Duke. "They often leave out important things that they think you already know."

I have watched my wife, who is a top child abuse detective, question children and perpetrators about abuse, and am always both awed and envious of her ability. Assigned to Indianapolis's Family Advocacy Center, and using the child-friendly atmosphere there, she is able to assume a completely nonthreatening appearance with children. She is able to talk with them on their level, use their vocabulary, and make them both believe in and trust her. Consequently, they are willing to tell her about what has happened. I have also watched her question child abusers and molesters, and she has a technique that seems to make them want to open up and tell her everything.

Although a very sophisticated woman, she is able, if need be, to put on the façade of being just a down-home country girl who knows the abuser or molester didn't mean to hurt the child. Within just a few minutes she has abusers and molesters crying and telling her everything about what they did. For some reason, when she puts on the country girl facade, child abusers and molesters don't seem to mind talking and telling her what happened, even when she turns on the tape recorder and advises them of their rights. They just start talking, and keep talking. To them she is someone who understands, someone whom they can pour their heart out to, and do. However, she can also be as sophisticated as the abuser or molester believes he or she is. Occasionally, child molesters will try to act as though being questioned by the police is below their station in life. They try to act as though they can't understand what all of the fuss and bother is about since they obviously wouldn't do anything that depraved. This ability of a detective to assume whatever role is needed is an invaluable talent because a child abuser or molester has a substantial interest in convincing everyone that the child is lying or fantasizing.

Of course, a victim of child abuse or neglect must first come to the attention of the police in order for the crime to be investigated and the perpetrators and victims questioned. In a survey of Boston parents, researchers found that in forty-eight families in which a child had been sexually molested only 56 percent of the parents reported the crime to the police. In another study, also in Boston, only 38 percent of 156 families reported the sexual abuse of their children. The reason most of the people didn't report the incident, the study found, was because they believed it to be a family matter, meaning that many of the unreported crimes involved family members as perpetrators.[11]

Just as disturbing to investigators as families who don't report child abuse are those cases in which the victim of abuse is too young to tell what happened, and there are no other witnesses. This many times leaves the investigator powerless to do anything. In addition, often the victim of child abuse and neglect is a handicapped child who is many times so handicapped as to be unable to testify. In these cases, if the police cannot get a confession, they have little power to do much else, and consequently little often happens.

In most family abuse investigations, however, not having

enough power and authority is not a problem. Most states give the police more than enough authority to resolve these incidents. The problem is that many police officers are reluctant to use this authority. The solution is that police departments must rigorously train officers about their responsibilities when dealing with family abuse. They must train the officers in the dynamics of family abuse and in their role in solving it. Also, police supervisors must rigorously ensure that officers fairly and impartially enforce family abuse laws.

Overall, the investigation of family abuse, most officers agree, is one of the worst parts of police work because the cases are so often fraught with strong emotion that they are seldom adjudicated to anyone's satisfaction. In a burglary or a robbery case, once the perpetrator is identified and arrested, the victim usually cooperates fully with the police, and wants to see the perpetrator properly punished for the crime. Family abuse cases, unfortunately, are seldom this clear-cut. The victims of abuse usually have strong emotional attachments to the perpetrators, and consequently seldom involve themselves in any criminal investigation wholeheartedly, if at all, regardless of the viciousness of the crime. Family abuse investigations, therefore, are seldom settled to anyone's satisfaction.

12

Family Abuse Prosecution

On a windy and cold November evening last year, Latasha Moore brought her twenty-month-old son, Robert, into a large inner-city hospital emergency room. The child suffered severe burns on his buttocks, the backs of both legs, and his hands and feet. When the medical personnel examined Robert, they found that the top layers of his skin were completely gone, as if they had been ripped off, and the bloody tissue below was now exposed. The examining physician, used to seeing cases of child abuse, recognized Robert's injury as a submersion burn, which occurs when a young child, and occasionally an elderly person, is intentionally submerged in scalding water. Submersion burns, the doctor knew, differ from accidental burns in that with submersion burns there are no splash burns on other parts of the body, such as on the face or chest, which would occur if a child accidentally fell or climbed into the water. The hospital personnel telephoned the police, and an on-call child abuse detective came to the emergency room.

After first speaking with the emergency room personnel, the on-call detective then began looking for Robert's mother, Latasha. The detective found her sitting with a man in the waiting room, and so the detective walked over and introduced herself, then asked Latasha to tell her what had happened.

"I was soaking some clothes in the bathtub," Latasha said, "you know, in hot water and bleach. Well, Robert, he just loves baths. He wants to take them all the time. So anyway, I went to the closet to get a towel and some more bleach and I guess Robert must've climbed into the tub."

"What did you do?"

"I reached in there and grabbed him out. Then I just kind of panicked and didn't know what to do. Luckily, a friend of mine who was coming over to help me with my car came to the door right then. I told him that Robert's burned and I need to take him to the hospital. So I wrapped him up in some towels and we brought him here."

The on-call detective had seen many burn cases, and had seen many submersion burns. While some accidents happened like Latasha claimed this one did, they were very few. Most cases of burn injury, the detective had found, weren't accidents at all, but intentional abuse. The detective also noticed that while Latasha said she had grabbed the child out of the scalding water she had no burns on her hands. While that was also possible, it too wasn't very likely. The on-call detective didn't say anything for several moments, but just looked at Latasha.

"This is just a tragic accident," Latasha said finally, seeming to wince under the detective's stare. "That's all it is. My baby was just in the wrong place at the wrong time."

Making several notes for whoever the assigned investigator would be, the on-call detective nodded at Latasha's last comment. This wasn't an accident. The detective was certain of it.

Two days later, Detective Monica Styles, the investigator assigned to the case, brought Latasha in for further questioning. Before beginning, and after advising Latasha of her rights against self-incrimination, Detective Styles showed Latasha some photos she had taken of Robert's injuries, and then bluntly told Latasha that she knew she was lying, that the story she had told at the hospital was not the truth. This wasn't an accident. It was a deliberate submersion.

Detective Styles simply stared at Latasha and waited. Suddenly, Latasha broke down crying, and after a few seconds said that the detective was right, that she had lied at the hospital, and that she would tell her what had really happened that night. Detective Styles again advised Latasha of her rights against self-incrimination, and then turned on the tape recorder.

"Latasha," Detective Styles began for the recorder, "you now want to revise the statement you gave to the police last Friday night at the hospital. Is that right?"

Still teary-eyed, Latasha sniffled a little and then nodded. "Yes I do."

"Is this because you didn't tell the truth the other night at the hospital?"

She sniffled and then nodded again. "Yes."

"Okay, Latasha, why don't you tell me what really happened to Robert."

"Well, first off, I want you to know I wasn't trying to protect anybody or anything like that when I lied. I just didn't want anyone to think that I was a bad mother. You see, that night I had to go to a meeting, you know, about my job. But before that, before I could go to the meeting, I had to go over to my aunt's house to drop off my daughter. She was going to watch her for me. I was planning on taking Robert with me to the meeting. But he wasn't cleaned up or dressed yet, so I asked Jerome if he'd watch him until I got back."

"Who's Jerome?"

"Jerome Kenney. He's my boyfriend."

"Does he live there with you?"

Latasha seemed to think for a moment, and then nodded. "Yeah, since July."

"How old is your daughter?"

"She's four."

"Okay, so you took your daughter to your aunt's and you left Robert there with Jerome. Then what happened?"

"Well, I got to my aunt's house. I wasn't there very long, just long enough for me to sit down and take my coat off. It wasn't any longer than that, and then the phone rang. It was Jerome. He said for me to get right back there because Robert's got burned. I asked him how he got burned. He said he was getting ready to give him a bath, and Robert, he jumped in the water real fast before he could check it. Something like that. He was excited and talking real fast."

Stopping for a second to take a breath, Latasha continued, "So I jumped in my car and got home as quick as I could. When I got there, Jerome already had Robert wrapped up in some towels and had his coat on. When we got into the car I unwrapped Robert and looked at him. When I saw how bad he was burned I just broke down. I started screaming and hollering and telling Jerome I should never have left my baby with him. I kept asking him why."

"What did Jerome say?"

"Nothing. He was real quiet. And I've noticed that he's been real quiet ever since that night. But I just had to know the truth. I had to know if he deliberately hurt my baby. But when he would finally talk, he just kept saying that he had run some water and then went into the other room and Robert must've climbed into the tub. He said he heard Robert hollering and when he ran in there and saw how burned he was he grabbed him up out of the water."

Detective Styles didn't say anything for a few moments, but just looked at Latasha. "I went to the hospital this morning and looked at Robert," the detective said finally. "You've seen him too. The way he's burned it doesn't look like he climbed into the tub on his own. It looks like he was set in the tub. Now think real hard about what Jerome said when he called you on the phone and told you that Robert was burned."

Latasha began crying again and just kept shaking her head. "I really don't remember. I mean, he was so excited and I was so excited. But I just can't see him deliberately doing this. He treats me really good." She stopped and seemed to think for a moment. "But still, you know, that's always been in the back of my mind."

"Has he ever hurt Robert or your daughter before this?"

"No, but then I've never left them alone with him. My daughter, she doesn't like him very much. I'm not sure why, but she doesn't like being around him. But Jerome's all right. I mean, he helps me with my bills and all, and I've known him for years. He's really only got one problem. He's kind of nutty about cleanliness and all, but that's not real bad. I mean, he really gets on my nerves sometimes because he's always cleaning up stuff around there. But that's not real bad."

"Latasha, why did you lie to the detective at the hospital?"

Wiping her eyes with a tissue, Latasha shrugged. "I guess because I was scared. I didn't want anyone to think I would leave my son with someone who might hurt him. I wasn't trying to save Jerome from anything. Really, I wasn't. I mean, I know that Jerome's done some pretty bad things in the past, and if he had done it deliberately, I didn't want anyone to know that I had left my son with him."

Detective Styles would later obtain a copy of Jerome's criminal record and find that he had indeed done some bad things in the past. His lengthy record included several arrests for burglary, several for theft, one for contributing to the delinquency of a minor, several for drug possession, one for resisting law enforcement, one for battery, and one for child molesting.

"I mean, nobody knew who was really there that night with Robert," Latasha continued. "So I just told them I was."

"Is Jerome still living with you?"

Latasha nodded. "Yes."

"Did you and Jerome discuss what you were going to say when you got to the hospital?"

"No, but he was sitting there right next to me when I started talking to the detective, and he didn't say anything when he heard what I told her. I was looking right at him, but he didn't say anything."

The next day, Detective Styles had Jerome come in for questioning. After being advised of his rights against self-incrimination, he told the detective the same story he had told Latasha, that he had drawn Robert a bath, but hadn't checked the water temperature, and must've made it too hot. He said he left the room for a few moments to watch the news on television, and when he returned he found Robert in the bathtub.

"When I went back in there," Jerome said, "I could see that

Robert didn't have any skin left, just blood. I didn't know what to do, so I grabbed some towels and wrapped him up. I don't know how long he was in the water."

"Didn't you hear him cry when he got into the hot water?" Detective Styles asked.

"No ma'am. He never did cry or scream or anything. He was just sitting there in the water shaking."

Detective Styles recalled from her questioning of Latasha that she had said Jerome told her he heard Robert hollering. She made a note of the discrepancy. "How did you manage to keep from burning your hands getting Robert out of the water?"

A few moments of silence passed before Jerome finally answered. "I guess he must've stood up or something."

Two days after this interview, Jerome called the detective back and said that he would like to talk with her again. He told her he might have left out a few things when he spoke with her earlier.

After once again advising Jerome of his rights against self-incrimination and turning on the tape recorder, Detective Styles said, "I understand you want to add something to your statement that you left out the other day when we spoke. Is that right?"

Jerome nodded. "Yes ma'am. I forgot to tell you the other day the reason I was giving Robert a bath. It was because when he came over to sit with me and watch TV I could smell that he had messed in his pants."

"Did that upset you?"

Seeming to think for a moment, Jerome finally said, "No, not really."

This was all the new information Jerome added to his previous statement, and then he simply repeated his earlier story of Robert climbing into the bathtub on his own. However, it was enough. The detective recalled Latasha's statement about Jerome's obsession with cleanliness, and felt certain she had now found the motive. Jerome, however, would not admit that he had intentionally placed Robert in the scalding water, but still insisted he had climbed in on his own. The burn patterns on Robert, though, Detective Styles knew from experience, indicated that Robert hadn't climbed in on his own but had been placed in the water. There were no splash burns that would have resulted from a small child climbing or falling into a tub of scalding water, just burns on his buttocks, backs of his legs, and hands and feet. These were clearly submersion burns.

A screening prosecutor, whose job it is to screen all cases for prosecutorial merit, agreed with the detective. A judge then approved a warrant for Jerome, and, after his arrest, set the case for trial.

❖ ❖ ❖ ❖ ❖

The above case is a typical incident of family child abuse, just like the many thousands of other cases of child abuse that police officers see every year across the United States. The reason I used this case in this chapter, however, is because, even though approved by the screening prosecutor, the prosecutor actually assigned to try the case in court decided that it likely wasn't winnable and dropped the charges against Jerome.

As often happens, a police department loads its child abuse detectives with cases, usually giving them many new cases a week to investigate. Once the detectives have gotten all of the witness and suspect statements taken, gathered all of the available evidence, presented the case to the screening prosecutor, and had the case filed for trial, the detectives then move on to other assignments, and can't give the case much more thought until they receive notice of a trial date. This can often be months, and much can happen during this time. Consequently, cases can be forgotten about, but luckily not Robert's case. When Detective Styles routinely checked on it, she found that the prosecutor had dropped the charges without telling her.

Livid, Detective Styles went to see the prosecutor, found that he still felt reluctant to prosecute the case, but could give her no concrete reason for it, only a feeling that it wasn't winnable. Detective Styles, however, felt she had a good case, and pressed hard for a trial, even going so far as to locate all of the witnesses to be certain they were still available. The prosecutor held fast for some time to his decision, but then at last agreed to go to trial, and refiled the charges against Jerome. When Jerome's attorney found that his client was going to have to go to trial on the case after all, he worked out a plea bargain with the prosecutor. Jerome would plead guilty to the burning of Robert and receive a twelve-year prison sentence.

Why didn't the prosecutor want to try this case, even though the screening prosecutor felt it was a good case, and even though Jerome and his attorney obviously felt the state had enough evidence to convict him? It's hard to say what it was about this case that the prosecutor didn't like, but police detectives find that many prosecutors don't like to try any type of family abuse cases. In child abuse cases particularly, such as the one above, there are usually no witnesses who can tell what really happened since the child victim is often very young and cannot talk. The cases, therefore, many times hinge on circumstantial evidence, something which makes many prosecutors feel uncertain. In addition, prosecutors can't depend on the statements and testimony of a child abuse victim's parents. The parents are many times torn between protecting their children and protecting the abusers, who are often spouses or intimate partners.

Unfortunately, if a prosecutor holds fast to a decision not to try a case, no matter how good a case it might be, the police are powerless to do anything about it, other than what Detective Styles above did. Prosecutors are elected officials who usually answer only to the voters at election time. These voters often have no idea, beyond the press releases put out by the prosecutor's office, what prosecutors are doing between elections. Occasionally, pressure from the news media may force a prosecutor to try a case he or she would rather not, but this is the exception. Usually there is very little oversight of a prosecutor's decision about trying or not trying a child abuse or other type of family abuse case. Because of this, every year thousands of family abusers escape punishment when the prosecutor's office declines to take the case.

According to the National Institute of Justice's research paper *When the Victim Is a Child*: "Prosecutional rates (i.e., the proportion of cases referred for prosecution that are subsequently accepted) appear to be extremely variable. Among five prosecutors' offices participating in a demonstration project for the Bureau of Justice Assistance (BJA), prosecution rates ranged from 38 percent to 100 percent.... Not surprisingly, prosecutors who accept only cases where there is a confession tend to enjoy remarkably high conviction rates. Among the five jurisdictions that participated in the BJA study, conviction rates ranged from 50 to 93 percent of the cases accepted for prosecution."[1]

A study reported in the Office of Juvenile Justice and Delinquency Prevention's research paper *The Child Victim as a Witness* stated: "[V]ictims in accepted [for prosecution] cases averaged almost 2 years older than victims in cases that were declined. Only 34 percent of cases involving pre-schoolers (age 4 to 6) were accepted, versus 69 percent of cases involving elementary school children (age 7 to 12), and 68 percent of cases in which the victims were teenagers (age 13 to 17)." The authors then go on to say: "Abuse of longer than one month's duration, use of force, and severity of abusive acts increased the likelihood of prosecution. Cases involving multiple incidents showed trends toward greater prosecution.... Almost ninety percent of cases were accepted when physical evidence was present, but under 60 percent when it was absent."[2]

A 1993 American Bar Association national survey found that 91 percent of the six hundred prosecutors surveyed said that the main reason for rejecting child sexual abuse cases was the problem of having a child witness. But still, 80 percent of the prosecutors said that they prosecuted substantially more cases of child sexual abuse than physical abuse. This is interesting because national statistics show that there is a significantly higher number of child physical abuse cases reported to the police every year than sexual abuse. The prosecutors had a number of reasons for this difference, with one of the major reasons being that the sexual abuse of a child is viewed as wrong by practically everyone, while physical abuse is often seen by many as the parental prerogative to discipline a child.[3]

"Most physical abuse cases are in a discipline context," said a prosecutor who handles child abuse cases. "Unless the injury is really serious, like a fractured skull, jurors often take the parents' side. They believe parents have the right to discipline their children."

On the other hand, even though prosecutors try more child sexual abuse cases than physical abuse cases, they still don't like trying these child sexual abuse cases. The reasons for this dislike include the fact that usually the only witnesses are the child and the alleged perpetrator, and often, particularly if the alleged perpetrators have good community standing, jurors don't want to convict them of something as repulsive as child molesting. For example, in 1992 the police charged Stephen A. Sharp, a presidential appointee to the Federal Communications Commission, with three separate incidents of child sexual abuse, including one involving a teenager over whom he had legal custody. At his trial, however, even though the jury said they felt there was ample evidence to convict Mr. Sharp of the child sexual abuse, two jurors at first refused to do so because of Mr. Sharp's "respected position in the community." After asking the judge for advice, the two jurors finally voted to convict Mr. Sharp.[4]

"When you're prosecuting a child sexual abuse case you're very often prosecuting someone who doesn't look the part," said Carol Orbison, a former prosecutor and now juvenile court judge. "The man often has a good job, a nice wife, and a fine home, while the victim is many times a runaway, a truant, or uses drugs."

Another reason prosecutors don't like trying child sexual abuse cases is because physical evidence of the crime is often inconclusive. Only recently have doctors become aware that a child's normal genital and anal condition is extremely variable. What were once considered sure signs of abuse is now recognized as possibly normal development for a child. An article in the September 1994 issue of the journal *Pediatrics* tells of a study of 236 cases in which a court had determined that child sexual abuse had occurred. A team of medical researchers from the Child Sexual Abuse Evaluation Program at Valley Medical Center in Fresno, California, inspected the medical files of these 236 children, including anal and genital photographs. In only 9 percent of the 236 cases could it be established that the medical evidence showed suspicion of sexual abuse, while in 77 percent of the cases, the children's genital and anal areas were deemed to be normal. Interestingly, though, in 72 percent of the 236 cases the accused abuser pleaded guilty, while another 14 percent were found guilty.[5] Explaining part of this discrepancy, child sexual abuse cases often involve oral sex or fondling, both of which leave no evidence, but which also make prosecutors unlikely to want to try the case.

In his book *The Battle and the Backlash*, David Hechler, an investigative reporter, tells of a prosecutor who refuses to take almost any child sexual abuse cases because their outcome is too hard to predict. The same prosecutor, interestingly enough, has a perfect 100 percent conviction rate in the cases he has taken to prosecute, which means he only takes those cases that have perfect evidence and perfect witnesses, something extremely rare. This also means that a lot of guilty people in this prosecutor's community are getting away with their crimes. But a prosecutor in another part of the country has a different outlook: "We try lots of cases that we lose. We try them for the sheer inconvenience of the defendant.... There's always a question in marginal cases about whether you'll get a conviction. And if I lose, well, I lose."[6]

From my twenty-eight years as a police officer I can say without reservation that this latter prosecutor's attitude is one of the keys to stopping family abuse in a community. Abusers must know that the community sees their behavior as criminal, and that if they decide to continue with it they must take the risk of being sent to prison. There should be no doubt in the minds of abusers what will happen if they continue their behavior. Unfortunately, this prosecutor's attitude is in the minority.

One of key reasons, however, why so many prosecutors don't like to try child abuse cases is because, as prosecutors, they are elected officials, and usually want to be reelected or elected to another office. A less than sterling conviction rate as prosecutor is often seen by them as damaging to their political aspirations, and convictions in child abuse cases are never certain.

Political reasons aside, however, many prosecutors don't like to try child abuse cases because, even if the child is old enough to testify and tell what happened, still certain problems are inherent. When young children have told a story a number of times, to a parent, to a child protective services worker, to a detective, and to a prosecutor, they many times assume the story is already known and will leave out parts of it when retelling it in court. Defense attorneys will usually jump on this and accuse the children of changing their story. In addition, children are easily confused by aggressive defense attorneys, and often feel intimidated by the courtroom and the proceedings, particularly since many times they must sit facing the family member they are accusing. A study reported in the journal *Child Abuse and Neglect* tells of an experiment in which children were questioned in a mock courtroom set up in a law school and at their own school about their memory of an activity. The children, researchers found, had better recall of the activity in their own school than in the courtroom.[7] For all of these reasons, many prosecutors just don't feel comfortable prosecuting a case in which the only evidence is a child's testimony.

"You never know how a child will react to a situation where there are many strange people listening to him or her tell an embarrassing story," said Judge Carol Orbison. "And you don't know how the child will react to having to tell it in front of the abuser."

My feeling on this is, like the prosecutor quoted above, just try the case, and if you lose, you lose. When a child shows the courage to come forward and tell about abuse, the prosecutor should have the courage to try the case. I think that with the proper publicity about what he or she is doing the public will understand that a prosecutor who tries most family abuse cases will have less than a perfect conviction rate. Presented in the right way, I believe the public will see that the prosecutor is not performing poorly because of the conviction rate, but rather is doing the job he or she was elected to do—protecting the public.

However, even if the prosecutor does decide to try the case, before children in most states can give testimony they must first demonstrate their competency as witnesses. The 1895 U.S. Supreme Court case *Wheeler v. United States* established that a child witness's competency depended on: "the capacity and intelligence of the child, his appreciation of the difference between truth and falsehood, as well as of his duty to tell the former."[8]

In the years since this case, the courts have established four measures of a child's competency to testify: capacity for truthfulness,
mental capacity, memory, and communication skill. Because of
these measures, the younger the child, the less likely he or she
will be competent to testify. This is why many child abusers,
particularly sexual molesters, pick very young children as their
targets.

Unfortunately, even children who pass the four measures
above are still often perceived by jurors as being less credible than
adult witnesses. A survey of seventy-four defense attorneys and
forty-seven prosecutors in Florida discovered that attorneys are
well aware of most jurors' negative perceptions of a child witness's credibility. The defense attorneys in the survey even said
that, because of this knowledge, they often use aggressive cross-
examination tactics that focus on children's vulnerability as witnesses.[9]

Yet, even more distressing than this deliberate attack on child
witnesses by defense attorneys is the large number of "expert
witnesses" who ride circuit around the country testifying in child
abuse cases for whichever side pays them. The field of child abuse,
and particularly child sexual abuse, is relatively new and there is
still much to be learned about it. Consequently, much of what
these expert witnesses testify to is unproven or controversial. Still,
these paid "experts" can often sway the court with their testimony, since they seem confident and decisive, while the children
seem frightened and confused.

Likewise, in cases of family abuse involving the elderly, often
the victims are so old, ill, frail, or senile that, like small children,
they many times cannot provide information about what has
happened. And again, since the abuser is often a family member,
it is difficult to get other family members to testify or give evidence against him or her. Also, since many elderly family members are bedfast, they cannot be brought into court to testify.

All of the above problems, incidentally, are true not just in
abuse and neglect cases, but also in cases of financial exploitation.
The prosecutor must prove that the perpetrator didn't have the
victim's consent to use or convert his or her property. This can be

particularly difficult if the victim is senile or very ill, and especially if the perpetrator is the victim's guardian or has power of attorney.

Of all types of family abuse, though, prosecutors especially don't like to try cases involving spouses and intimate partners who abuse each other. The reason for this reluctance is that, because of the crowding of the court docket, the trial usually takes place months after an abusive incident, and the passing time often dulls the victim's original intention to prosecute. Because of this, prosecutors usually feel reluctant to try spousal or intimate partner cases in which the victim and perpetrator continue to live together. This arrangement, prosecutors find, far too often leads to a change of heart, dropped charges, and an uncooperative victim.

Although most cases brought to trial without cooperation from the victim usually fail to convict the abuser, this is not always true. The Pulitzer Prize-winning series of articles about domestic violence in Kentucky, published by the *Lexington Herald-Leader*, tells of the case of Mabelle and Danny Brown. In 1988, Danny beat Mabelle so badly she suffered facial fractures and brain injuries that kept her in the hospital for thirty-nine days and left her partly paralyzed. Despite this, Mabelle refused to cooperate in the prosecution of Danny. The prosecutor went ahead anyway, and eventually convicted Danny.

"The attack speaks for itself, and her permanent injuries speak for themselves ...," said Keith McCormick, assistant commonwealth's attorney. "We weren't trying the case based on whether or not Mabelle wanted a trial—the question was whether or not the commonwealth's law was broken when Mabelle was beaten."[10]

Of course, while the law recognizes a husband–wife immunity against compelled testimony, a spouse waives this right if he or she communicates information about a crime to the authorities. Once a spouse does report a crime, then it is possible that the spouse can be compelled under the threat of contempt to testify against the other spouse. This, however, very rarely happens. A recent article in *The New York Times* tells of the growing use of testimony by experts in the field of family abuse in those court cases where the victims have changed their minds and recanted their earlier accusations of abuse. These experts explain to the jurors why people who have been severely and brutally abused would refuse to cooperate in a trial, and why severely abused people would want to protect their abusers by recanting.

"It's hard for jurors to understand why they should take a case seriously if the victim is unwilling to come forward and testify," said Holly Maguigan, a professor at the New York University School of Law. Use by prosecutors of these experts can help overcome this misunderstanding by jurors.[11]

Few prosecutors are so vigilant, however, and many family abuse victims come to feel that their prosecutor's office is set up not to protect and help them, but rather to discourage them from using it. Since prosecutors see so many family abuse cases dropped, they often make the victims go to great lengths to convince them that they are serious about prosecuting. Few other criminal cases, though, particularly those involving strangers, are prosecuted or not prosecuted on the basis of whether or not the victim may have a change of heart. Prosecutors seldom make robbery or burglary victims convince their office that they are serious about prosecuting, even though many of these cases are dropped. The same should hold for family abuse cases.

How do prosecutors make victims prove they are serious? In some cities spousal and intimate partner abuse cases require a "cooling off" period before charges will be filed. Others require extensive paperwork, or that the victim and perpetrator separate. Some cities have even been known to require the victim to pay a fee to bring charges. In many other cases, because of the questions asked by the prosecutor's office, the victims begin to feel that they are being held responsible for their own victimization. When asked why they are still with the abusers or why they haven't done something about the abuse before this, many victims become discouraged and withdraw their complaint.

Is asking these kinds of questions proper and ethical? No. These questions have the tendency to blame the victim rather than the abuser, which can only perpetuate abuse in a community. However, most prosecutors operate under only the barest of oversight, and so there is very little individual victims can do.

Worse still, in some jurisdictions, even if the prosecutor does decide to prosecute a spouse or intimate partner for abuse, the charges filed are many times not as severe as the crime was. Often, for example, a felony assault will be tried as a misdemeanor. In this way, the case can be tried in a lesser court, with less trouble and less expense. Unfortunately, this is within the prosecutor's authority, even if it doesn't serve the public interest.

Denise Markham, supervisor for the Domestic Violence Advocacy Project in Chicago, estimates that 90 percent of the family abuse cases in Cook County are filed as misdemeanors, regardless of the severity of the injuries, including those that should make the crime a felony.[12] A National Crime Survey discovered that over a third of the domestic violence cases filed as misdemeanors would have been felonies if committed by strangers. A *Los Angeles Times* analysis of California statistics for 1990 through 1992 found that while two-thirds of the people arrested for felony spouse abuse went to court, 80 percent of these cases were treated as misdemeanors. This, of course, makes the victims feel that the criminal justice system does not take their case seriously.

"I think spousal battery is frequently dropped to a misdemeanor for reasons of expediency and insensitivity on the part of law enforcement and the courts," said Susan Frascella, chairwoman of the Southern California Coalition on Battered Women.

"It's probably too high," said Los Angeles County District Attorney Gil Garcetti, speaking of his office's misdemeanor filing rate. According to the *Los Angeles Times* study, 90 percent of Los Angeles County's spousal abuse cases are filed as misdemeanors.[13] I would certainly have to agree with Mr. Garcetti. It sounds high to me too.

In addition to all of these problems, prosecutors also find that, except in the most extreme cases, jurors often don't want to convict in domestic violence cases. Hearing the testimony about a family's dirty laundry, about squabbles and intrafamilial fighting, often comes too close to home. Also, jurors question why the victims didn't just leave, and wonder whether or not the victims played a part in antagonizing the abusers. Only intensive public education in the reality of family abuse will change this attitude.

It should be obvious from what I have shown in this chapter that a critical problem exists in the prosecution of family abuse cases in our country. Much of this problem stems from the fact that prosecutors don't like to try these cases because they are difficult to win. However, this can be changed. An alert, knowledgeable public which makes their prosecutor justify decisions about trying or not trying family abuse cases could solve 90 percent of the problem. If a community demands full prosecution for family abusers, then losing cases does not become a political liability.

Readers may wonder how the public can make their prosecutor responsible and answerable to them. It's not difficult. Any group concerned about the problem of family abuse can act as an oversight committee for their prosecutor. It doesn't take any type of election or appointment, just a commitment to solving the problem. While asking for statistics and figures about the family abuse prosecution rate will likely make a prosecutor nervous, he or she is a public servant and the public has a right to this information. Once a prosecutor knows that his or her actions are being closely watched and monitored, he or she will be much more willing to serve the public's interest rather than personal political aspirations. The public must demand that family abuse cases not be treated as any less serious than crimes involving strangers. The injuries do not hurt less, and the consequences are not less severe. Most of all, a prosecutor should never be allowed to view a family abuse case as a political liability. To do so lessens the victim's worth in the eyes of the law.

13

Signs of Family Abuse

"Ma'am," I heard an officer on the police radio tell the dispatcher, "we need a supervisor here at 1718 North Capitol on a resister."

I pulled my radio microphone off the dash clip. "Edward 3 to Control, I'll take that."

A few moments later, Edward 18, the only sergeant working on the sector that day, contacted me on the radio, and said thanks. While resisting-arrest reports are usually handled by sergeants, I volunteered to take it for him since I knew he was on his dinner break. I had been promoted to lieutenant a few months before and, as part of this promotion, had moved into headquarters as the new Field Training Officer Program Coordinator, basically a desk job, but a job that was just a temporary stop. Soon afterward, I would take over as the Commander of the Planning and Research Branch, while my ex-partner would become the Police Department Executive Officer. He would then eventually be promoted to Deputy Chief of Operations, and I would step into his job as the Police Department Executive Officer.

While I realized at the time that I should be happy I was suddenly making giant leaps upward in the hierarchy of the police department, my enthusiasm was dampened a bit by the fact that in order to move upward I had to leave street duty behind and take a number of administrative jobs. I had been the Field Training Officer Program Coordinator now for only a few months, and already I missed street work. So, whenever Edward sector had a shortage of street supervisors, as they had that day, I volunteered to work.

After receiving acknowledgment from the dispatcher that I was assigned to the resisting-arrest run, I began searching through my forms for the necessary paperwork. Whenever a person in Indianapolis resists arrest with sufficient vigor that he or she, or the officer, is injured, a report by a supervisor is made, and one copy goes to the Deputy Chief of Operations and the other to Internal Affairs. This is done because, while any officer can have a resisting-arrest case, when an officer becomes involved in a large number of them this usually signals problems with the officer. Internal Affairs and the Deputy Chief's Office want copies in order to keep track of them.

When I pulled into the 1700 block of North Capitol, I saw an ambulance sitting at the curb in front of a police car. I parked my own Crown Victoria behind the other police car, and when I stepped out into the extraordinarily warm fall air I saw a man, obviously handcuffed behind his back, sitting in the rear seat of the police car in front of me. He had a blood-soaked bandage over his right eye. I then walked up to the open ambulance, cringing from the antiseptic smell, and saw a medical technician working on a young woman's face that looked as though she had gone a couple of rounds with George Foreman on one of George's good days. Her left eye was already swollen shut, the right one fast on the way to being shut. I could also see she had a spot on her right cheek that was just turning bluish-purple, and that her bottom lip had a huge split in it.

"No, I don't want to go to the hospital," she told the med tech. "I just want to get away from that son of a bitch!"

"Hi, Lieutenant."

Officer Jack Greene walked around from the other side of the ambulance and gave me a wave. Close behind followed his rookie, the excitement obvious in the young officer's eyes, his breathing short and raspy. The knuckles of the rookie's right hand, I noticed, were skinned and bloody.

In those days, Edward sector was the field training sector for

the Indianapolis Police Department. For four months after graduation from the Police Academy rookies rode on Edward sector
with field training officers like Jack Greene. The field training
officers would watch over and instruct the rookies on how to
apply the knowledge they had gained at the academy in the real
world of police work. The field training officers evaluated the
rookies every day, and failing marks usually meant dismissal from
the police department.

"What happened here, Jack?" I asked.

"Well, Lieutenant, we got a run here on a domestic disturbance." He hooked a thumb at the ambulance. "Her and her husband I guess are in the middle of a divorce, and he's not supposed
to be anywhere near her. Anyway, she says he came to her door a
little while ago and told her he wanted to talk about the divorce.
So she let him in and right away they got to arguing. I'm not sure
what their argument was about, but he really beat the hell out of
her. When we pulled up, he saw us and took off running. My
rookie here is pretty damn fast though and chased him down."

Jack let out a loud breath. "I was close behind, Lieutenant, but
I couldn't keep up with them. Anyway, Mr. Sheldon, that's his
name, Arnold Sheldon, obviously didn't want to go to jail and he
took a swing at my rookie. I saw it all. My rookie cracked Sheldon
just once and the fight was over."

I nodded. "Okay, let me go talk to Mr. Sheldon." I turned and
walked over to Jack's police car and opened the rear door. Resisting arrest reports required that we attempt to get a statement from
the resister. Although usually it was something like, "Go take a
flying leap," we were still required to try.

"Hi, Mr. Sheldon, I'm Lieutenant Snow." I advised him of his
rights against self-incrimination, noting the strong smell of cheap
wine. "I think you're aware that the officers are going to charge
you with resisting arrest. Would you like to tell me what happened?"

Mr. Sheldon didn't even look up at me. He just stared at the
floor and frowned, then finally shook his head.

"Okay, thank you." I shut the door, and then walked back
over to the ambulance, where the medical technician was having

Mrs. Sheldon sign a medical release since she didn't want to go to the hospital. "Mrs. Sheldon," I said, "I'd like to talk with you for a second."

I walked with her back up onto the porch of her house, where she took a seat on a wooden bench swing. "Since my officers had to pop Mr. Sheldon," I told her, "I need to make a special report. Would you tell me what happened."

"That son of a bitch beat the hell out of me for nothing! This is the exact reason I'm divorcing his ass. He's been beating on me for four years."

"How long have you two been married?"

"Four years."

In the twelve years I had been on the police department at that time I had been on hundreds and hundreds of similar runs. But before my promotion I had been helping Dr. David Ford of Indiana University at Indianapolis gather statistics for his study of conjugal violence. His research assistants had ridden with me numerous times, and listening to them questioning conjugal violence victims had gotten me interested in the subject. I sat down on the rather hard, rough brick ledge that ran around the porch.

"He's been beating on you since your honeymoon?" I asked.

"Just about. I think the first time he hit me couldn't have been more than a month or so after we were married."

"Was he a nice guy when you two were dating?"

Mrs. Sheldon gave a half-shrug. "He wasn't too bad then, just kind of moody. I mean, if he'd see me even glance at another guy he'd get all pouty and stuff. And he was always worried that whenever we weren't together I was out with some other guy. It seemed like every minute he had free he was either calling me or coming over to be with me. But he wasn't mean then." She stopped and seemed to think for a moment. "Except for one time. He got real drunk one time when we were dating and he came over to my apartment. When I told him I didn't want to go out with him, he shoved me down the stairs." Mrs. Sheldon gave another small shrug. "But he was really drunk and he swore he didn't know what he was doing."

I just had to ask this. "After all of that you married him anyway?"

She looked kind of sheepish for a second. "I thought he'd change. He promised that after we were married everything would be great. And I thought that once we were married he'd quit worrying about other guys." Mrs. Sheldon let out a loud breath. "Hell, in the last four years the only person he hasn't accused me of sleeping with is the paperboy, and that's probably only because he hasn't thought of it."

I remembered something I had heard many victims of domestic violence tell Dr. Ford's research assistants, and so I asked, "Do you know if your husband came from a violent family?"

Mrs. Sheldon let out another harsh breath. "Are you kidding? His dad still beats the hell out of his mom all the time. We were over there a couple of months ago and he accused her of wanting to sleep with his brother. And hell, they're all probably in their sixties."

"How about you?" I asked. "Did your mother and father fight?"

She gave a little humorless laugh. "Like cats and dogs."

❖ ❖ ❖ ❖ ❖

Mrs. Sheldon's notion that Mr. Sheldon would change after their marriage is a common belief among victims of family abuse. However, most researchers in domestic violence find that the likelihood of this happening is very remote. An abuser's problems are usually very deeply rooted in the person's personality, and unless he or she voluntarily seeks counseling or other help, these problems almost inevitably culminate in family abuse. What Mrs. Sheldon saw of her husband before they were married had all of the signs of a future case of family abuse. She should have dumped him and looked for another mate. And even more than most, she should have been alert to the signs of family abuse since she had her own family background to use as a reference. Unfortunately, however, few people do use their own childhood experiences with abuse as reference when picking a spouse or intimate partner. Most mistakenly believe their lives will be different or that their future partner will change.

But what about people who have come from a nonviolent family? Those people who have always been nurtured and loved by family members, and so have no frame of reference? How can these people recognize a likely future abuser? What are some of the signs of probable future family abuse that they can look for?

The first sign is that, like Mr. Sheldon, many family abusers exhibit extreme jealousy of their spouses or intimate partners. This often manifests itself from the very start of a relationship, practically from the first date. Driven by compulsive jealousy, they constantly check on their partners, making them account for every second they are away, and often accusing them of having desires for, or actually having affairs with, every person imaginable. Any type of male–female contact becomes a secret and illicit sexual liaison.

"When I was six months pregnant," a formerly abused woman told me, "a man at a gas station said to me, 'It's a nice day, isn't it?' When my husband saw this he came out of the station, grabbed me by the hair, and began beating my head against the car door."

Abusers occasionally even beat their victims until they admit to imagined infidelities, which then, of course, only fires up the abusers' paranoia and certainty that their partners are unfaithful and want to leave them. This is known as the "Othello syndrome," named after the Shakespearian character who murdered his wife, Desdemona, because of his certainty she had been unfaithful to him. In actuality, of course, Desdemona was innocent.

Interestingly, many people often find this close attention paid to them and their every move very flattering at first. Wanting to be with them and know where they're at every second seems intensely romantic. It makes the person receiving the attention feel needed and seems to demonstrate that the other person obviously cares intensely for them. However, this close attention can quickly become suffocating after marriage, particularly when the victims find they must account for and report everything they do. What once seemed nice—the abusers wanting the victims to spend every minute with them and only them—soon begins to feel imprisoning. Eventually, because of this extreme jealousy, many victims literally do become prisoners.

Along with being intensely jealous, these men, who have a poor self-image and feel very insecure, often feel the need to overcompensate for their insecurities. This type of man many times believes that he has to act tough and masculine all of the time, and that if he doesn't act tough and masculine, people will see him for the weakling he really believes himself to be. Seeing any of the traits I have discussed so far in a possible future intimate partner should send up warning flags—this type of person often becomes extremely dependent on his spouse or intimate partner, and will go to almost any length to keep the person in the relationship, from begging and giving gifts to threats and violence.

Another very hazardous kind of intimate partner is the man who has strict traditional ideas about family relationships. Such men believe that the man should always be in charge and be the head of the family, and that the man's decision is final. This type of man will also usually have strict ideas about the role of women, most often seeing them as subservient. This outlook can lead to abuse because this type of man, believing himself to be rightfully in charge, usually also believes he has the right to force compliance to his ideals, force that includes abuse.

When looking for signs of the likelihood of future family abuse, a key one is a history of witnessing family abuse. Children who witness family abuse very often grow up to do the very same thing, even though they may have sworn that they never would. One of the most famous mass murderers in American history, Charles Whitman, the sniper who climbed to the top of the clock tower on the campus of the University of Texas at Austin in 1966 and shot several dozen people, had witnessed his father regularly beat his mother. Although Whitman swore to himself again and again that he would never be like his father, in the months before he became a mass killer from his perch atop the clock tower he started realizing that he had become exactly like his father. He had already beaten his wife several times. While Whitman hated himself for it, he claimed he couldn't stop it.[1]

Anyone looking for signs of possible future abuse should be aware that any violence between a couple before marriage makes it almost a certainty that there will be more violence after the marriage. While the abusers may apologize profusely, or, like Mr. Sheldon above, claim they weren't responsible because they were drunk, this violence shows the person's method for handling stress or disagreements. It clearly demonstrates that violence, rather than discussion and working out solutions, is the person's first choice when experiencing stress or opposition.

This violence before marriage, incidentally, also includes violence against others. A person who regularly resorts to violence in order to solve problems or to vent frustration, who regularly becomes involved in fistfights with others, who is always angry at someone and has a hair-trigger temper, will eventually act the same against a spouse or intimate partner. Anyone contemplating a long-term relationship with another person should try to see that person when under stress or when highly frustrated. How that person deals with it will indicate how he or she will treat a spouse or intimate partner.

As I talked about in previous chapters, researchers have found that almost all family abuse has one goal: control. So, consequently, a very good sign of a likely future family abuser is a person who always wants control. There are several questions you need to ask yourself about any possible intimate partner. Does the person you're dating always have to have his or her way? Does he or she always decide where the date will be and what you'll be doing? Does he or she decide what you will wear? Does the person want to decide whom you associate with? If the person doesn't get his or her way, does he or she become sullen and angry? Does the person you're dating try to keep you away from your friends, or insist that they really aren't your friends, and that he or she is the only one you can count on? If so, this is a person attempting to control you, and a person to stay far, far away from.

"It was all about control," an abused woman told me, speaking about her marriage. "Even on things we had agreed about already, he would change them because he wanted control."

Excessive alcohol or drug use is another warning sign of possible future family abuse. While such alcohol or drug use doesn't really cause family abuse, and should never be accepted as an excuse or rationalization for abuse, it does lower a person's inhibitions against it. Also, research shows that substance abuse and aggression toward others very often go together. A study talked about earlier with college students showed this relationship. Students in the study who thought they were being given alcohol acted more aggressively than they did when they thought they were being given a nonalcoholic drink (though both were nonalcoholic). It appears it is the expectation of the effects of alcohol, more than the actual effects, that cause aggressive and abusive behavior.

Abusive behavior may also become a possibility for a woman if she enjoys a higher social or financial status than her spouse or intimate partner, or when she has higher educational achievements than him. Often, an insecure man in this type of unequal relationship, feeling inferior, will use the only resource he has to "equalize" or "overcome" his spouse's or intimate partner's higher status: abuse. Police see this happen often when such men are laid off from their jobs and the wives then seek employment to support the family. The men, feeling inadequate, many times become violent and abusive.

A person with wild mood swings, extreme emotional highs and lows, is also not likely to make a good spouse or intimate partner. People who can be kind and sweet one moment, and then cruel and mean the next, will be hard to live with, and will likely become meaner and more cruel the longer they are in a relationship. This includes the people who, outside the relationship, appear friendly and charming, but who can be cruel and abusive to those close to them.

In the book *Battered Women: Living with the Enemy*, an abused woman says: "You would love him if you met him. To people outside, he was nice, he was in control, he seemed strong, and the type we respect in our society. But he was also very moody, and at home you never knew what was bothering him."[2]

The author of *Next Time, She'll Be Dead* states: "Batterers can be perfectly agreeable, straightforward, or conciliatory to police officers, bosses, neighbors, co-workers, or friends when they think it's in their best interests. If they don't use those interpersonal skills with their wives, it's because they think it's *not* in their best interests; they *choose* not to."[3]

Keeping the above two quotes in mind, people who find themselves falling emotionally for another person might find it worthwhile to investigate that person's past relationship history. While a certain amount of negativism will undoubtedly come from a former lover or spouse if the breakup was not congenial, several reports of any of the traits mentioned so far in this chapter should be cause for serious concern, even if the person being investigated doesn't seem anything at all like what is reported. Keep in mind that the person might be treating you well now only because it is in his or her best interests to do so. Don't be foolish enough to believe that your relationship with a person is so special or so different that the same thing that has happened to other intimate partners will not happen to you.

Interesting correlations have also been found between the company a person keeps and that person's attitude toward a spouse or intimate partner. Lee H. Bowker, in research reported in *Police Studies*, found "a strong correlation for 1,000 men between severe wife assault and three measures of social embedment in male culture: exclusive contact with male friends, time spent in bars without the wife, and reading of pornography."[4]

Dr. Richard Gelles of the University of Rhode Island, after examining data from the National Institute of Justice and other sources on domestic violence, says: "Many of the factors are economic. Severely abusive men are more likely than their nonabusive peers to be unemployed or to hold blue-collar jobs, or to have family incomes of less than $15,000 a year. They are likely to be from 18 to 30 years old, to use illicit drugs like cocaine or engage in binge drinking, and to have dropped out of high school."[5]

Readers should keep in mind, however, that Dr. Gelles is

talking about probabilities and percentages. While a higher percentage of lower-income people may be abusive, this certainly doesn't mean a financially well off person cannot be. Also, Dr. Gelles is talking about *severely* abusive men. Overall, family abuse knows no social class, and all of the warning signs, no matter whom they come from, should be taken very seriously and acted upon.

All of the examples I've given so far in this chapter are warning signs to look for in a possible mate or intimate partner before committing yourself to a long-term relationship. But what about friends or family members who you think might be victims of abuse? You naturally may not feel comfortable asking anything or taking any actions unless you are fairly certain. Are there signs or indications you can look for? Yes.

A very common sign of abuse between spouses and intimate partners is the "clumsy" person. This is the person who always seems to have a black eye, bruises, or other injuries, and who always seems to have a story about tripping over or running into something. While we all occasionally have these type of accidents, too many of them usually means abuse.

This type of family abuse victim may also often fail to show up at prearranged functions. This can come from either the abuser's attempt to control the victim, to decide whom he or she will associate with, or from the victim's attempt to hide the injuries he or she has suffered. Also, very often a sign of an abusive relation ship is the woman who wears turtlenecks and long sleeves in warm weather or who uses heavy makeup in order to cover up bruises or other injuries.

"I lied to everyone about my injuries," a formerly abused woman told me. "I used to wear long-sleeved shirts in the summer so that my father wouldn't see the bruises."

A couple involved in an abusive relationship can also often be spotted through the abuser's actions toward the victim when they are out together in public. The abusers will many times ridicule the victims in front of their friends. When seen in public, the victims, who may have once been very outgoing, may now seem timid and afraid around the abusers, seldom speaking or drawing attention to themselves. Abusers may also try to alienate the victims' friends with insults or a bad temper, hoping that the friends will not want to associate with the victims any longer, thereby further isolating them. Social isolation is a common characteristic of abusive homes. When there is little or no outside social intercourse, the abuser doesn't have to worry about disapproval and informal sanctions by friends and neighbors, or the formal and legal sanctions possible from the criminal justice system.

Unlike physical and emotional abuse of spouses and intimate partners, the physical abuse and neglect of children can often be easier to detect. Children, when they reach school age, must go out and be seen by teachers, school administrators, and other children, and they are usually less enthusiastic about hiding the abuse and injuries. While children will many times injure themselves playing, these injuries are usually scrapes and cuts on the bony protuberances, such as knees and elbows. Children don't usually whip themselves with electrical cords hard enough to raise welts, they don't burn themselves with cigarettes, they don't put pressure bruises on their arms, and they don't bite themselves hard enough to leave wounds.

Signs of neglect of children, of course, include youngsters who appear thin and malnourished, who look gaunt and underweight, who wear tattered or filthy clothing, and who have obvious medical problems unattended to. Neglected children are also often left for long periods without supervision and attention, and consequently appear to be clinging and attention-craving because of the emotional neglect they are suffering.

The signs of intrafamilial sexual abuse of children can be much more subtle, and consequently more difficult to detect. Still, a person should be suspicious whenever a young child's underwear is torn, stained, or bloody, or a child complains of itching or pain in the genital area. It should also be of concern when a child is suddenly afraid of a family member. In addition, young child sexual abuse victims often act much more sexually mature than they should for their age, or will seem to have an inappropriate knowledge of sex. This includes children sexually flirting with other children or adults, expressing desires and emotions far above their age, and talking about sexual matters they should be unaware of.

Children who are being sexually abused by family members may also show behavioral problems and changes. These include withdrawal, depression, sleep disturbances, nightmares, and eating disorders. The children may suddenly become obsessed with taking baths or showers. Often the children begin losing interest in school activities, and start having academic problems. Children being sexually abused can also become sexually aggressive toward other children.

"Things that were important to a child will no longer be," said Detective Michael Duke. "A sexually abused child who was once interested in school or sports will often no longer care about them."

Of course, the sexual abuser of a child will also show signs of the abuse. The abuser will be very protective of the victim since he or she naturally does not want the victim questioned about the abuse. The abuser and the victim will also seem to have developed a new closeness. Anyone who has seen two people who share an intimate secret that others close to them are unaware of will know what this relationship looks like. Also, incest, it has been found, often occurs in families where there is a very dominant father figure, a man who views the other family members as his to do with as he sees fit.

Intrafamilial abuse of the elderly can many times be the hardest kind of abuse to detect because elderly family members are often the hidden generation. Many people do not feel comfortable around elderly people, and so they avoid them. In addition, families often segregate the elderly to back bedrooms, and consequently they are not always readily visible to home visitors. But there are signs of abuse of the elderly that can be detected for those who look.

While elderly people injure easier than younger people, unexplained bruises, welts, and black eyes are serious indicators of physical abuse of the elderly, as are injuries in the shape of buckles or electrical cords or belts. Bilateral bruises, or bruises that appear on opposite sides of the body, indicate that an elderly person has been grabbed or shaken. Bruises that encircle an elderly person's arms or legs indicate that the person has been forcibly restrained. In addition, an abused elderly person will often appear easily frightened and seem withdrawn and unwilling to speak.

Signs of sexual abuse of the elderly include genital itching, irritation, and infection. Also alarming should be any torn, stained, or bloody underwear, as should be elderly family members showing distress when being bathed or having their clothing changed. The sexually abused elderly person will often demonstrate an inappropriate sexual relationship with a family member by acting coy or flirting.

Neglect of an elderly family member can often be very hard to detect because many elderly people are naturally thin and frail. However, a few clear signs of neglect are bedsores, poor hygiene, prescribed or necessary medicine not available, untreated injuries, and absence of personal items.

The signs of financial abuse are usually the clearest and easiest to detect of all signs of elder family abuse. These include an unusually large amount of banking activity, such as daily ATM withdrawals, particularly for a frail elderly person. Receipt of nonpayment notices for bills can indicate that someone has misappropriated the funds for these bills. Bank statements and canceled checks suddenly being sent to another family member could be meant to hide illegal financial transactions. Also, expensive items belonging to the elderly person suddenly missing may be a sign of financial abuse.

Abuse doesn't have to be in your future. No one contemplating a long-term intimate relationship wants to knowingly enter into one that will eventually turn violent and abusive. The effects of such a relationship can be crippling both physically and psychologically, and can even be deadly. Anyone, therefore, who is considering a long-term relationship with another person should look closely at this possible partner. While none of the signs in this chapter say that future or present abuse is an absolute certainty, these signs should be given the serious concern they deserve.

14

Personal Solutions to Family Abuse

In March 1989, twenty-nine-year-old Lisa Bianco felt her domestic troubles were finally over. With degrees in business and psychology, and now employed as a program director at the Elkhart County Women's Shelter in northern Indiana, she seemed to have her life back on course. Two years before, a court sentenced her former husband, Alan Matheney, to eight years in prison for his severe beating of her and his kidnapping of their two daughters, with whom he attempted to flee to Canada. Although Matheney had made repeated and recent threats on Bianco's life from prison, he remained safely locked up.

"Once I heard her counseling another woman," said Michalyn M. Chilcote, executive director of the shelter. "I remember her (Bianco) saying ... that as long as he is in jail, she didn't have any fears."[1]

On 4 March 1989, despite the fact Matheney had made recent and repeated threats on his former wife's life, prison officials didn't consider him a major offender and granted him an eight-hour furlough from prison. A condition of Matheney's furlough, however, was that he was restricted *on his honor* to stay in the Indianapolis area. In addition, a 1979 law, which began the furlough program as a reward to prison inmates for good behavior,

required that a notification of any release be made to the fur-
loughed inmate's victim. Bianco, even though she reportedly told
her mother that she didn't trust the system, had nevertheless filed
a written request that she be notified of any release of Matheney.
She wasn't notified.

Released into the custody of his mother, Matheney didn't stay
in the Indianapolis area as he had promised, but instead immediately drove to the northern Indiana town of Mishawaka, where
his ex-wife, Lisa Bianco, lived. Matheney first visited the home of a
friend, stole a .410 shotgun, and then went to his ex-wife's house.
Catching Bianco by surprise, he reportedly chased her from her
house, and then, in view of his two daughters and neighbors,
Matheney bashed in Bianco's skull with over twenty blows from
the butt of the shotgun, killing her. Afterward, he calmly waited
for the police to come and arrest him.

"It seemed like it didn't faze him in the least," said Sergeant
Norval Williams, who took Alan Matheney into custody. "He had,
you might say, completed a mission he set out to achieve, and now
that he had done what he wanted to do he was ready to turn
himself in, and more or less ready to pay his dues."[2]

In the aftermath of the murder, state officials disciplined the
two Department of Corrections workers who approved the furlough and were supposed to notify Bianco of Matheney's release.
The new governor of Indiana, Evan Bayh, in office for only two
months, immediately suspended the furlough program and demanded an investigation into what went wrong.

"This is an outrage," Governor Bayh said. "This individual
shouldn't have been eligible and shouldn't have been let go. I'm
quite angry about it."[3]

Speaking about what had gone wrong, Department of Corrections spokesman Vaughn C. Overstreet said: "We didn't want
him in the South Bend area. We thought he was going to Indianapolis."[4]

Interestingly, when Matheney showed up at his initial court
hearing he had a black eye. He was reportedly beaten by other
inmates who were upset that he had caused the furlough program
to be discontinued.

❖ ❖ ❖ ❖ ❖

While corrections is not my area of expertise, I find it difficult to understand why anyone would believe it was safe to release on furlough a person incarcerated for a violent crime, especially when this person had made repeated threats against someone. And as to why the Department of Corrections workers didn't notify Bianco of Matheney's release, again this is beyond my understanding, but I suspect that, like most abusers, Matheney could make himself very charming and likeable to people not involved in a relationship with him. The workers probably thought he was a nice guy who wouldn't hurt anyone.

Quite to the contrary, Alan Matheney was a cold-blooded, ruthless person, who felt absolutely justified in murdering his ex-wife. He demonstrated this by not fleeing after the murder. But was he always this vicious and brutal with Lisa Bianco? Of course not. When Lisa first met Alan, a plumbing contractor, and agreed to marry him, she didn't know or believe he would eventually turn into a maniacal killer. She thought they were about to start a wonderful life together. The level of violence that eventually culminated in Lisa Bianco's murder typically takes years to develop. In the book *Battered Women: Living with the Enemy*, the author states: "But keep in mind that abusive relationships do not begin as abusive. In fact, many of these guys are very charming and loving and give the women a great deal of attention."[5]

Actually, most victims aren't even aware when the family abuse really begins because it usually starts out as something very small, such as a minor incident of verbal or emotional abuse. Much too often, however, if unchecked, this then progresses in seriousness to minor physical abuse, such as slapping or shoving, and eventually to more and more serious violence, which can finally become so serious that murder is the outcome. This increase in seriousness happens, experts believe, because at each stage the abusers get away with using the abuse. They suffer little or no negative consequences because of it. But most important, the abusers find that not only is the abuse not punished, but it also gets them what they wanted. Using violence, the abusers always get their way. This makes the use of abuse tremendously reinforcing, building it from minor violence to major assaults.

"Commonly, the battered woman is unaware prior to her marriage that her partner is abusive," said Jessica L. Goldman in the book *Violence Against Women*. "A woman struck for the first time reacts in disbelief and anger. The batterer may be repentant, asking for forgiveness and promising that the violence will not happen again. The woman loves him and, therefore, believes his apologies and considers the incident an aberration. But the battery continues and a cycle begins."[6]

How can a person use this information to recognize, resist, and prevent family abuse? By acting on it.

"If the early danger signs are present, end a relationship even if you love someone," said the author of *Battered Women: Living with the Enemy*.[7]

"The *first time* physical or verbal abuse occurs, leave," said Pamela Thomas in an article in *Black Elegance*.[8]

According to the authors of *The Compatibility Quotient*: "If you're a woman and the man you think you want to marry lays a hand on you in anger—or even threatens to strike or rough you up—stop everything! This arrangement simply won't work."[9]

"End the relationship early, at the first act of violence," said Dr. David Ford, who has studied conjugal violence for over twenty years.

"The most effective means of stopping violence is not to permit it from the start," said the authors of *Domestic Violence: No Longer Behind the Curtains*.[10]

"Although many women minimize the abuse that is inflicted on them, domestic violence tends to escalate, and experts maintain that it is crucial to confront reality before it is too late," said an article in *Parents Magazine*.[11]

"Any act of violence should be taken seriously...If you ignore the abuse, you give your unspoken approval to violence and increase the chance of it happening again," said Dr. Kathleen H. Hofeller, author of *Battered Women, Shattered Lives*.[12]

"Understand that an abusive partner will almost always get worse if there is not intervention or if he does not seek help," said Laura B. Randolph in an article in *Ebony*.[13]

While it may seem that I have overdone the advice above, this is a crucial point to make because this is the most important action that can be taken personally to prevent family abuse. It is, admittedly, a tough solution, but family abuse of any type, against any victim, must be met at its first appearance by negative consequences against the perpetrator of the abuse. He or she must see, and see very plainly, that this type of behavior will not accomplish what he or she had hoped it would. If a victim does not take action immediately the abuse will almost certainly continue and likely escalate.

"Many women have said that, in retrospect, once their husbands discovered they could get away with being violent, it seemed to lower their inhibitions against future and more severe abuse," said Dr. Kathleen H. Hofeller in her book *Battered Women, Shattered Lives*.[14]

Also, confronting the abuser the very first time abuse occurs makes it easier if it becomes necessary, in order to end the abuse, to sever the marriage or relationship. It is much easier to end a marriage or a relationship before there is a large emotional commitment, before there are children, before there is considerable joint property, and especially before there is a feeling of ownership of the victim by the abuser.

While some of the experts quoted above advise leaving and ending the relationship at the first act of physical violence and this is good, solid advice—often, as I have stated, the abuse doesn't start that clearly. Many times, physical abuse doesn't begin until months, and even years, into a relationship. The abuse may instead begin with emotional or verbal abuse. Or it may be an act of forced sex against a spouse, which until recently wasn't even against the law. How many people have the courage to end a marriage because a spouse yelled at them or called them a name? Or because of a sexual encounter that the partner will likely claim he thought was by mutual consent? How many people have the courage to give up a spouse, a home, financial security, and their social position because of emotional abuse? Probably not that many. Still, it is important to remember that while a person might think that a breakup of the relationship is too drastic for very minor initial abuse, one should never allow the abuser to believe that this behavior gained whatever it was he or she wanted. To do so only invites further, and usually escalating, abuse. A key personal solution to family abuse is to be certain that no acts of abuse are ever ignored, no matter how small, but instead acted upon immediately. The abuser must see that this behavior, even though minor, gains nothing, and actually costs him or her.

The victims of any type of physical violence, on the other hand, as the experts above recommend, should address such abuse immediately and much more forcibly than minor verbal or emotional abuse. Whatever action a person takes, however, including a breakup of the relationship, should receive the support of friends and family.

"Early intervention must be supported by family, friends, neighbors, and the criminal justice system," said Dr. David Ford of Indiana University at Indianapolis. "Unfortunately, this support of early intervention is unlikely because the violence is so minor that breaking up a marriage seems like overreacting."

As Dr. Ford says, family members and friends will often discourage a victim from breaking up a relationship over what to them seems a very minor incident, such as a slap or a shove. The criminal justice system, unfortunately, acts much the same. Even if a couple is ordered into counseling by the court, few social service agency counselors would advise breaking up a marriage over minor violence. They and family and friends will say such things as "you've got to work to make the relationship a good one"; " 'til death do you part"; "the course of true love never runs smooth"; or "the children need two parents." Keep in mind, however, that these are the same people who, when the violence becomes severe, will ask you why you stayed so long in the relationship. Take action immediately.

Interestingly, though, many victims not only ignore the early warning signs of family abuse, but stay in progressively abusive relationships because of mistaken beliefs about what is best for their children. Many of them believe children should always have two parents, even if one of them is abusive. Consequently, these victims simply put up with the abuse, even when it escalates to serious physical battery. They feel that they are suffering for the good of their children. Actually, the opposite is true. Research shows that abuse in a family often flows over to the children, and even for those children who don't become victims of abuse themselves just witnessing abuse in a family can have terrible psychological consequences. The likelihood, for example, of eventually becoming an abuser or an adult victim of abuse is significantly higher for a child who witnesses abuse than it is for one who actually suffers it. Children are only hurt by having an intact family that practices abuse. Some families are just not worth saving.

"If my mother had had the guts to leave with us when she first knew my father was a dangerous man, she would have saved me a lifetime of torture," said a woman interviewed in a *Parents Magazine* article about domestic violence. "Growing up with a stepfather or no father would have been minimal compared to what staying with an abusive father does to you."[15]

In addition, many adult victims who stay in abusive relationships erroneously believe that their children do not know about the abuse. Researchers, however, have found that in most homes where abuse occurs between the spouses the children are very much aware of it.

As damaging psychologically to children as staying in an abusive relationship can be, many social service agencies still have as their prime directive the necessity of keeping the family together at all costs. For this reason they often recommend family counseling for families in which there is an abuser. There are many problems, however, with this approach. It implies everyone in the family has a problem, when actually the problem is the abuser. Also, what many agencies don't seem to realize or want to recognize is that there are some families that can't be saved. The abuser is too entrenched in a pattern of abuse to ever change, and will likely only become worse. Keeping the family intact under such circumstances only gives the abuser more opportunity to hurt others and only makes the victims of the abuser suffer when they don't have to.

In support of this, authors Daniel G. Saunders and Sandra T. Azar in the book *Family Violence* said: "A major argument against a family focus is the implicit or explicit blame that may accrue to the victim. Simply having the victim in treatment may imply that the victim is equally responsible for the abuse.... There is increasing evidence, however, that much family violence, particularly wife abuse and child sexual abuse, is the product of offender characteristics rather than family dynamics."[16]

Besides mistaken concern for the children, a number of adult victims of family abuse also decide to stay in abusive relationships because they believe that the abusers will eventually change on their own. This, however, is highly unlikely. Why would the abusers want to change? They are suffering no negative consequences and always getting their way. In addition, spouse abusers, when questioned by the police or other authorities, inevitably blame the victims, not themselves, for the abuse. They see their actions as totally right and justified. The victims, they claim, brought the abuse onto themselves by nagging, by poor housecleaning, by spending too much money, etc. Or, in other types of family abuse, the abusers will claim, for example, that their parents really wanted them to have their money or property, that their daughters were just asking for it by wearing sexy clothing, and a million other rationalizations. Abusers seldom change their behavior unless there is heavy external pressure to do so, along with the likelihood of extreme negative consequences if they don't.

"There are no studies that document 'natural' or spontaneous desistance (voluntarily stopping family violence)," said Dr. Jeffrey Fagan, "without intervention by the victim or as a result of some form of sanction or treatment."[17]

A large number of abuse victims who announce that they intend to end an abusive relationship are often persuaded to stay in the relationship when their partners offer to go to counseling or treatment. However, as the authors of *It Could Happen to Anyone* warn: "Indeed, batterers frequently resort to counseling as a means of manipulating their female partners and not as a means of changing their own behavior ... men do not come into therapy because they think personal growth is 'far out,' and they can't wait to change. They come in either because their partner left, or they really believe she will leave, or because God speaks to them through the SWAT team."[18]

The actual chances that a batterer will change after going through counseling are dependent on the batterer's own commitment to truly wanting to change. Anyone who has dealt with an alcoholic, for example, knows that an alcoholic cannot be changed unless he or she wants to and seeks to change. An abuser is very similar. Forcing an abuser to go to counseling is seldom beneficial.

"Our success rate for long-term abstinence is around 25 percent," said David Adams, program director for Emerge, a counseling program for men who batter.[19] In researching the subject, I haven't found any programs claiming much more success than this.

However, victims should be warned that even in these 25 percent of the cases in which counseling has actually stopped the physical violence, abuse, in other forms, often still continues. A study done by the Domestic Abuse Project of Minneapolis found that even in those cases in which physical violence had stopped in the six months following their treatment program, threats and intimidation had not. The abusers had not really changed. They still wanted dominance over their victims. They knew, however, that violence would get them into trouble, and so instead they used emotional abuse and threats as a means of control.

An important piece of advice, therefore, for people at risk of abuse is that they should never allow themselves to be put into a position where potential abusers have complete control and dominance over them. This includes being put into positions where they do not have access to money, transportation, and friends who will help them if they want to leave the relationship. One of the things that abusers typically do is to take all of these things away from victims in order to make the victims totally dependent on them. The authors of *Domestic Violence: No Longer Behind the Curtains* say: "[M]ost who leave without asking for help usually have a strong personal support system of friends and family and often a

job so they are not economically dependent on their abusive husbands or companions."[20]

An important personal solution to family abuse, therefore, is,
before entering into any marriage or other long-term relationship,
a person should always consider the possibility (even though
perhaps remote) that the relationship will become abusive and
violent, and consequently always have an exit plan in place. A
person should always be prepared to be able to leave a relationship at a moment's notice, which is just how quickly abuse and
violence can suddenly flare up. But at the same time, people at risk
for abuse should also know the volatility level of their partners.
Do they keep firearms or other weapons in the house? Would they
use them if provoked? If so, a secretive exit would be wiser.

Most victims when they are first abused by their partners are
surprised and stunned. And because they never expected it, they
aren't prepared and don't know what to do. Therefore, anyone
entering into a long-term relationship should be aware of this
possibility, and should have a plan for what to do if it does
happen. An exit plan should contain a method for obtaining
money for the expense of moving, a safe place to go to, and
transportation there. This plan should also be constantly updated
to account for changes in the relationship. People at risk for abuse
shouldn't let good times allow them to let down all defenses, and
consequently become a trapped victim.

In an article in the *Los Angeles Times* by Robin Abcarian, a
volunteer for a battered women's hotline is quoted as saying: "I
can't believe how many women have no friends or support. It just
blows me away. Lots of my calls are from phone booths: 'I have my
life ... my kids, my van, and no money.'"[21]

An exit plan, incidentally, often must be able to be carried out
alone, because family and friends, as the hotline worker above has
found, may not always be supportive or helpful. Family and
friends may see the abuser only in his or her "outside the relationship" appearance as friendly and charming, and consequently
will believe the victim is overreacting. Also, by helping the victim
they are taking sides against this friendly, charming person. On
the other hand, often family members and friends could see the

abuser clearer than the victim, and may have opposed the relationship from the beginning. Since the victim obviously didn't
take their advice then, they may not feel inclined to help the victim
now. And even on those occasions in which the family does confront the abuser and he or she admits the abuse, what usually
follows next is a tearful plea about how much the abuser loves the
victim and will do anything to make the relationship work. Few
family members can listen to this kind of plea without some belief
that maybe the relationship can work. Of course, what inevitably
happens is that, after forgiveness by the victim, the cycle of abuse
begins again.

Some readers, especially those in the beginnings of a loving,
caring relationship, might say that the idea of always having an
exit plan ready and regularly updated is dooming the relationship
from the start. By not believing in a relationship, by assuming
from the beginning that it will not work out, you are setting
yourself up for a self-fulfilling prophesy. But this isn't necessarily
so. I would hope that everyone who moves into a home has a fire
emergency plan. I would hope that everyone in the family knows
how to escape from the home quickly in the event of a fire. Does
having a fire escape plan mean you have doomed your home to
burn down because you believe it is possible there might eventually be a fire there? No, it just means you are prepared for a
possible emergency, which is all you are doing when making exit
plans from a relationship. It is sort of like being trained in first
aid. People hope they'll never have to use this training, but if an
emergency does occur, because of the training, they will know
exactly what to do. There will be no hand-wringing and wondering what to do. Also, knowing that one is not trapped and has
other options gives a person confidence, independence, and freedom, regardless of circumstances.

While it is, of course, easiest for a person simply not to tolerate family abuse, and leave or take action at its first appearance,
what about victims who didn't do this and now find themselves
trapped in a severely violent relationship? What can they do?

An important fact these people should be aware of is that it is against the law in every state for one spouse to physically assault the other, as it is for unmarried intimate partners. Therefore, if a person is assaulted, and the violence has reached the point where this person fears for his or her safety, call the police. Readers should also be aware that, while it is against the law of every state to assault a spouse or intimate partner, not every state mandates that an arrest be made in these cases, and many leave it up to the discretion of the police officer. It is therefore imperative that people at risk for abuse find out what the laws of their state are in relation to family abuse. This is important because police officers often don't arrest, even in situations where an arrest is mandated by law, simply because they think the people they are dealing with don't know what the law is, and the officers don't want to be bothered with an arrest that they believe will likely never amount to anything anyway. In a situation such as this the victim needs to be respectful but assertive with the officers. If officers realize that a person knows the law, and will not be put off, they are much more likely to enforce the law as it is supposed to be. If the officers still don't arrest, even though the circumstances require one, it is time to ask for a supervisor. And if the officers refuse to call for one, dial 911 and ask the dispatcher to send one.

And yet, while I wholeheartedly advise calling the police in family abuse incidents, when dealing with the police I caution to do so in a calm, rational manner. Officers resent people trying to intimidate them or people demanding that they do something, because the public is often badly misinformed about what an officer must or must not do. Usually, police officers will vehemently resist any such pressure, particularly if the officers know they don't have to do what the person is demanding. Many times, the police arrive at the scene of a domestic disturbance and both people involved show signs of injury, though one turns out to have injuries sustained defending against the abuse. The real victim, of course, knows that he or she is right and mistakenly believes the officers should know this too. These victims naturally become incensed when the police don't do what to them is a clear duty, but all the officers see is two people screaming at each other.

Even worse, often the abuser, though injured by the victim defending him- or herself, is calm and rational, while the real victim, reacting to the abuse, is screaming and ranting.

A person's demeanor toward the police, therefore, is paramount to getting the police to do what he or she wants. Often, though it is not correct, many victims believe that the police take the part of the abuser because they talk first and mostly to him or her. The police are not taking the abuser's side, but before any action can be taken the officers must find out what happened. The officers, therefore, often talk to the abuser first because he or she appears calm and rational, while the victim many times is hysterical, something certainly understandable for someone who has just been brutally assaulted by a loved one. Therefore, even though livid over the assault and injuries, and no one could expect an abuse victim to be calm and nonchalant, victims must try to do all they can to appear rational and speak intelligibly. The officers need to hear the victim's side.

It is also important to show police officers any bruises or injuries suffered in the abuse. These are needed for probable cause to make an arrest. Also, victims should not be afraid to ask the officers to make a report. This paper trail can be useful later if proof is needed to substantiate the abuse for custody hearings, protection orders, etc. Indianapolis, like many other cities, requires that police officers make reports whenever citizens ask them to. But most officers won't unless asked to. In addition to this, victims should be certain to get the officers' names or badge numbers. Victims can use this information to substantiate the abuse if they need to supply proof that the police were called. Again, I caution to do this in a calm, rational manner. Victims don't have to loudly demand names and badge numbers from the officers. Nothing turns police officers away from a person's side quicker than someone making an implied threat by demanding badge numbers when the numbers are already clearly visible. Victims simply need to look at and remember what's on the officer's badge or name tag, or politely ask.

When dealing with police officers it is important to remember that practically every police department in the United States has some mechanism for citizens to use if they want to complain about officers not doing their jobs. If you feel officers answering a family abuse call didn't do what they should have done it is imperative that you use this complaint procedure. If no one ever complains, then administrators of a police department can only assume that their officers are doing their jobs properly. Police officers are public servants, paid by the public. They should be responsive to your needs.

If abuse victims who fear for their safety staying in the home have called the police because of an incident of abuse and the officers won't make an arrest, even when state law mandates it, these victims should ask the officers to escort them out. Very few officers will refuse to do this because they know it will usually end the fighting, at least for that night. The officers know that if they leave the couple together, they will very likely have to come back. But in preparation for this, victims must have a place to go. Therefore, besides researching the laws in their state, victims also need to know where the shelters in their community are, what their requirements are, and where to go if they are full.

On the other hand, if the police do make an arrest and the victim fears that this will only increase the violence of the abuse, I advise the victim to take immediate action. Use the time the abuser is in custody to get out and go somewhere safe. Even if the abuser is released without bail it will still take several hours for the travel time, paperwork, and administrative details. Remember, there are resources in every community for the victims of family abuse, but they are only available if the victims know about them. People at risk for abuse, or those who care about them, should research what assistance is available in the community ahead of time so that once out of an abusive environment victims won't be facing the future without any help.

Abuse victims should never believe, however, that just because they have left their abusers they are now safe. Abusers who have been able to control their victims, often for years, through violence are usually committed to getting these people back the same way. Researchers have found that the most dangerous time in a violently abusive relationship is when one partner makes the other one aware that he or she intends to end the relationship. As talked about earlier, this is the time when most murders and severe assaults between intimates take place.

Spouses or intimate partners who have had their way in relationships, often for years, through intimidation and violence many times panic when they must suddenly face the prospect that they are actually not in control after all, that the people they thought were their property are now about to slip away from them. Since violence has always worked in the past, and increasing violence has not yet met with many adverse sanctions, the natural impulse for these abusers is simply to use more intense violence. This increasing violence, incidentally, can often lead to murder, particularly if it becomes apparent to the abusers that they are going to permanently lose the control they have enjoyed for so long. A fact supporting this is that, in 1994, over 28 percent of the women murdered in the United States were murdered by husbands, ex-husbands, or boyfriends, while just over 3 percent of the men murdered were killed by wives, ex-wives, or girl friends. (The disparity between these numbers is not as great as it appears since many more men are murdered each year in the United States than women.)[22] Researchers in King County (Seattle), Washington, in a study of gunshot deaths, uncovered another important statistic of which family abuse victims should be aware. They found that those who kept a gun in the home were eighteen times more likely to use it to kill a household member than an intruder.[23]

So, as both research and bitter experience show, when a victim finally decides and announces the intention to leave an abuser, extra precautions must be taken. Since this is an extremely dangerous time, I would strongly advise against any confrontation at the time a victim leaves. For violently abusive relationships, a secretive exit is far safer.

How do victims protect themselves from revenge-minded partners once they are out of the house and into new living quarters? First of all, while having some sort of court-issued restraining or protective order is helpful, it can never protect a person in any real sense. A restraining order helps establish the fact of a victim's abuse and his or her fear of the abuser on paper. It also gives the police grounds to make an arrest if the victim is ever harassed. However, people at risk should *never* depend on one of these orders to really protect them. In some cases, an order enrages the abusers even further since they see it as flaunting the fact that the victims are no longer under their control. These abusers can often become even more violent when served with them. I'm always amazed at the number of people who believe that these orders are like some sort of invisible armor that will protect them. Not so. Not so at all. Hundreds of the intimate-partner murders that occur every year occur in spite of protective or restraining orders. In the worst cases, the only thing these orders do is make it easier for the police to figure out who the murderer is after a dangerous abuser finally goes too far.

If victims fear after a separation that their abusers will stalk them at work, they should make the people there aware of the problem, with instructions to call the police if the abuser shows up. A copy of any restraining or protective order should be on file at the victim's place of employment. Also, victims should try to break their usual patterns so the abusers cannot predict where they will be. Take different routes to work, if possible use different entrances at the place of employment, and don't always go to the same place for lunch.

Victims also need to make their new home as burglarproof as possible. In 1992, 86 percent of the people killed by spouses were murdered at home.[24] This is reason enough to leave a violent relationship, and also reason enough to want to assure that an ex-spouse or intimate partner cannot easily gain access to a new home. Victims must be certain that if their abusers do mean to forcibly come into their new home it will be difficult and time-consuming, giving them time to escape or call the police. My book *Protecting Your Life, Home, and Property* (Plenum Publishing Corporation, 1995) offers dozens of tips and methods for making a residence, and a person when outside the home, safer and more secure.

"After I left my husband, he kept threatening to kill me," a former abuse victim told me. "He kept saying that he was going to shoot me through the window. I hid out for eighteen months after leaving him."

Another particularly dangerous and vulnerable time for violence is when an ex-spouse picks up the children for visitation. Abuse victims should never believe that an ex-spouse would not do anything violent in front of the children. That certainly didn't stop Alan Matheney in the incident at the beginning of this chapter, nor does it stop dozens of other similar murders every year. It is preferable to choose a spot for picking up the children that lessens the chance of violence, such as at the ex-partner's parents, in front of a police station, and so forth. But abuse victims shouldn't depend totally on this. While I find it nightmarishly frightening that parents would be forced to hand over their children to someone they fear is capable of murder, gaining total custody of children is a civil matter and out of my area of expertise. Duluth, Minnesota, however, has a program that addresses this problem.

Duluth began a program in 1989, which is now also used in several other cities, that addresses the problem of child visitation by possibly violent ex-spouses. Called the Duluth Visitation Center, this is a facility whose staff oversees child exchanges, and is also a facility that can be used as the site of child visitation, if so ordered by the court. For this purpose the center maintains age-appropriate resources, including a nursery, a play area for small children, and a gymnasium for older children. I will talk more about this concept in the next chapter, as it is a facility needed in every community, but I mention it here because in order for these facilities to be built there must be pressure from citizens for them.

But what about readers who are not victims themselves, but may have a friend or neighbor who they suspect might be the victim of family abuse? Alternately, what can readers do if they accidentally stumble onto what appears to be family abuse? It is tempting for most people to just ignore what they see or deny it is real, and so do nothing. This is exactly what the abuser wants. All the abuser asks is that outsiders do nothing.

Yet, what if readers don't want to just do nothing? What can they do to help? First off, don't be surprised if both the victim and the abuser deny the abuse. Most abusers do not see themselves as bad people. They often feel totally justified in using violence, and, if they can't deny it, will blame the victim for causing it. Most victims of family abuse, on the other hand, feel that their situation is unique, are ashamed that it is happening, and many will simply not admit it is happening. In the book *Violence Against Women*, author Jessica L. Goldman said: "Battered women are unable to escape from abusive relationships without outside help. A battered woman may also deny that the abuse occurs. The woman, ashamed of the abuse, denies the reality to herself, thereby avoiding acknowledgement of the reality to others." The author then goes on to say: "Practical considerations can also serve to bind the woman to the husband. In battering relationships the man characteristically dominates the woman in all aspects of the relationship, particularly the area of family finances."[25]

As Goldman makes clear, what abuse victims really need are family members or friends who will help lessen their fear, dependency, and isolation. By making victims aware that you are there to listen and help if needed, they may begin to see a way out. Family abuse victims often feel they are cut off from all help, and having this reassurance from someone can possibly make the difference of whether or not they take action. If a person does eventually come to you and tells a story of long-term abuse, the worst thing you can do is ask the person why he or she has put up with it for so long or why he or she hasn't left the abuser before this. Victims aren't looking for someone to blame or judge them. Victims need a sensitive, reassuring listener who will not pressure them to do something they aren't ready to do right then. Victims need friends who will build up their self-esteem. Victims might also need help with transportation, money, or shelter. But most of all, the victim needs a supportive friend, who will stay a friend even if the victim decides to go back to or stay with the abuser. Victims often do this because they may fear that the abuser will harm their children if they leave, and they may do this because they have no money and no job skills, and so believe they cannot support themselves and their children without their partner. Leaving a relationship, even an abusive one, is not that easy. Studies have shown that victims leave an average of five to seven times before permanently dissolving the relationship. It is only once he or she is totally free that a victim can look back and objectively evaluate what he or she did.

"Being alone and struggling is better than being involved in an abusive relationship," a former abuse victim told me. "When you're in an abusive relationship you're always walking on eggshells."

Police officers find that victims who do stay in an abusive relationship often do so because they have developed what is known as "learned helplessness." What this means is that the years of abuse have beaten the victims down. The abusers have convinced the victims that they are worthless, helpless, and cannot do anything without them. Often, officers go to a family disturbance, and, once they have separated the parties, they offer their help to the victims. They may, for example, offer to arrest the assailants. No, the victims don't want that. The officers may then offer to take the victims and any children to a shelter. No, they don't want that. The officers may then offer to help the victims obtain a protective order. No, they don't want that. After enough refusals of help, most officers can't figure out why the victims even called the police since they don't seem to want any of the assistance the officers have offered. This is what starts police officers mistakenly believing that many abuse victims really like the abuse. Why else, the officers believe, would they stay and why else would they refuse all offers of help?

Dr. David Ford, in his study of conjugal violence, obtained interesting, and disturbing, feedback from police officers about their attitudes toward abuse victims with learned helplessness. For example, 54 percent of the police officers he questioned agreed with the statement: "If a woman does not leave a man who beats her she should not expect the police to protect her." Forty-seven percent of these officers agreed with the statement: "A battery arrest is not called for if the woman plans to stay with an abusive man." What this says is that half of the officers surveyed have no sympathy for family abuse victims who will not help themselves.[26]

As a police administrator, Dr. Ford's findings cause me considerable concern. What the findings say is that half of all the police officers answering family abuse runs really don't understand the dynamics of them, and consequently don't serve the best interests of abuse victims. This can only be corrected by intensive and regular training on family abuse. I'm always amazed that we spend so much time teaching our new officers how to fire a weapon, something an officer usually does only a few times during an entire career, yet spend so little time educating them on family abuse, which officers deal with every day of their careers. This must change.

Since family abuse doesn't involve just adult partners, we must also take steps to protect children from abuse in the family. The best personal solution to stopping child abuse within a family, both physical and sexual, is, first, to recognize it is happening, which may not always be readily apparent, and then to take action immediately. This usually means notifying the police or other authorities. Like abuse between spouses, abuse of children will not stop if it is ignored. And while few family members relish the thought of making their problems public, particularly something as unseemly as child sexual abuse, secrecy is what allows family abusers to continue with their abuse. The abusers of children often know that what they are doing is wrong, but as long as they can do it without suffering any negative consequences they will continue to do so.

In order for parents to know what is happening with their children, however, children must feel that they can come and speak with their parents about anything, that their parents will take the time to listen to them, and, most important of all, that their parents will be supportive of them. Child abuse detectives many times find that children have tried to tell their parents about abuse or attempted abuse. These children, however, were scared or embarrassed, and the parents just didn't have time for a child who wouldn't say what's on his or her mind. Because of this, many

children tell someone other than their parents about being molested. If parents want their children to tell them about abuse, the
children must feel that they have their parents' attention, support,
and understanding. Unfortunately, often they don't. I had a case
once that vividly illustrates this point.

❖ ❖ ❖ ❖ ❖

One afternoon, while working as a uniformed district officer,
I came across a car parked in a part of a railroad yard where
derelicts usually slept and where we occasionally found drug
paraphernalia. The flurry of clothing and bare skin as I pulled up
to the car told me I had happened onto a couple of lovers. After
giving the couple time to get dressed, I walked up to their car to
tell them that where they were parked was a dangerous spot. The
man in the car was fifty-two years old. The other person was his
thirteen-year-old niece.

After arresting the uncle, I took the young victim to the hospital. On the trip she told me of her two years of sexual abuse. The
young girl's mother (the arrested man's sister) was an invalid
whose livelihood depended totally on her brother. The sexual
abuse began through threats to throw the mother out of the house
if the niece didn't submit.

Since I registered the girl as a rape victim, and she was only
thirteen, the hospital needed a relative to come and okay the examination. The arrested man's wife arrived shortly afterward. The
woman's first words to me were: "It's impossible. She couldn't
have been raped. She was with my husband."

I sat the victim's aunt down and told her the story of what I
had found out so far. She didn't believe a word of it. Not a word.
Her husband was a deacon of the church, she said, a loving father
of four children, and vice president of a local heating oil company.
There was just no way. She told me she was sorry but she just
didn't believe it.

Fortunately, at that moment they wheeled the young victim
past us on her way to the examination room, and the look on the
girl's face was enough to convince the aunt that perhaps her
husband might not be the pillar of the community she thought he

was. Still, despite the aunt's conversion, the child's mother insisted to me that her daughter was a slut, and had very likely enticed her uncle. Eventually, she sent the young girl out of state so that she couldn't testify against her abuser. Is it any wonder the young victim had not told anyone about the abuse for two years?

❖ ❖ ❖ ❖ ❖

In an article in the September 1994 *Journal of Interpersonal Violence*, titled "Telling the Secret: Adult Women Describe Their Disclosures of Incest," the authors found in a survey of 228 incest victims that their disclosure of incest to a parent was more often met with disbelief and blame than support and protection. Unfortunately, the police also often find this to be the case.

Given this trend, if concerned parents or others see any of the signs of child abuse I listed in the previous chapter, they must be supportive and understanding when talking with the children. Also, when talking with these children, avoid being judgmental or showing horror, shock, anger, or disgust. This is likely what the abuser told the child would happen if he or she told. Most importantly, when talking with victims of child abuse, parents and others must open their minds for the worst. No story is too outrageous, and any family member could be a child abuser. My wife, a child abuse detective, almost daily tells me stories that still shock me after twenty-eight years as a police officer. Once you do have suspicions, though, don't immediately begin accusing people. Instead, listen to the child's story with an understanding ear and then look into what he or she has said. There are cases, though rare, in which children accuse innocent people of abuse.

To prevent child abuse, particularly sexual abuse, parents and others need to be suspicious of any family member who wants to spend a lot of time alone with children, and who always tries to get the parents and other adults out of the way. In addition, be cautious of the family member who constantly wants to baby-sit children. While this person could be simply someone who loves children, too often the motives are more sinister. Also, children must be taught that while they should be respectful and polite to adult family members, they have a right to say no to anyone who wants to touch them in a way they don't like, and that if they are touched in a way they don't like they must tell someone about it.

Most important of all, parents and others must notify the police of any child abuse. Many families are reluctant to do this because they fear the publicity will hurt the family and further traumatize the child. Remember, however, secrecy is what allows child abusers to thrive and continue. Also, a number of studies have shown that children are not permanently harmed, as many parents fear, by taking part in a criminal investigation and trial for child abuse. Still, many families, rather than wanting to involve the authorities and lay their family problems out in the open, instead pressure a family sex offender into treatment. This, however, is not as good an idea as it sounds. Many of the people who work with child molesters believe there is no cure.

Brian Ross, manager of the Sex Abuse Treatment Program at Midtown Mental Health Center, said: "There is no cure. A child molester will always be a potential child molester. The only thing that stops them is death. Like a person attending Alcoholics Anonymous, a previous child molester is just abstaining, not cured."

Interestingly, the advice columnist Ann Landers once stated (and later retracted) that the only cure for child molesters was castration. Brian Ross, however, tells of attending child molester therapy sessions in which two of the molesters had been castrated (due to cancer) but nevertheless still continued molesting children.

Therefore, I cannot overstate the importance of family members making children feel that they can come and talk about anything, and that no matter what they say they will be believed and supported. This is important because children can be experiencing sexual abuse but show no outward signs of it. Also, you want your child to come and talk with you the very first time an improper touch or suggestion occurs, before it has had time to progress to more serious abuse.

As with child abuse, elder abuse is also often a difficult problem for family members to deal with. Many times, relatives are so happy that someone in the family is taking care of an elderly family member that they will overlook minor abuse, because they know that if they say too much they might have to be the one to take care of the elderly person. Also, families often segregate elderly people to back bedrooms and other places out of sight of those visiting the house, thus making the detection of abuse more difficult. But like all other types of abusers, abusers of the elderly must be confronted and shown that what they are doing is wrong and will not be tolerated. This can only be accomplished, though, if the abuse is detected.

Family members, therefore, should always be concerned when elderly people seemed frightened or unusually quiet around the caretaker, and should be concerned when the caretaker attempts to limit access to the elderly family member. This is often to hide the effects of abuse from visitors. Family members should also be on the lookout for financial abuse, which many experts say is one of the fastest growing types of elder abuse. Has the caretaker suddenly bought things he or she couldn't afford before? Has he or she paid off long-term bills? Is property of the elderly family member suddenly disappearing?

Considering the high level of care many elderly family members need, a personal solution for elder abuse is for other family members to watch the stress level of the caretaker. To prevent abuse and protect the safety of the elderly family member, if it appears the stress is at high levels, someone should step in and help. Sometimes giving the caretaker a short break or some financial support can go a long way.

While I have talked so far in this chapter about a number of personal solutions to family abuse, what can be done community-wide by individual citizens to help prevent family abuse? Actually quite a lot.

To truly stop family abuse it must be treated for what it is: a crime. Far too often, though, the criminal justice system treats family abuse as less than a crime, and more as a personal problem that should be worked out within the family. As long as this attitude continues, abusers will suffer no punishment for their actions, and will be encouraged by the criminal justice system to continue their crimes.

What can individual citizens do to pressure the criminal justice system to treat family abuse as the serious crime it is? This is not as difficult as it seems. It can be done by holding the members of the criminal justice system responsible for their actions. In my career, I have witnessed several examples of this being done very effectively. While the following two examples brought reform in areas other than family abuse, what these people did can also be used to fight for more serious treatment of family abuse by the criminal justice system.

Here in Indianapolis we have a neighborhood close to the downtown area that had once been very affluent, full of large, beautiful Victorian homes. In the 1950s and 1960s, the neighborhood fell onto hard times, and the big homes were cut up into cheap apartments. Then in the 1970s, an influx of people from the suburbs, who bought and refurbished the homes, revitalized the area. The only problem was that the neighborhood, when it had fallen onto hard times, had also become a haven for prostitutes. However, even after the neighborhood was revitalized, the prostitutes did not want to leave because they feared their customers would not be able to find them. Consequently, the residents came to the police and asked us to help them with the prostitution problem. And so we tried. But, while the police would make arrests of the prostitutes who used this area, the legal system, we found, treated their cases as nuisances at best, a nominal fine being the most serious punishment ever meted out.

One of the residents of this revitalized neighborhood finally decided she had to do something personally, and so she formed a court watch with her neighbors. These residents worked with the police, found out which prostitutes were arrested in the neighborhood, when their trial was, and then would sit in the court and report back to the neighborhood association what the prosecutors and judges did. Since the members of this neighborhood association and all of the readers of its newsletter were voters, they soon began getting the attention of the judges and prosecutors, who are elected officials. Before long, whenever a prostitute went to trial where there was a court watcher present, the case received serious attention.

In another instance, when I was the captain of detectives for the North District of Indianapolis we had a serious problem with a large number of illegal gambling establishments. The neighborhood residents complained almost daily to the police about these establishments because they brought an unsavory collection of people into the neighborhood, and minor crime, particularly thefts, was always high around one of these establishments. However, while my detectives would make arrests at these locations, the local prosecutor came to the decision that it was too much trouble and expense to prosecute any of these arrests, and so his staff would always turn loose any people we arrested at one of these illegal gambling establishments. We solved this problem by inviting the prosecutor to a neighborhood meeting, where he met with a large gathering of irate voters. He immediately changed his policy and began prosecuting our arrests.

This very same pressure can work with family abuse, and can stop criminal justice officials from treating family abuse as a minor affair. No judge or prosecutor wants to be known as being soft on crime, or as someone who thinks that something voters obviously take very seriously is a joking matter. And no elected official wants to be mentioned in a report to voters as not doing his or her job. Using a court watch system or other means, individuals can assure that family abusers are treated like what they are: criminals. Once this stigma is attached to their actions, the actions become less attractive and rewarding. Also, it should go without saying that judges or prosecutors who continue to refuse to treat family abuse as a serious matter should be voted against. And, of course, while most police officers are not elected officials, their bosses—mayors and city council members—are.

Another personal action that can be taken which will help fight family abuse communitywide was revealed recently in the local newspaper, the *Indianapolis Star*. The paper published an article about a group of women in southern Indiana who have started a secret network of "safe houses" for battered women. These are private residences open to the victims of family abuse. Called Crisis Connection, the organization, which has twenty-two volunteers and serves about 220 families annually, began because of the scarcity of shelters in rural areas. To gain access to this network, an abuse victim calls an 800 number, speaks with a hotline volunteer, and, if needed, a member of Crisis Connection meets the victim and any children at a neutral location and drives them to the safe house. The victim must agree not to contact the abuser while at a safe house, and not to reveal its location.[27]

An article in *The Washington Post* tells of a couple, Daniel and Sherry Carrigan, living in Fairfax County, Virginia, who volunteer as emergency foster parents. When the county suddenly has an abused child who needs a place to stay, officials place the child with volunteers such as the Carrigans.[28] Without volunteers like this, many counties would be without any safe place to put youngsters in danger. Last year, Fairfax County placed 140 endangered children into these emergency foster homes.

As can be seen from the advice given in this chapter, it is far better and safer to never let relationships degenerate to the point where the victims find that extricating themselves becomes physically dangerous and often life-threatening. Action should be taken at the first incidence of abuse. However, even for those who find they are in a relationship that has progressed to the point of being dangerous, there are still solutions, though admittedly tough solutions. No one is totally powerless against family abuse. There are many sources of help, governmental and private, for anyone who is being abused. Stopping family abuse, however, is not something that can be left up to only the authorities or private organizations to do. Everyone must become personally involved. Our first and most urgent job is to change society's attitudes. We must all see and treat family abuse for what it is: a crime.

15

Governmental Response to Family Abuse

In October 1982, Charles Thurman assaulted his estranged wife, Tracey, while she visited some friends at their home in Torrington, Connecticut. The friends, outraged at the attack, called the police and requested that they keep Mr. Thurman off their property. On 5 November, Mr. Thurman returned to the same home and dragged his son out of the residence. Afterward, Tracey and the owners of the property attempted to file a complaint against Charles, but the local police refused to take it.

On 9 November, Charles Thurman screamed threats at Tracey as she sat in her car. A local police officer reportedly witnessed the incident, but did nothing until Charles finally broke out the windshield of Tracey's car. The officer then arrested Charles, and the next day a judge convicted Charles of breach of the peace. As a part of its sentence, the court ordered Charles to stay away from Tracey and the home of her friends.

On 31 December, Tracey again visited her friends at their home, and once again Charles showed up, making threats against Tracey. Tracey called the police department, advising them of the situation and of the court order that Charles continued to violate. The police refused to do anything.

Many times between 1 January 1983 and 4 May 1983, Tracey called the Torrington Police Department to report threats made by her estranged husband. During these calls she also requested that Charles be arrested because he continued to violate the terms of the court order. The police refused to arrest him.

On 5 May, Tracey reported to the local police a threat Charles had made to shoot her. A detective took the complaint and then told Tracey to come back in three weeks, and at that time they would seek a warrant against Charles. On 6 May, still fearing that Charles meant to harm her, Tracey applied for a restraining order against him. The court issued the order and made the local police department aware of it.

On 27 May, Tracey went to the Torrington Police Department and requested that her estranged husband be arrested for violation of the restraining order. An officer told her that she would have to come back after the Memorial Day holiday.

On 31 May, Tracey returned to the Torrington Police Department, as the officer requested her to do, but this time an officer told her that the only person who could help her was on vacation. She would have to wait until he returned. Tracey's brother-in-law then called the police department to complain about their treatment of Tracey. An officer assured him that Charles would be arrested on 8 June. Charles, however, was not arrested.

On 10 June, while Tracey once more visited her friends at their home in Torrington, Charles, in violation of the restraining order, appeared at the residence and demanded to speak with Tracey. Tracey called the police and asked that they come and arrest Charles. After waiting fifteen minutes for the police to arrive, Tracey finally went outside to speak with Charles, hoping to persuade him to leave without hurting anyone.

Charles, however, had apparently come there with the clear intention of hurting someone. Suddenly brandishing a knife, he attacked Tracey, repeatedly stabbing her in the chest, neck, and throat, until finally she fell bleeding to the lawn. About ten minutes later, the first police officer finally arrived. Charles still stood on the front lawn holding the bloody knife. The officer, however, did not attempt to arrest Charles or give Tracey first aid. The officer instead just watched as Charles kicked Tracey in the head, then ran into the residence and grabbed his son, carrying him back outside and dropping him onto the wounded Tracey, kicking her in the head again. Even when three more police officers arrived, they still didn't restrain Charles, but permitted him to wander around and continue to threaten Tracey. They finally did arrest Charles, however, when he tried to attack Tracey as she lay on a stretcher.

Tracey recovered from her wounds and sued the city of Torrington for their failure to protect her. The court awarded her $2.3 million. The city appealed the lawsuit and lost. In its decision upholding Tracey's lawsuit the United States District Court said: "Today ... any notion of a husband's prerogative to physically discipline his wife is an 'increasingly outdated misconception.' As such it must join other 'archaic and overbroad' premises which have been rejected as unconstitutional."

The court went on to instruct police departments that: "A man is not allowed to physically abuse or endanger a woman merely because he is her husband. Concomitantly, a police officer may not knowingly refrain from interference in such violence, and may not 'automatically decline to make an arrest simply because the assaulter and his victim are married to each other.' Such inaction on the part of the officer is a denial of the equal protection of the laws."

As a possible reason, but certainly not any kind of excuse, for the police department's inaction against Charles, during most of the time of his stalking of Tracey, Charles worked as a counterman and short-order cook at a diner in Torrington. Reportedly, many local police officers hung out and ate there. According to the court record, he boasted to the officers who visited the diner that he intended to kill his wife.[1]

❖ ❖ ❖ ❖ ❖

The very next year after Tracey won her case against the city of Torrington, the state of Connecticut passed a law making it mandatory that police officers arrest in domestic violence situations where evidence of an assault (a physical attack) exists. Presently, twenty-seven states require that arrests be made in domestic violence situations where certain conditions (usually evidence of an assault) are present.[2] But does this really solve anything? Does it really decrease the incidents of family abuse?

From 1980 to 1983, the Minneapolis Police Department, under the direction of Police Chief Anthony Bouza, a very outspoken and progressive leader in the law enforcement field, participated in an experiment conducted by the Police Foundation. The goal of this experiment was to discover what effect various police strategies, including arrest, had on the crime of domestic violence. The experiment incorporated three possible strategies that police officers would use when responding to incidents of domestic violence where an assault had occurred: the police would order the assailant out of the home for eight hours, attempt to mediate the dispute, or arrest the assailant. Depending on a random assignment, officers participating in the experiment would each night use just one of these three strategies.

The results of the experiment showed that, of the three strategies, being arrested and consequently spending a night in jail reduced by half any repeat violence against the same victim during the following six months, as compared to the strategies of mediation and ordering the assailant away. The results of this experiment first appeared in an article in the Science section of *The New York Times*, and following this were reported in over 300 other newspapers and discussed on numerous television news programs.

The leader of the experimental team, Dr. Lawrence Sherman, now at the University of Maryland, and for a time the chief criminologist in Indianapolis, warned, however, that these results could be unique to Minneapolis and might not carry over to all communities. And so, from 1985 to 1991, replication experiments were carried out in Omaha, Charlotte (North Carolina), Milwaukee, Metro-Dade (Miami), and Colorado Springs. What happened in these other communities?

According to the book *Policing Domestic Violence* by Lawrence Sherman, "The results are complex, but they clearly challenge the central premise of mandatory arrest laws: that arrest always works best. The replications in Milwaukee, Charlotte, and Omaha even produced evidence that arrest *increased* the frequency of future domestic violence by the suspects. On the other hand, the replications in Colorado Springs and Metro-Dade produced victim-reported evidence that arrest did reduce the risk of future violence."[3] The options of mediation and sending the assailant away did not significantly or dramatically deter future violence in any of the cities. The only difference the designers of the experiments could find between the "arrest works" and "arrest doesn't work" cities was their racial composition.

In Omaha, Nebraska, the experimental design differed a bit from other cities in that, in Omaha, when an abuser had left before the police arrived a warrant was issued for his or her arrest. The experimenters found this to have a stronger deterrent effect against future violence than any of the other methods (on-site arrest, mediation, and sending away), possibly because the abusers knew that if they had any contact with the police after this they would certainly be arrested.

Although the findings of these studies were not consistent, many states, on the strength of the finding in Minneapolis, began passing laws that mandated arrest in domestic violence situations where an assault had occurred. Dr. Sherman, however, warned that arrest was not necessarily a "miracle cure." Arrest would only work to stop future violence with those abusers who had a "stake in conformity," with those who feared what effect an arrest would have on their social standing. In other words, the batterer with no stake in conformity, who often holds a menial job at best, or is unemployed, does not worry about any stigma arising from being arrested, and may even gain status in his social group from it. This person also has little to fear about losing a job, since his or her employment record is often spotty at best. Consequently, the idea of arrest holds little threat for the abuser, and will likely not deter, and may even increase, future violence. Because of this, Dr. Sherman felt that the best policy would be for officers to be given the authority, but not the mandate, to arrest, even in those situations where they might not have actually witnessed the assault. By 1988, however, 90 percent of the police agencies in cities of over 100,000

people either encouraged or mandated arrests in domestic violence cases where an assault had occurred.[4]

Interestingly, family abuse is probably the only crime where it
has been necessary to show that arrest will deter further occurrences of the crime, or that an arrest is really needed. We don't do
this for robbery, burglary, or stranger assault. As a matter of fact,
we often know that arresting a burglar, for example, will not keep
this person from committing more burglaries the first chance he
gets, but this certainly doesn't stop us from wanting to arrest him.
The fact that it took the Minneapolis experiment to finally convince many in the criminal justice field that arrest was a viable
option for handling violent family abusers speaks volumes about
the old beliefs and prejudices regarding family abuse.

One community, however, Duluth, Minnesota, a city of 90,000
located on Lake Superior, took charge long before the Minneapolis
study. In 1982 they started a program called the Domestic Abuse
Intervention Project, a program that has been studied and copied
all over the world. While calling for mandatory arrests when there
is evidence of an assault during a domestic altercation, the Duluth
program also tracks the abuser through the criminal justice system
to be certain no part of the system breaks down. The first-time
offender in Duluth, if found guilty, is usually sentenced to a jail
term, but then put on probation pending the completion of a
twenty-six-week batterer's counseling program.

Is the Duluth program successful? It's hard to say. While most
residents of Duluth now realize that family violence is a crime, one
study shows that five years after completing the batterer's program 40 to 60 percent of the batterers are still batterers, either with
the same victim or a new one. And, as I talked about in the
previous chapter, many of the "cured" abusers may have stopped
the physical abuse out of fear of what will happen to them if they
don't, but they haven't stopped abusing. They have simply
switched to verbal and emotional abuse. So the real success rate is
probably much less than the 40 to 60 percent Duluth claims. This
low percentage of success for the Duluth program may be low,
however, because Duluth depends so heavily on counseling to
stop the abuse. Counseling, though a good idea, often doesn't

work in practice. The problem with most counseling is that it doesn't treat family abuse as a crime, but more as a family problem, and often all members of the family are asked to attend the counseling. This is not meant to offer support to the victims, but to treat the abuser and victims as one unit that needs to be fixed. However, we don't ask people who assault strangers or those who abuse other people's children to go into therapy with their victims and attempt to work out the problem. We try them and put them in jail, as we should family abusers.

"What works?" asks Murray A. Straus of the Family Research Laboratory at the University of New Hampshire, talking about treatment for batterers. "The research generally shows: not much."[5]

Dr. Neil S. Jacobson of the University of Washington in Seattle adds: "The therapies most commonly used in treating wife batterers assume that among their major problems are managing their anger and controlling their violent impulses. But new data suggest that for many of the worst offenders, violence is not impulsive, and their fury is paired with cool control."[6] According to Dr. Jacobson, many batterers don't just strike out impulsively, but instead coolly use violence as a control mechanism.

But most important, batterers forced into a treatment program, as they are in Duluth, are not going to have the same commitment to change as would batterers who had sought out the help themselves. Instead, often batterers forced into treatment will do just the minimum they have to do in order to get through the program and stay out of trouble with the court. Clearly, this is not change. "Counseling is the American way to heal a problem," said Pittsburgh sociologist Edward W. Gondolf, who develops batterers' programs. "She'll think, 'If he's trying, I should support him,' while he's thinking, 'I'll go to the program until I get what I want—my wife back.' But his being in counseling may increase the danger for her because she has got her guard down."[7]

If counseling programs are not that effective, then what do I think should be done?

After twenty-eight years in law enforcement, after witnessing hundreds and hundreds of family abuse incidents, and after interviewing dozens of people who work in the field of family abuse, I find that there are a large number of changes that must be made in America if we are to stem the tide of family abuse. There are laws that must be enacted, laws that must be changed, and laws that must be enforced if family abuse is to be brought under control. In addition, there are a number of programs working in various parts of the country that need to be transplanted to every part of the country.

First off, I find I must agree with Dr. Sherman. While I certainly feel that an arrest should be made in the vast majority of family abuse cases where an assault has taken place, I do not support mandatory arrests. The reason for this is that officers sent to handle a family violence situation usually encounter two people with completely different versions of what happened. Quite often, both parties bear the bloody signs of an assault, and both are screaming that the other one assaulted them first. The officers, having no way of knowing which injuries were the result of an assault and which were sustained in self-defense, are unable to sort out the truth. Most officers have seen enough cases to know better than to just assume that the man has to be the assailant and the woman the victim. So, in cases where arrests are mandated by law, the police find themselves often having to arrest both parties and then being forced to take the children to the community children's shelter. This doesn't work out to anyone's advantage. Both parents get a criminal record, and the children temporarily become wards of the state, which can be especially traumatic for young children.

Officers must be given the discretion not to make an arrest in certain, but very limited, situations, because situations where an arrest is not the best answer will always occur. But, on the other hand, officers should not be allowed to go to the scene of a family abuse incident where someone has been assaulted and just leave without doing anything.

Quite often, even in those jurisdictions where arrests are mandated, officers still do not make them. The reason for this, I believe, has little to do with an officer's personal beliefs about family abuse, regardless of what many advocates of mandatory arrest may claim. It usually has to do with paperwork and bother. Whenever a person is arrested an officer must complete a considerable amount of paperwork, send the person to jail, file charges, and later appear in court. If the officer just warns the combatants in a family violence situation to cool it and then leaves, he or she has saved a lot of paperwork and a lot of time and trouble.

The answer then, as Dr. Sherman suggests, is to require a written report whenever an officer decides not to make an arrest in a family abuse situation where there has been an assault. With this policy, police departments could monitor their officers' performance and should become concerned whenever an officer begins submitting these reports regularly. Like officers who suddenly begin amassing too many resisting-arrest charges, officers who turn too many abusers loose would be brought in for counseling and afterward kept under a closer watch. This policy would both allow for those situations in which arrest is not the best answer and also drastically reduce the number of guilty people being turned loose when they should be arrested. This is important because, whenever possible, the abuser in a family violence situation should be arrested. Family abuse only continues because the perpetrators seldom suffer any negative consequences. If the abusers know that they will likely be arrested if they commit family abuse, many of them will be much less inclined to do so. Perpetrators of family abuse must be shown that their behavior is unacceptable and that society will not tolerate it.

Along with this policy, though, police departments must also train their officers in the dynamics of family abuse. Officers need to know why it occurs, why the abusers and victims act as they do, and what the best response by the police is. This training should also include speakers from the various shelters and other organizations who can help officers assist family abuse victims. We have had training of this sort in Indianapolis, and as part of it have had both abuse victims and former abusers speak to us. Every police department in the United States needs this training so that their officers can intelligently deal with family abuse problems.

A strong involvement by the police, however, though useful, will not be enough to solve this problem. Perpetrators of family abuse must also be strenuously prosecuted. This, though, seldom occurs, and is one of the reasons police officers often don't make arrests in family abuse situations. "Without a policy of strong prosecution, efforts by law enforcement agencies have little impact," say the authors of the Bureau of Justice Assistance research paper *Family Violence: Interventions for the Justice System*. "The chief prosecutor should be solidly behind the development of a family violence intervention program and committed to the full participation of the prosecutor's office."[8]

Dr. David Ford, in the book *Legal Response to Wife Assault*, adds to this: "In exercising broad discretion at various decision points, the prosecutor is most influential in shaping the course of events for both victim and defendant." Dr. Ford then goes on to say: "The prosecutor's discretionary authority enables seemingly arbitrary action consistent with his or her unique interests, sometimes at the expense of the public or specific victims. For example, their screening function (deciding which cases to prosecute) allows prosecutors to manage their own work loads."[9]

Many prosecutors don't like to try family abuse cases, research shows, because the outcome of these cases is always so uncertain. This comes about because often jurors, and many times even judges, feel reluctant to convict family abusers for reasons having to do with personal beliefs about a spouse's or a parent's "inherent rights." This reluctance to convict, of course, then affects a prosecutor's conviction rate. Most prosecutors like to keep their conviction rates very high, often to use as proof of their qualifications for other elected offices. However, if we are ever to be able to bring the problem of family abuse under control, prosecutors must stop thinking politically and instead begin thinking humanly. Prosecutors must forget about percentages, and just try the cases. Of course, they will lose some of them. But they will also win a lot of cases that they would never have tried, and consequently will convict many abusers who would have been turned loose. Prosecutors must remember that they were elected *to be a prosecutor*, and not elected to prepare themselves for higher office. Readers should be aware, therefore, that any prosecutor who brags of a high conviction rate is not the "super public servant" this conviction rate is supposed to prove he or she is. Instead, this prosecutor is a fraud and is not doing the job he or she was elected to do. This prosecutor is picking and choosing only the best and easiest family abuse cases to prosecute, and consequently allowing a lot of abusers to go free. These kind of prosecutors must be turned out of office through organized campaigns by voters concerned about family abuse.

Family abuse, incidentally, is also one of the few crimes in which the victims must demonstrate that they are personally worthy of having their cases prosecuted. Indeed, often a prosecutor will only take cases of family abuse after weighing not just the criminal and legal aspects of the case, but also the personal attributes of the victims. My wife, Melanie, a child abuse detective, recently had a case of child sexual abuse that the prosecutor turned down for prosecution because the father of the victim (who had no connection with the abuse) was an alcoholic. I certainly can't explain this decision, but regularly, my wife reports, child abuse cases are turned down by the prosecutor because the victims have had problems at school or have previously engaged in what the prosecutor considers "improper behavior." Citizens need to closely monitor their prosecutors. What does any of this have to do with the fact that a crime, a serious crime, has been committed against a child? If someone robs a store where the police know that the store owners are involved in selling stolen merchandise, or if someone kills a bad person, the prosecutor doesn't decline the case because of the character of the victim. Why should family abuse be different? This must change.

There are some communities, however few, in which the local prosecutor *is* committed to trying family abuse cases. To facilitate the prosecution in these communities the prosecutor's office often uses a system called "vertical prosecution." This means that the same prosecutor is assigned to the family from beginning to end. Vertical prosecution is especially well received by victims because in many cities, at different stages of the prosecution, different prosecutors step in and take over the case, often with little or no knowledge about what has gone on before. This can be very disheartening to the victims, who many times feel a connection to the person they've worked with for some time. Being shuffled around makes family abuse victims feel that the prosecutor's office has little real interest in their case. Vertical prosecution is needed in every community.

One final piece of the criminal justice system must be re-formed if we are to stop family abuse: judges. Even if prosecutors firmly believe in prosecuting family abuse cases, and are willing to commit their office's resources to it, this will have little effect if the perpetrators of the family abuse find that, even after a trial and conviction, little happens to them. And unfortunately, this is many times the case. Judges far too often take family abuse cases lightly, and judges seldom mete out any lengthy punishment, even in cases of serious injury. Many judges still believe that family abuse is a private family concern that does not merit judicial punish-ment. While supposedly wise and just, judges are actually very often ignorant about such things as family abuse, and, like many people, hang onto and believe in old myths.

A judge in Fulton, Kentucky, after hearing testimony that a husband repeatedly beat his wife, ordered as his solution that the couple attend church services together. Another time he ordered an abusive couple to go out drinking together with the husband as designated driver. A judge in Cincinnati, Ohio, after hearing testi-mony about abuse of a woman by her boyfriend, ordered the couple to get married. (The judge quickly rescinded the order, however, when a reporter from *Inside Edition* showed up in his court.) In Johnson City, Tennessee, a judge sentenced a mother and father to ten years in prison for sexually molesting their own children. The judge in the case then offered the mother (but not the father) probation if she would agree to be sterilized. In Washing-ton, D.C., a man stabbed his wife seven times with a butcher knife, killing her. A judge later released the man pending the grand jury's decision about the murder because the judge said "he posed no significant threat to the public." Before the murder the man had been arrested twice for assaulting his wife. In New York City, a local judge has received heavy censure for his reportedly light-handed treatment of family abusers, including reducing the bail of a man who had repeatedly attacked his girlfriend. This man, while out on the lowered bail, then murdered her.

I recall witnessing this type of judicial thinking myself one day while waiting in court for a case. A woman told the court she had been followed, harassed, and beaten several times by a former boyfriend. After a short trial, the judge found the man guilty, but then sentenced him only to probation. As the woman was leaving the courtroom, obviously upset over the light-handed handling of her case, the judge said very loudly that if the victim and abuser got married he would drop the probation. This brought a roar of laughter from the courtroom, which is, I suppose, what the judge wanted.

In an article in the *Los Angeles Times*, domestic violence victims' advocate Lisa Foux is quoted as saying: "What we don't have is proper accountability for judges." She describes them as: "Uneducated gods who will make unthinking remarks and jokes that undermine the victims and reinforce batterers."[10] These types of attitudes, however, are changing.

In 1993, the Nevada Supreme Court used its judicial power to close all of the courts in Nevada for the day of 18 or 19 October 1993. On these days the Supreme Court required every judge in Nevada to attend a seminar on domestic violence.

"I believe that this will be an enormous aid to victims of domestic violence," said Kathleen Brooks of the Assistance for Domestic Crisis in Las Vegas. "What I see as one of the drawbacks for victims ... is that law enforcement officials and judges don't understand the dynamics of domestic violence and don't give the victim the support and protection that she needs."[11]

Judges, probably more than anyone else in the criminal justice system, have the power to affect an abuser's thinking about what he or she is doing. A strong admonishment, along with a stiff sentence, will make an abuser know that what he or she is doing is not socially acceptable.

I believe this training should be given to every judge in every state, but that it is just as important to train and educate prosecutors about family abuse. They hold the true power as to what can be done about family abuse in a community. Actually, every worker in the criminal justice system, including the police, needs to have yearly training in domestic violence, child abuse, elder abuse, sexual abuse, and financial abuse.

In addition to this training for all members of the criminal justice system, I also believe every major community should have a family abuse advocate system. This is a group of people, often volunteers, who assist family abuse victims. The criminal justice system can be daunting to anyone not familiar with its intricate workings. To help with this problem, in communities that have such a system, an advocate is assigned to a family abuse victim when he or she enters the system, and then assists the victim, up through the trial if necessary, showing the victim how to get done whatever needs to be done.

The first thing done by many victims of family abuse is to gain protection through the use of restraining or protective orders. (As I have stated before, victims of family abuse who fear for their lives or safety should *never* depend on a protective order to really protect them. Particularly when the level of violence has reached the life-threatening stage, these orders can often be of little value, and can even endanger the victims even more.) However, protective orders can be very useful against abusers in a less advanced state of their abuse. According to the National Institute of Justice's research paper *Civil Protection Orders*: "Our research suggests that protection orders can provide a workable option for many victims seeking protection from further abuse. Furthermore, it appears that when protection orders offer only weak protection, the principal explanation may lie in the functioning of the justice system rather than the nature of protection orders as a remedy."[12] This is so true. I often find that officers don't like enforcing protective orders for the same reason they don't like making arrests in most family abuse situations: because they know that even if they arrest the violator of the protective order the judge will not do anything substantial to him or her.

I'm really not sure why so many of the judges who issue protective orders are so often reluctant to punish abusers who violate them. This is especially difficult to understand because if someone opposed a judge's order in the courtroom, as the abusers who violate protective orders do outside of the courtroom, most judges would not be reluctant at all to throw the person in jail for contempt of court, which is exactly what a violation of a protective order is. I've only seen it happen twice in my career, where a person openly opposed a judge in the courtroom, but both times the judge did not hesitate to use his authority to punish the person. For some reason, however, many judges do not see a violation of a protective order as quite this serious.

The only answer to this problem, therefore, which will make protective orders actually protective, is near-mandatory sentencing for violators of protective orders. Most judges dislike mandatory sentencing because it does not allow them to make the exception in cases where an exception is applicable. Therefore, judges, like police officers in arresting family abusers, should be forced to explain and justify why they are not sentencing a family abuser who violates a protective order in the cases where they don't. Abusers must know that if they violate a protective order they *will* be sent to jail, and that this is not just a possibility but a near certainty. This will make all but the most desperate abuser stop and think seriously about violating a protective order. The National Institute of Justice research paper cited above states: "In jurisdictions such as Duluth and Philadelphia, where judges have established a formal policy that offenders who violate an order will be apprehended and punished, often with a jail term, both judges and victim advocates report the highest level of satisfaction with the system."

Colorado Springs, Colorado, has a protective order system that I believe should serve as a model for all communities. If a police officer in Colorado Springs responds to a family abuse situation in which he or she believes a protective order is necessary, the officer telephones an on-call judge and explains the situation. If the judge agrees that an order is necessary, the officer then fills out a blank protective order form, and, on authority from the judge, serves it on the abuser, ordering him or her off the property. This order lasts until the end of the next court day, giving the victim time to apply for extended relief.

In addition to the Colorado Springs program, I would also recommend a new program instituted in New York City that adds a bit more protection to protective orders. Working with ADT Security Systems Corporation, the Brooklyn District Attorney has devised a program whereby those abuse victims who are deemed to be in the most danger, even though having a protective order, are given small emergency pendants to wear around their necks. If the victims suddenly find themselves in danger from their abusers, they press a button on the pendant and the police are summoned to the victims' house.

Also needed in every state is a statewide registry of restraining and protective orders. Far too often when a victim crosses a county line the local police have no way of being certain a restraining order presently exists. The state of New Hampshire, however, goes even further than this and makes protective orders issued by courts in other states enforceable in New Hampshire as long as the order is valid in the issuing state. The new Violence Against Women Act has included a similar provision in its expanded protection of women. However, before being enforced nationwide, this provision is being tested in a selected area.

Even the New Hampshire law, though, still isn't enough protection because in many jurisdictions protective orders have a time limit set on them. Protective orders can usually be renewed only once, and then they expire. This does not make sense to me. Protective orders should not expire—period. An abuser doesn't become less dangerous because a year or two has passed. In the Lisa Bianco case discussed in the previous chapter, Alan Matheney sat in prison for several years, but never lost his desire to hurt Lisa. Stalkers have been known to harass their victims for years. For the safety of abuse victims this expiration of protective orders needs to be changed.

A new law passed in New York involving protective orders does give a bit more safety to abuse victims. Under this law, a person violating a protective order can be charged with first-degree criminal contempt, a felony, if that person has within the past five years violated a previous order of protection, or if the person injures the victim while violating the order. To make protective orders work, every state should make the first violation of a protective order a misdemeanor with the strong likelihood of jail time as punishment, and the second violation a felony. People served with protective orders must understand exactly what these orders mean: that the served person must leave the victim alone or be willing to suffer the inevitable negative consequences.

In addition to having a law similar to the New York law, I also believe every state should have a law such as the one Indiana has concerning repeat assaults. In Indiana, an assault becomes a felony when it is committed by a person previously convicted of another assault against the same victim. In 1996, this law was amended so that a previous assault now does not have to be against the same victim, but only occur during a family violence incident. As a felony, the assault is then punishable by a term in prison rather than a fine or jail. A recent article in *The New York Times* about two people involved in a violent relationship vividly describes the problem of not having such a law: "Despite evidence that Ms. Komar endured more than a year of repeated beatings that twice sent her to the hospital, her injuries did not, under state law, amount to charges against Mr. Oliver more serious than misdemeanors. Under state law," the article said, "assaults are treated as felonies only when they cause debilitating injuries, such as broken bones."[13] Mr. Oliver eventually murdered Ms. Komar.

Along with the above laws, I also believe an important addition to every state's laws should be one making the neighborhood around battered victims' shelters "no-combat" zones. What this means is that any person who goes to a shelter with the intent to harm or intimidate someone is guilty of a felony. Abusers must be aware that going to a shelter to further terrorize victims will likely end in a prison sentence for them. This is important because citizens must never feel that they are hopelessly trapped in an abusive relationship. There should always be somewhere they can go where they will be safe and can get help.

If a state, however, is going to commit itself to making all of this protection available to the victims of family abuse, it must also provide a means for the victims to start a new life without the abusers. Communities must be willing to help victims of family abuse gain economic independence from their abusers through short-term financial assistance, vouchers for day care, subsidized housing, job training, etc. Without this, we are only giving the victims false hope by protecting, but not really helping them. How can all of this be funded? Part of it could come from increased marriage license costs. In 1978, Florida placed a surcharge on marriage licenses that goes to support battered women's shelters. Perhaps getting married should be made a bit more expensive in all states so that couples would have to give it a little more thought. This extra expense could then be put to good use.

Also to assist family abuse victims, I believe every community in America should have a family advocacy center. This idea, which originated in Huntsville, Alabama, brings together in one facility all of the agencies in a community that deal with family abuse problems, such as the police, the prosecutor's office, child protective services, adult protective services, and others. Having all of these agencies working together in the same facility decreases the duplication of effort that often occurs when two or more agencies are investigating the same family or incident. Also, by being physically situated in the same facility, each agency's resources are immediately available to the other agencies. Ideally, a family advocacy center would not be located at the police department or at any other government facility, but in a separate building. In Indianapolis, for example, the family advocacy center is located in a downtown office building. Police departments and other government buildings have the tendency to appear very austere, sterile, and intimidating, which consequently frightens many victims and makes them less than totally cooperative. A family advocacy center, on the other hand, appears much more user-friendly, with bright wallpaper, toys for the kids, and an absence of most police and government paraphernalia.

"Every community needs the coordinated effort that a family advocacy center provides," said John Nolan, head of the Indianapolis Family Advocacy Center. "Cases of family abuse can be handled much more efficiently and effectively in a community with a family advocacy center."

Following on this idea of a combined effort, another necessity in every community is a Family Court. This court would ideally handle cases of child abuse and neglect, divorce, spouse and elderly abuse, child custody issues, and other family-related matters that require a court setting. The advantage of this concept is that it can solve the problem of a single family having several cases that all have the same root cause pending in several different courts. Judge Robert Page in an article in *Juvenile & Family Court Journal* stated: "The primary advantage claimed for a family court system is the unification of all complaints, petitions, and case types within one case processing and management system in order to provide a more efficient, less costly and damaging, consistent and longer lasting resolution of the problems presented."[14] This is an excellent family abuse prevention concept needed in every community.

Minnesota has already had a very progressive family abuse program in place for some time, and serves as a model for how the criminal justice system should work. In some jurisdictions in Minnesota, family abuse advocates track family violence cases from the initial call to the police through the prosecution to the sentencing. If something goes wrong with the case, the advocate attempts to find out what part of the system failed in its job. This type of scrutiny makes members of the Minnesota criminal justice system very reluctant to take family abuse cases lightly.

Duluth, Minnesota, has also established a very innovative program for handling child visitation problems involving abusive spouses. Called the Duluth Visitation Center, this facility, opened in 1989, serves as an exchange point for child visitation purposes, while also having facilities available if the family wants to use the center for the visitation. A parent in Duluth, who fears violence, and who has a protective order against a spouse, can request the judge to specify that all child exchanges take place at the center or that the visitation itself take place at the center. Judges also often order parents to attend the center's group parent sessions.

The staff of the visitation center, when receiving a new family, draws up a contract for each parent, specifying the terms of the visitation arrangements, such as no abusive language or actions, the visitation must take place at the center, etc. This facility in

Duluth spares the custodial parent the problems and dangers that could occur if an abusive former partner had to come to his or her new home in order to pick up the children. The staff of the center, in addition, are trained to watch for signs of possible abuse brewing, and either step in themselves or, if necessary, call the police. To help reduce the violence of family abuse, a visitation center is needed in every community in America.

In 1994, President Clinton signed the Violence Against Women Act. This law makes it a federal offense to cross a state line to abuse a spouse. Soon afterward, Chris Bailey of St. Albans, West Virginia, severely beat his wife, Sonya Bailey, then stuffed her into the trunk of his compact car and drove for six days through West Virginia and Kentucky before finally taking Sonya to a hospital. She was still in a coma several months later. On 1 September 1995, Chris Bailey, prosecuted under the Violence Against Women Act, received a life sentence in prison.

While the Violence Against Women Act is certainly a welcome addition in the battle against family abuse, another law that I believe needs to be passed and enforced in every jurisdiction is one that prohibits a person under a restraining order, or who has been convicted of family violence, from purchasing or carrying a firearm. Far too often, family abusers stalk their victims while brandishing firearms. We don't allow former mental patients and those convicted of a felony to buy or carry a gun because they have already demonstrated their dangerousness. Well, family abusers are just as dangerous, and in some cases even more so.

"The bill would make it clear that if you are not responsible enough to keep from doing harm to your spouse or your children, then society does not deem you responsible enough to own a gun," said Congressman Robert Torricelli, speaking about a law he sponsored that would complement the Brady Bill.[15] California, which already has such a law in effect, recently attempted to amend the law to allow judges to temporarily take away guns already owned by people under restraining or protective orders.

Local governments can also assist in the fight against family abuse. A study done in Indianapolis, for example, recently found the city to be in need of more emergency shelter beds and transitional housing for the victims of family violence. In November 1995, the mayor of Indianapolis, Stephen Goldsmith, announced that the Mayor's Commission on Family Violence had arranged with the Indianapolis Hotel/Motel Association to offer free emergency shelter to the victims of family violence. In addition, in April 1996, the city of Indianapolis purchased a former health care facility, which will be renovated and turned into a transitional shelter for domestic violence victims. The Mayor's office is also presently working with local businesses to find available buildings for more housing.

"One of the fundamental responsibilities of government is safety," said Mayor Goldsmith in a letter to me. "Violence inside the home can be the most frightening, and, in the long run, the most damaging violence. Local government bears a special responsibility to actively intervene to reduce this threat."

Businesses also have a responsibility to provide safety. Family abuse inevitably spills over into the working lives of abusers and victims, and no individual, or business, is immune from its negative effects. Abusers often follow family members to their place of employment to continue the abuse. In Houston, Texas, for example, a woman who had a restraining order against her former boyfriend notified her place of employment about it. They did not, however, take her fears seriously, and her boyfriend came to her place of business and gunned her down, killing her. The victim's family sued, and her employer and the business's property management company settled out of court for $350,000.

Judge Ruth Reichard, who oversees domestic violence cases in Marion County, Indiana, and who constantly hears about how family violence spills over into the workplace, stated in an article in the *Indianapolis Star* that she believes all businesses should have a family violence safety plan. This plan would include keeping a copy of any restraining order on file, and requesting that the police patrol the area more often when the victim is working.[16] A *Los Angeles Times* article reports that a bill put forth recently in the California state legislature would allow businesses to obtain restraining orders in those cases in which the victims are too frightened to get them.

According to an article in *The Wall Street Journal*, more and more businesses are responding to the problem of family violence spillover by developing protection and antiabuse programs. Polaroid Corporation, for example, taps the phones of employees who fear they will be attacked, provides an escort for these employees to and from their cars, and even posts guards at the employees' homes.[17] Liz Clairborne, Inc., holds seminars, on company time, about family abuse. All businesses in America need to follow these companies' lead.

Stalking, which I talked about in Chapter 7, is a behavior increasingly practiced by perpetrators of family abuse, and another area where reforms can help increase the safety of victims. In 1993, in response to this increasing danger, the Congress of the United States directed the U.S. Department of Justice to develop a model antistalking law that would encourage states to adopt antistalking measures. This model law, recently completed, recognizes that stalking is often characterized by a series of increasingly serious acts, and, because of this, the law recommends that states establish a continuum of charges so that the police can intervene and arrest stalkers in the early stages of the crime. The law also recommends that serious, obsessive stalking be made a felony; that stalkers, once released from custody, be monitored very closely to prevent a resumption of their activities; and that all criminal justice officials receive training about stalkers and their crime. These recommendations should be included in every state's antistalking law.

A further method to help prevent abuse from occurring in the first place, even beyond strict laws, is to rip away the shroud of secrecy that family abusers hide behind. Many times, even serious family abusers appear as fine, charming individuals to the community at large. Fewer people would want to be family abusers if they knew that the community was going to find out what kind of people they really are. Recently, *Editor & Publisher* magazine featured an article about *The Caledonian-Record* in St. Johnsbury, Vermont. This 10,500-circulation newspaper began printing final abuse orders granted by the Family Court. These are orders that are issued once the case has been heard and a decision made by the judge as to what should be done about the abuse. These orders identify both the victim and the abuser in family violence cases, the reason the victim requested the order, and what the judge ruled.[18]

This idea is receiving mixed reviews because some people fear that victims may be reluctant to pursue such orders if they know their names will be published in the newspaper, and there is certainly the problem that this can just further punish the victims by exposing their problems to the public. However, the merits of this idea, I feel, outweigh any disadvantages. Secrecy is what allows family abusers to continue abusing. If potential abusers knew that their neighbors, friends, and co-workers would discover what kind of people they really are, they would be much less inclined to become abusers. And by the time a victim has asked the criminal justice system to intervene, as many of the victims in these orders have, the problems and danger of the abuse have reached levels where privacy is a minor matter.

"In other words, it's not enough to lock the guy up; he needs to be looked down on by his family, friends, and co-workers," said Sergeant Sandy Kline, head of Houston Police Department's Family Violence Unit. "These formal and informal sanctions work in tandem."[19]

In support of this idea, the Family Violence Prevention Fund has recently begun a publicity campaign aimed at showing family abuse for what it is: a crime. The campaign's theme is "There is no excuse for domestic violence." The group in 1994 sent ads condemning family violence to 22,000 media outlets. "[I]f we remain silent, our silence will breed even more fear and continue creating a sanction for abuse," said Esta Soler, the Fund's executive director.[20]

The seriousness of the family abuse problem is also being proclaimed yearly by the President during October, which is Domestic Violence Awareness Month. I believe we need much more of this type of awareness heightening so there is no mistake in the public's mind that family abuse is wrong and will not be tolerated by society. This has worked for other "socially acceptable" crimes. In the last few years, for example, there have been some very effective publicity campaigns against drunk driving. Locally, for instance, television spots run during prime time have used real police officers with the message that if we catch you driving under the influence you will be arrested. The same awareness campaign is needed with family abuse.

Another area for reform lies in family abuse cases involving children. An extremely serious handicap in far too many jurisdictions is the statute of limitations for child abuse. In some states if prosecution is not brought within a few years of the abuse then the abuser can never be tried, no matter how horrible the crime. The problem with this is that the more horrible the abuse is the more likely it is that the child will suppress the memory of it, or be reluctant to tell anyone about it. Also, many times children cannot press charges, or even bring the abuse to anyone's attention, because they are very young and still under the strict control of the abuser. There should be no statute of limitations on child abuse.

On the other hand, even if the case is prosecuted within the statute of limitations, being forced to testify in court can be, at least temporarily, traumatic for children. While studies have shown that children do not suffer permanent, long-term harm from testifying in child abuse cases, at the very least children can be frightened and intimidated by the formal courtroom proceedings and by having to sit facing their abuser. Consequently, they often become less than convincing witnesses. The U.S. Supreme Court, however, has ruled that innovations in the courtroom, such as closing the court proceedings to outsiders or allowing the young victims not to have to confront their abusers (through the use of screens blocking the view or by having the victims testify on closed-circuit television), can be used only when it is shown that the children will suffer serious emotional trauma if they are forced to testify in the traditional courtroom environment. The problem, however, is often not so much any serious trauma that the children may suffer, but, as I have stated, the children being so intimidated by the court proceedings or by having to sit facing their abuser that their testimony is poor and halting at best.

Some states have attempted to address this problem. In Rhode Island, for example, mental or emotional harm resulting from testifying is a rebuttable presumption for children thirteen and under. This means that the defendant, if he or she wants to confront the child in court, must show that the child will not be harmed by it. In other words, the defendant must show that the child is so mature and stable that the mental and emotional stress of testifying will do no harm. This law also keeps defense attorneys from putting terrified youngsters on the stand and aggressively cross-examining them until they make a mistake, and then jumping on this mistake as proof the children are liars.

Many of these problems, though, can be corrected by judges and prosecutors who are knowledgeable and trained in handling child witnesses. If the sight of the alleged perpetrator will intimidate the child witness, but the effects are not so severe as to justify circumventing the Sixth Amendment right of facing an accuser, the prosecutor can handle this by simply standing between the child and the perpetrator, or by instructing the child to always look at a supportive family member when testifying. They can also encourage the child to tell the judge if the defendant begins making faces at him or her. As to the intimidating effects of a harsh cross-examination on a child, a judge always has the authority to stop a defense attorney from badgering a witness. All judges, prosecutors, and other court personnel need to receive training in dealing with young witnesses.

In most court proceedings, "hearsay," or repeating what someone told a witness, rather than having the person who actually said it testify to it, is usually forbidden. However, there have been notable exceptions in child abuse cases, since children are often too young to testify in court, yet may still have said something to someone that would identify their abuser. In *Ohio v. Roberts*, the U.S. Supreme Court ruled that before an out-of-court statement can be used as evidence, the state must show the declarant's unavailability to testify.[21] With very young children this is not difficult, and, as a result, many states have created hearsay exceptions for young child abuse victims. All states should.

The state of Utah has gone even further and included in its code of criminal procedure a Bill of Rights for Children. This document includes the right of children to be free from physical and emotional abuse during their involvement with the criminal justice system, the right not to be questioned about being responsible for inappropriate acts adults may have committed against them, the right to have interviews held to a minimum, and the right to be informed of community resources available to them. This is a document that should be included in every state's code of criminal procedure.

Additionally, several states have also instituted programs in which a child victim has a designated "friend of the court" who assists the child victim through the judicial procedures. Some jurisdictions have the court appoint a "guardian ad litem," whose job it is to look out for the child's best interests. Since these people work with the judicial system, they know what will happen and can prepare the child for it. Several large communities have even set up "court schools." For example, the Los Angeles "Kids in Court" program has group discussions of what occurs in court, tours of the courtroom, role-playing, and talks by court personnel, including judges, prosecutors, defense attorneys, and so forth. Having a child victim go through this kind of program can greatly lessen the anxiety and stress of testifying in court.

Alternately, some communities want to prevent the need for children to have to testify in court at all, and so attempt to intervene before family abuse occurs. The state of Hawaii, for example, has instituted a very innovative program aimed at lessening child abuse and neglect cases. The program, called Hawaii Healthy Start, targets prospective abuse and neglect victims from birth and follows them to age five. Mothers are screened for a number of variables that denote possible future abuse and neglect, including not being married, having a partner unemployed, unstable housing, a history of substance abuse, a history of depression, and other signs. The program then begins a series of weekly visits by program members, who assure that the mother knows where and how she and her child can receive the community services they need. The program's goals are to reduce family stress, improve parenting skills, enhance the child's heath and development, and prevent abuse and neglect. Preliminary findings have indicated that the program is successfully meeting its goals. Programs such as this should be in place in every community.

Strangely though, a large number of programs and organizations that work to prevent family abuse also have as their prime directive the need, if at all possible, to keep the family together. From a police officer's point of view—someone who has seen the damaging and deadly results of family abuse much too often—this is an extremely naive belief, usually based on the assumption that even being with bad parents is better than taking a child out of a home. A *Los Angeles Times* article quotes child advocate Kathryn Turman as saying: "Only a certain proportion of families can be fixed. Do we have three or four or five years to experiment with a family? Not when the children are being damaged."[22] Turman said she believes that the movement to keep the family together at all costs is based on the myth that enough therapy can make the violence and the pain go away. This simply isn't so.

My wife, Melanie, as a detective who works regularly with abused children, has told me many times that she sees this as one of the worst injustices occurring constantly in her job. Often children are taken out of a horrible home and put into a foster home, where the foster parents love and nurture them, but then several months or years later, the children are pulled out of the foster home and put right back into the same horrible home, where more abuse often occurs. In the National Institute of Justice research paper *The Cycle of Violence*, author Cathy Spatz Widom says of a study about children put into foster care: "These findings (about taking children away from their parents) challenge the assumption that it is necessarily unwise to remove children from negative family situations ... there is no evidence that those who were separated from their families fared any worse on the arrest measures (being arrested later in life) than those who remained home."[23]

The truth of the matter is that there are many children better off in foster care because some families are simply not worth saving. Some families are so violent and so degenerate that keeping them together is sentencing the children to be victims. The only real answer for these families is to remove the abusers and prosecute them, and, if this is not possible, to remove the children. Consider, for example, the Search family discussed in Chapter 4, the family who would all join in on the beatings of the mildly retarded daughter, Dolly. Could anyone really be so naive as to believe that Dolly was actually better off with her natural parents, the Searchs, who eventually murdered her, than she was with her foster family, who loved and nurtured her?

So far in this chapter I have talked almost exclusively about legal and governmental changes that will help in the fight against family abuse, but private organizations can also be of tremendous assistance. The American Medical Association (AMA), for example, has for a number of years recognized that the members of its organization have a responsibility to report child abuse. It has also recently reminded its members of the need to do more than just medically treat victims of spouse or partner abuse. Additionally, the AMA has recommended that all medical schools have comprehensive courses on family violence and that all hospitals have written protocols for handling cases of family violence.

"Training on domestic violence of any kind has been sadly lacking in medical schools," said Dr. Mark Lachs of the Yale University School of Medicine, "and there is no doubt that elder abuse is the most unexplored area of domestic violence." Indeed, new guidelines issued by the AMA state: "Physicians are ideally situated to play a significant role in the detection, management and prevention of elder abuse. A physician may be the only person outside the family who sees the older adult on a regular basis, and he or she is uniquely qualified to order confirmatory diagnostic tests ... to recommend hospital admission or to authorize services such as home health care."[24]

Dr. Palma E. Formica, a trustee of the AMA, says: "We hope to encourage physicians to become more acutely aware of elder abuse and to intervene when necessary. We've talked a lot about abuse by care givers, but we have not been willing to admit the prevalence of elder abuse by family members."[25]

But to help even more to stem elder abuse, communities need to have short-term help available for the caretakers of the elderly. In every community there must be some place caretakers know they can get help if they feel they are being overcome by the stress of caring for the elderly. This can be through a helper coming to the home to assist them or through a center where the elderly person can be left for a few hours while the care givers take a break or take care of necessary business.

Finally, to make the elderly more aware of the legal rights they have, the Indiana State Bar Association yearly publishes a book titled *Legal Reference for Older Hoosiers* (Hoosiers is a nickname for the residents of Indiana). This free, 200-page book contains legal information important for elderly family members. It contains chapters on Social Security law, veteran's benefits, Medicare, civil commitment, nursing homes and alternatives, landlord–tenant issues, guardianships, probate and estate planning, and many other legal issues that often arise for the elderly. Offering this kind of service, I feel, should be considered by every state bar association.

As the reader can see from all of the suggestions I have given in this and the preceding chapter, much needs to be done if we are to meet and stop the increasing threat of family abuse in America. The problem, however, certainly isn't hopeless. Americans simply need to become much more aware of the problem, and demonstrate a strong commitment to ending it. This, though, can only come about by having citizens and government officials willing to take action.

A Final Thought

There have been many books about family abuse written by psychologists, sociologists, family counselors, and others, but few by police officers. I find this void in the literature troubling because of all professionals who deal and work with family abuse, police officers are the closest to it. Unlike other professionals, police officers don't hear about family abuse weeks later in an office setting, where the victims are now dressed up and calm, and where the passing time has dulled the pain. Instead, police officers deal with family abuse victims while they are still bleeding and hurting, and they often confront the abusers in their seldom-seen guise of control-craving bullies. Yet, because so little has been written about family abuse by police officers, few people see the problem as realistically as police officers do.

The literature on family abuse reflects this void: written by social scientists far removed from the scene of the crime, family abuse is treated as a large, nebulous psychological problem, social problem, or family problem. It becomes a complex societal issue with many causes and no solution, and for which no person is really to blame. While this sort of literature is undeniably useful to academics, it doesn't lead to the practical and urgently needed solutions our country must have if we are to fight this growing problem.

Before we can begin to solve the problem of family abuse,

however, a radical change in attitude must occur. The attitude I want to change through this book (along with the academic view of family abuse) is the one held by many people, including some in the criminal justice system, that family abuse is a private family matter to be worked out within the family. If we are ever to stop family abuse, we must change this. The public must see family abuse not as a private matter, but as a crime. Treating family abuse as a crime lets the perpetrators know they will no longer be allowed to feel safe in the anonymity of the family—instead, they will be exposed and punished.

My hope for the future is that readers will become not only more aware of the seriousness of family abuse as a crime, but also insistent that their elected officials see the problem in the same way and treat it as such. Elected officials with this criminal view of family abuse are much more likely to embrace the changes in laws and social programs needed to fight it. This is the only answer to the problem. If we are ever to stop family abuse and give every American the freedom to live as he or she wants, without fear and intimidation, we must see and treat family abuse for what it is: a crime.

Appendix

While nearly every community in the United States has resources available to help victims of family abuse, finding these resources is not always easy. Fortunately, there are several hotlines that can assist family abuse victims in locating these resources:

1-800-799-7233
1-800-787-3224 TDD

These numbers will put a caller in contact with the National Domestic Violence Hotline. This hotline serves all of the United States, and provides callers with crisis counseling and referrals to local agencies and organizations that can help them.

1-800-422-4453

This number will put a caller in contact with the Child Help USA Hotline. This hotline also serves all of the United States, and provides callers with crisis counseling and local referrals. This hotline serves both children and adults abused as children.

Notes

Chapter 1

1. Anna Quindlen, "The Role of Guns in Domestic Violence," *Indianapolis Star* (2 June 1994), p. A-7.
2. Don Colburn, "Domestic Violence," *Washington Post Health* (28 June 1994), p. 10.
3. Don Colburn, "When Violence Begins at Home," *Washington Post Health* (15 March 1994), p. 7.
4. Fact sheet compiled by the National Coalition Against Domestic Violence, Denver, Colorado.
5. Carla Rivera, "U.S. Child Abuse at Crisis levels, Panel Says," *Los Angeles Times* (26 April 1995), p. B-1.
6. Matt Kelley, "Woman Tells Foes of Execution to Let Hers Proceed This Week," *Indianapolis Star* (15 January 1996), p. E-1.
7. U.S. Department of Justice, *Violence between Intimates* (Washington, D.C., U.S. Government Printing Office, 1994).
8. U.S. Department of Justice, *Murder in Families* (Washington, D.C., U.S. Government Printing Office, 1994).
9. U.S. Department of Justice, *Crime in the United States* (Washington D.C., U.S. Government Printing Office, 1995), p. 19.
10. U.S. Department of Justice, *National Assessment Program: 1994 Survey Results* (Washington, D.C., U.S. Government Printing Office, 1995), p. 2.
11. "Cost of Crime (Not Including Drugs) Said to Top $450 Billion," *Law Enforcement News* (15 May 1996), p. 1.
12. Erik J. de Wilde et al., "The Relationship Between Adolescent Suicidal Behavior and Life Events in Childhood and Adolescence, *American Journal of Psychiatry* (January 1992), p. 45.
13. M. Angeles Cerezo and Dolores Frias, "Emotional and Cognitive Adjustment in Abused Children," *Child Abuse and Neglect* (November 1994), p. 923.
14. Cathy Young, "Abused Statistics: Domestic Violence; Like Hydra Heads or Spreading Kudzu, the False Statistics Keep Proliferating," *National Review* (1 August 1994), p. 43.
15. Lawrence Sherman et al., *Policing Domestic Violence: Experiments and Dilemmas* (New York, Free Press, 1992), p. 6.

16. Laura B. Randolph, "Battered Women: How to Get and Give Help," *Ebony* (September 1994), p. 112.
17. Select Committee on Aging, U.S. House of Representatives. *Elder Abuse: An Examination of a Hidden Problem* (Washington, D.C., U.S. Government Printing Office, 1981), p. 1.
18. Sherman, p. 31.
19. *Violence between Intimates.*
20. Patsy Klaus and Michael Rand, *Special Report: Family Violence.* U.S. Justice Department (Washington, D.C., U.S. Government Printing Office), pp. 1–2.
21. Jennifer Dixon, "2,000 Children Die Each Year from Abuse, Neglect, Study Says," *Indianapolis Star* (28 April 1995), p. A-4.
22. Barbara Ehrenreich, "Battered Welfare Syndrome," *Time* (3 April 1995), p. 82.

Chapter 2

1. U.S. Department of Justice, *When the Victim Is a Child* (Washington, D.C., U.S. Government Printing Office, 1992), p. 4.
2. *Domestic Violence: No Longer Behind the Curtains* (Wylie, TX, Information Plus, 1991), p. 71.
3. Diana Russell, "The Secret Trauma," in *Domestic Violence: No Longer Behind the Curtains,* p. 69.
4. Jessie Anderson et al., "Prevalence of Childhood Sexual Abuse Experiences in a Community Sample of Women," *Journal of the American Academy of Child and Adolescent Psychiatry* (September 1993), p. 911.
5. *Domestic Violence: No Longer Behind the Curtains,* p. 69.
6. Donna Britt, "An Ugly Family Secret Revealed," *Washington Post* (12 November 1993), p. D-1.
7. Ronald Summit, "The Child Abuse Accommodation Syndrome," *Child Abuse and Neglect* (1983), p. 177.
8. Ibid.
9. Kathleen A. Kendall-Tackett and Arthur F. Simon, "A Comparison of the Abuse Experiences of Male and Female Adults Molested as Children," *Journal of Family Violence* (March 1992), p. 57.
10. Susan E. James, "The Secret Scar: Evaluating For Sex Abuse," *Addiction & Recovery* (May–June 1993), p. 10.
11. U.S. Department of Justice, *Victims of Childhood Sexual Abuse—Later Criminal Consequences* (Washington, D.C., U.S. Government Printing Office, 1995), p. 5.
12. William Barbour, Karin L. Swisher, and Carol Wekesser, editors, *Violence Against Women* (San Diego, CA, Greenhaven Press, 1994), p. 170.

Chapter 3

1. Carlos Sanchez, "Lorena Bobbitt Tells of Forced Sex," *Washington Post* (9 November 1993), p. A-1.
2. "Husband Tells Court of Sexual Mutilation by Wife," *The New York Times* (10 November 1993), p. A-20.

3. Mary Lou Tousignant and Carlos Sanchez, "Virginia Woman Says She Cut Husband in Self-Defense," *Washington Post* (25 June 1993), p. D-1.
4. "Husband Tells Court of Sexual Mutilation by Wife," p. A-20.
5. Stephen Labaton, "Husband Acquitted of Assault in Mutilation Case," *The New York Times* (11 November 1993), p. A-18.
6. Jan Hoffman, "Acquittal in Sex Mutilation Case Alarms Women's Advocates," *The New York Times* (12 November 1993), p. A-16.
7. David Margolick, "Does Mrs. Bobbitt Count as Another Battered Wife?" *The New York Times* (16 January 1994), p. 5.
8. Ola W. Barnett and Alyce D. LaViolette, *It Court Happen to Anyone* (Newbury Park, CA, Sage, 1993), p. 60.
9. Lonnie R. Hazlewood, Anson Shupe, and William A. Stacey, *The Violent Couple* (Westport, CT, Praeger, 1994), p. 56.
10. Diane Russell, *Rape in Marriage* (New York, Macmillan, 1982).
11. *Violence between Intimates*, op. cit.
12. Lloyd Ohlin and Michael Tonry, editors, *Family Violence* (Chicago, University of Chicago Press, 1989), p. 188.
13. Louis J. Shiro and Kersti Yllo, *Bar Bulletin* (September 1985).
14. *Violent Relationships: Battering and Abuse Among Adults* (Wylie, TX, Information Plus, 1995), p. 21.
15. "Bishops Denounce Abuse of Spouses," *The New York Times* (30 October 1992), p. A-12.
16. *Domestic Violence: No Longer Behind the Curtains*, pp. 93–94.
17. Jose Torres, *Fire and Fear*, quoted by William Nack and Lester Munson in "Sports' Dirty Secret," *Sports Illustrated* (31 July 1995), p. 66.
18. Hazlewood, p. 117.
19. Mary J. Quinn and Susan K. Tomita, *Elder Abuse and Neglect* (New York, Springer, 1986).
20. *Improving the Police Response to Domestic Elder Abuse* (Washington, D.C., Police Executive Research Forum, 1993), p. I-9.
21. *Summary of the Statistical Data on Elder Abuse in Domestic Settings FY90 and FY91*, quoted in *Violent Relationships* (Wylie, TX, Information Plus, 1995), p. 132.
22. Lenore Walker, *Terrifying Love* (New York, Harper Collins, 1990).

Chapter 4

1. Louis Sahagun, "Murder Case Opens Eyes to Horrific Tale of Child Abuse," *Los Angeles Times* (9 September 1993), p. A-1.
2. "When Violence Begins at Home," p. 7.
3. Shari Rudavsky, "AMA Urges Questioning on Abuse," *Washington Post* (17 June 1992), p. A-1.
4. *Domestic Violence: No Longer Behind the Curtains*, p. 12.
5. "Battered Women and the New Hampshire Justice System," as quoted in *Domestic Violence: No Longer Behind the Curtains*, p. 96.
6. *Violent Relationships: Battering and Abuse Among Adults*, p. 36.
7. Barnett, p. 16.
8. Pam Maples, "Under The Gun," *Indianapolis Star* (11 July 1993), p. F-1.

9. Judith Sherven and James Sniechowski, "Women Are Responsible Too," *Los Angeles Times* (21 June 1994), p. A-12.
10. Hazlewood, p. 79.
11. Kathleen H. Hofeller, Ph.D., *Battered Women, Shattered Lives* (Palo Alto, CA, R&E Research Associates, 1983), p. 89.
12. *Violence between Intimates* (Washington, D.C., U.S. Government Printing Office, 1994), p. 2.
13. Lenore Walker, *The Battered Woman Syndrome* (New York, Springer, 1984).
14. Barbour, p. 180.
15. *Study of National Incidence and Prevalence of Child Abuse and Neglect: 1988*, as quoted in *Domestic Violence: No Longer Behind the Curtains*, p. 12.
16. Rajiv Chandrasekaran, "Confronting Tragic Effects of Shaking a Baby," *Washington Post* (15 August 1994), p. A-14.
17. Annette Fuller Reynolds, "Affectionate 3-year-old Is Progressing," *Indianapolis Star* (28 May 1995), p. J-10.
18. *Domestic Violence: No Longer Behind the Curtains*, p. 62.
19. Karen Murphy, "Family Depicted As Monstrous Abusers," *Indianapolis Star* (12 March 1995), p. B-1.
20. U.S. Department of Justice, *Child Abuse: Prelude to Delinquency?* (Washington, D.C., U.S. Government Printing Office, 1986), p. 8.
21. Naomi A. Adler and Joseph Schutz, "Sibling Incest Offenders," *Child Abuse and Neglect* (July 1995), p. 811.
22. Steve Bates, "Elderly Abuse Rises Sharply," *Washington Post* (7 March 1993), p. 1.
23. *Violent Relationships: Battering and Abuse Among Adults*, p. 134.
24. Karl Pillemer, "The Dangers of Dependency: New Findings on Domestic Violence against the Elderly," *Social Problems* (February 1985), p. 212.

Chapter 5

1. *Growing Old in America* (Wylie, TX, Information Plus, 1994), p. 107.
2. Roger T. Anderson et al., "The Investigation and Outcome of Reported Cases of Elder Abuse: the Forsyth County Aging Study," *The Gerontologist* (February 1994), p. 123.
3. Joseph P. Shapiro, "The Elderly Are Not Children," *U.S. News & World Report* (13 January 1992), p. 26.
4. Mathis E. McRae, "Policing the Guardians: Combatting Guardianship and Power of Attorney Fraud," *FBI Law Enforcement Bulletin* (February 1994), p. 1.
5. Jeff Barnard, "Adoptive Parents Are Found Guilty of Racketeering," *Indianapolis Star* (23 November 1995), p. A-11.

Chapter 6

1. J. Madeleine Nash, "When Love Is Exhausted," *Time* (6 April 1992), p. 24.
2. Timothy Egan, "Old, Ailing and Finally a Burden Abandoned," *Washington Post* (26 March 1992), p. B-1.

3. Nash, p. 24.
4. Ibid.
5. *Current Trends in Child Abuse Reporting and Fatalities: Results of the 1994 Annual Fifty State Survey* (National Center on Child Abuse Prevention Research, Chicago, 1995), p. 15.
6. *Child Abuse: Prelude to Delinquency* (Washington, D.C., U.S. Government Printing Office, 1986), p. 8.
7. Matthew C. Johnson and Jeffrey Leiter, "Child Maltreatment and School Performance," *American Journal of Education* (February 1994), p. 154.
8. Ron Harris, "Gregory's File: A Childhood of Neglect, A Life of Crime," *Los Angeles Times* (23 August 1993), p. A-1.
9. "Reno Says Child Neglect at Root of Much Trouble," *Indianapolis Star* (4 October 1993), p. D-2.
10. Anne C. Roark, "More Children Are Victims of Violence, Studies Find," *Los Angeles Times* (5 November 1992), p. A-1.

Chapter 7

1. Bonnie Johnson, "A Love Betrayed, A Brief Life Lost," *People* (13 February 1989), p. 87.
2. Ibid.
3. Ronald Sullivan, "Hedda Nussbaum, Filing Suit, Testifies to Personal Agony," *The New York Times* (27 October 1994), p. B-3.
4. Ronald Sullivan, "Witness Says Numerous Injuries to Nussbaum Were Nearly Fatal," *The New York Times* (5 November 1988), p. 31.
5. Johnson, p. 88.
6. Susan Brownmiller, "Madly in Love," *Ms.* (April 1989), pp. 62–63.
7. Ronald Sullivan, "Nussbaum Testifies to Not Hearing Noise," *The New York Times* (13 December 1988), p. B-3.
8. Ann Landers, "Wife Batterer Warns of Potential Murder," *Indianapolis Star* (27 December 1995), p. D-8.
9. David Finkelhor, "Common Features of Family Abuse," *The Dark Side of Families: Current Family Violence Research* (1983).
10. W. J. Goode, "Force and Violence in the Family," *Journal of Marriage and the Family* (1971).
11. Christopher R. Goddard and Janet R. Stanley, "Viewing the Abusive Parent and the Abused Child as Captor and Hostage," *Journal of Interpersonal Violence* (June 1994), p. 258.
12. "Wife Abusers' Volatile Brew," *Science News* (27 August 1994), p. 143.
13. Randolph, p. 112.
14. Maria Henson, "A Death Foretold," *Lexington Herald-Leader* (2 December 1990).
15. *Violent Relationships: Battering and Abuse Among Adults*, p. 49.
16. Susan Baugh, "County Prison Combats Domestic Violence with MENDS Program, *Corrections Today* (August 1994), p. 84.
17. Stuart Silverstein, "Stalked by Violence on the Job," *Los Angeles Times* (8 August 1994), p. 1.

18. U.S. Department of Justice, *Female Victims of Crime* (Washington, D.C., U.S. Government Printing Office).
19. Patricia Phelan, "Incest and Its Meaning: Perspectives of Fathers and Daughters," *Child Abuse and Neglect* (January 1995), p. 7.

Chapter 8

1. Welton W. Harris II, "Woman Who Had Been Involved in Lawsuit with Robert Montgomery, Sr. Also Had Restraining Order Against Him," *Indianapolis Star* (21 October 1995), p. A-1.
2. Jeff Swiatek, "Killer Called Longtime Abuser," *Indianapolis Star* (22 October 1995), p. A-1.
3. Barnett, p. 51.
4. *Crime in the United States*, p. 19.
5. Jill Smolowe, "When Violence Hits Home," *Time* (4 July 1994), p. 18.
6. Anna Kosof, *Battered Women: Living with the Enemy* (New York, Franklin Watts, 1994), p. 75.
7. Ann Jones, *Next Time, She'll Be Dead* (Boston, Beacon Press, 1994), p. 95.
8. Smolowe, p. 18.
9. Don Terry, "Killing of Woman Waiting for Justice Sounds Alert on Domestic Violence," *The New York Times* (17 March 1992), p. A-14.
10. Joseph B. Treaster, "Man Shoots Wife to Death As She Holds Their Infant," *The New York Times* (7 June 1994), p. B-3.
11. U.S. Attorney General's Task Force on Family Violence (Washington, D.C., U.S. Government Printing Office, 1984), p. 1.
12. *Current Trends in Child Abuse Reporting and Fatalities*, op. cit.
13. Robert L. Davis and Eugene E. Sabotta, "Fatality After Report to a Child Abuse Registry in Washington State, 1973–1986," *Child Abuse and Neglect* (September–October 1992), p. 627.
14. Anne C. Roark, "More Children Are Victims of Violence, Studies Find," *Los Angeles Times* (5 November 1992), p. A-41.
15. Sandra Evans, "Increase in Baby Killings Attributed to Family Stress," *Washington Post* (23 June 1992), p. A-1.
16. "Twin Charged in Sister's Beating Death," *Indianapolis Star* (24 November 1995), p. B-3.
17. George McLaren, "Young Killer Testifies Against Friend," *Indianapolis Star* (2 July 1996), p. B-1.
18. U.S. Department of Justice, *Murder in Families* (Washington, D.C., U.S. Government Printing Office, July 1994).
19. U.S. Department of Justice, *Spouse Murder Defendants in Large Urban Counties* (Washington, D.C., U.S. Government Printing Office, September 1995).

Chapter 9

1. *Domestic Violence: No Longer Behind the Curtains*, p. 61.

2. Murray Straus, *Behind Closed Doors: Violence in the American Family*, as quoted in *Domestic Violence: No Longer Behind the Curtains*, p. 114.
3. Hazlewood, p. 80.
4. Brent Staples, "Learning to Batter Women," *The New York Times* (12 February 1995), p. E-14.
5. Leslie Bennetts, "How Domestic Violence Hurts Kids," *Parents Magazine* (November 1994), p. 44.
6. *Growing Old in America*, p. 109.
7. Geraldine Baum, "The Forgotten Victims," *Los Angeles Times* (20 July 1994), p. E-1.
8. Ibid.
9. U.S.Department of Justice, *Victims of Childhood Sexual Abuse—Later Criminal Consequences* (Washington, D.C., U.S. Government Printing Office, 1995), pp. 4–5.

Chapter 10

1. Brooks Jackson, "Storm Center: John Fedders of SEC Is Pummeled by Legal and Personal Problems," *Wall Street Journal* (25 February 1985), p. 1.
2. "D.C. Wives Unlikely to Report Beatings," *Fort Worth Star-Telegram* (11 July 1979), p. 1.
3. Gail Buchalter, "If You Are Battered," *Parade Magazine* (26 March 1995), p. 14.
4. Dick Lipsey, "Doctor Is Charged with Murder in Her Kids' Arson Deaths," *Indianapolis Star* (24 November 1995), p. A-13.
5. "Dr. Provisor's Husband Charged in Home Incident," *Indianapolis Star* (1 October 1995), p. C-4.
6. *Violent Relationships: Battering and Abuse Among Adults*, p. 63.
7. Candace A. Hennekens, *Healing Your Life: Recovery from Domestic Abuse* (Chippewa Falls, WI, ProWriting Services and Press, 1991), p. 14.
8. Daniel Goleman, "Surprising Portrait of Psychotherapists As Abuse Victims," *The New York Times* (9 September 1992), p. C-13.
9. "Man Charged With Butchering Wife After Spat," *Indianapolis Star* (31 August 1995), p. A-17.
10. Diana Jean Schemo, "Amid the Gentility of the East End, A Town Confronts Domestic Abuse," *The New York Times* (13 August 1992), p. B-7.
11. Carol Lawson, "Violence at Home: They Don't Want Anyone To Know," *The New York Times* (6 August 1992), p. C-1.
12. "Ex-Minister Indicted In a Choking Attack on His Wife in 1985," *The New York Times* (26 August 1992), p. A-16.
13. "Personality Parade," *Parade Magazine* (3 September 1995), p. 2.
14. "LaToya Jackson Claims Beating, Leaves Husband," *Indianapolis Star* (10 May 1996), p. D-2.
15. Bill Brubaker, "Violence in Football Extends Off Field," *Washington Post* (13 November 1994), p. A-1.
16. William Oscar Johnson, "A National Scourge," *Sports Illustrated* (27 June 1994), p. 92.

17. Peter H. Neidig, Harold E. Russell, and Albert F. Seng, "FOP Marital Aggression Survey," *National FOP Journal* (Fall/Winter 1992), p. 25.
18. *Domestic Violence: No Longer Behind the Curtains*, p. 105.
19. Ronnie Priest, "Child Sexual Abuse Histories Among African-American College Students: A Preliminary Study," *American Journal of Orthopsychiatry* (July 1992), p. 475.
20. Ohlin, p. 270.

Chapter 11

1. Sherman, p. 37.
2. David A. Ford, "The Disinclination of Police Officers to Arrest Wife Batterers: A Survey of Police Attitudes Toward Warrantless Probable Cause Arrests for Conjugal Violence," Paper presented at the annual meeting of the Law and Order Society Association, Washington, D.C., 1987.
3. Bonnie L. Yegidis and Robin Berman Renzy, "Battered Women's Experiences with a Preferred Arrest Policy," *Affilia Journal of Women and Social Work* (Spring 1994), p. 60.
4. *Violent Relationships: Battering and Abuse Among Adults*, p. 68.
5. U.S. Department of Justice, *Domestic Violence* (Washington, D.C., U.S. Government Printing Office).
6. David A. Ford, "Wife Battery and Criminal Justice: A Study of Victim Decision-Making," *Family Relations* (October 1983), p. 469.
7. David A. Ford, "Prosecution as a Victim Power Resource: A Note on Empowering Women in Violent Conjugal Relationships," *Law & Society Review* (February 1991), p. 316.
8. Sherman, p. 35.
9. "Wife Battery and Criminal Justice: A Study of Victim Decision-Making, p. 471.
10. Gail Goodman and Karen Saywitz, "Understanding and Improving Children's Testimony," *Children Today* (January–February 1993), p. 13.
11. *When the Victim Is a Child*, p. 4.

Chapter 12

1. *When the Victim Is a Child*, p. 9.
2. U.S. Department of Justice, *The Child Victim as a Witness* (Washington, D.C., U.S. Government Printing Office, October 1994), p. 96.
3. U.S. Department of Justice, *Prosecuting Child Physical Abuse Cases: A Case Study in San Diego* (Washington, D.C., U.S. Government Printing Office, June 1995), p. 1.
4. Robert F. Howe, "D.C. Lawyer Convicted of Sexually Abusing Youth," *Washington Post* (5 September 1992), p. B-1.
5. "Physical Proof Rare in Child Sex Abuse," *Washington Post Health* (20 September 1994), p. 5.
6. David Hechler, "The Battle and the Backlash," in *Domestic Violence: No Longer Behind the Curtains* (New York, Macmillan, 1989), p. 82.

7. Rebecca Nathanson and Karen J. Saywitz, "Children's Testimony and Their Perceptions of Stress In and Out of the Courtroom," *Child Abuse and Neglect* (September–October 1993), p. 613.

8. *Wheeler v. United States*, 159 U.S. 523 (1895).

9. *When the Victim Is a Child*, p. 26.

10. Maria Henson, "A Strong, Clear Voice," *Lexington Herald-Leader* (3 March 1991), p. 1.

11. Adam Nossiter, "New Witness for the Prosecution," *The New York Times* (9 June 1996).

12. Barbour, p. 86.

13. Bettina Boxall and Frederick M. Muir, "Prosecutors Taking Harder Line Toward Spouse Abuse," *Los Angeles Times* (11 July 1994), p. A-1.

Chapter 13

1. Martin Waldron, "Whitman Told Doctor He Sometimes Thought of 'Shooting People,'" *The New York Times* (3 August 1966), p. 1.

2. Kosof, p. 59.

3. Jones, p. 89.

4. Lee H. Bowker, "Battered Wives and the Police: A National Study of Usage and Effectiveness," *Police Studies* (1984), p. 84.

5. Daniel Goleman, "An Elusive Picture of Violent Men Who Kill Mates," *The New York Times* (15 January 1995), p. 22.

Chapter 14

1. George Stuteville, "Beaten Women Mourn Their Slain Counselor," *Indianapolis Star* (9 March 1989), p. A-1.

2. Ibid.

3. Marc D. Allan, "State Suspends Workers Who Freed Slaying Suspect," *Indianapolis Star* (7 March 1989), p. A-1.

4. James L. Patterson, "Prisoner on Leave Charged in Wife's Death," *Indianapolis Star* (5 March 1989), p. A-1.

5. Kosof, p. 35.

6. Barbour, p. 96.

7. Kosof, p. 41.

8. Pamela J. Thomas, "Which Way Out?" *Black Elegance* (January 1996), p. 74.

9. Steven S. Simring and Sue Klavans Simring, *The Compatibility Quotient* (New York, Fawcett, 1990), p. 152.

10. *Domestic Violence: No Longer Behind the Curtains*, p. 122.

11. Bennetts, p. 44.

12. Hofeller, p. 93.

13. Randolph, p. 112.

14. Hofeller, p. 89.

15. Bennetts, p. 44.

16. Ohlin, p. 530.

17. Ohlin, p. 380.
18. Barnett, p. 18.
19. David Holmstrom, "Programs Aim to Help Men Who Batter Women," *Christian Science Monitor* (11 January 1994), p. 2.
20. *Domestic Violence: No Longer Behind the Curtains*, p. 117.
21. Robin Abcarian, "Telephones and Tender Voices," *Los Angeles Times* (13 July 1994), p. E-1.
22. *Crime in the United States*, p. 19.
23. "When Violence Begins at Home," p. 7.
24. *Violence between Intimates*, p. 6.
25. Barbour, p. 95.
26. "The Disinclination of Police Officers to Arrest Wife Batterers: A Survey of Police Attitudes Toward Warrantless Probable Cause Arrests for Conjugal Violence."
27. "Rural Volunteers Offer Safe Havens for Battered Women," *Indianapolis Star* (14 November 1995), p. D-4.
28. Tamara Jones, "When Home Is Where the Hurt Is," *Washington Post* (9 July 1995), p. F-1.

Chapter 15

1. *Thurman v. City of Torrington*, 595 F. Supp. 1521 (1984).
2. Ted Gest and Betsy Streisand, "Still Failing Women?" *U.S. News and World Report* (19 June 1995), p. 54.
3. Sherman, p. 3.
4. Ibid., p. 14.
5. Sandra G. Boodman, "The Formidable Task of Treating Batterers," *Washington Post Health* (28 June 1994), p. 11.
6. Daniel Goleman, "Standard Therapies May Help Only Impulsive Spouse Abuse," *The New York Times* (22 June 1994), p. C-11.
7. Jan Hoffman, "When Men Hit Women," *The New York Times Magazine* (16 February 1992), p. 23.
8. U.S. Department of Justice, *Family Violence: Interventions for the Justice System* (Washington, D.C., U.S. Government Printing Office, 1993), p. 7.
9. N. Zoe Hilton, editor, *Legal Response to Wife Assault* (Newbury Park, CA, Sage, 1993), p. 135.
10. Boxall, p. A-1.
11. Maria L. LaGanga, "Nevada Judges Must Attend Domestic Violence Forum," *Los Angeles Times* (9 September 1993), p. A-1.
12. U.S. Department of Justice, *Civil Protection Orders* (Washington, D.C., U.S. Government Printing Office, 1990), p. 1.
13. Matthew Purdy and Don Van Natta, Jr., "Before the Murder, A Judicial Journey," *The New York Times* (14 March 1996), p. B-1.
14. Robert W. Page, "Family Courts: An Effective Judicial Approach to the Resolution of Family Disputes," *Juvenile & Family Court Journal* (1993).
15. "No Guns for Abusers," *Washington Post* (6 November 1993), p. A-24.

16. Judith Cebula and Kathleen Schuckel, "Victim Isn't Only One Affected by Domestic Violence," *Indianapolis Star* (21 October 1995), p. A-2.

17. Joseph Pereira, "Employers Confront Domestic Violence," *Wall Street Journal* (2 March 1995), p. B-1.

18. Dorothy Giobbe, "Publicizing Domestic Violence: Newspaper's Policy of Identifying Victims of Domestic Violence from Court Papers Creates a Debate in a Small Vermont Town," *Editor and Publisher* (18 December 1993), p. 13.

19. Deirdre Martin, "Domestic Violence," *Law Enforcement Technology* (October 1994), p. 38.

20. Barbara Vobejda, "Group Sets National Drive Against Domestic Violence," *Washington Post* (1 July 1994), p. A-20.

21. *Ohio v. Roberts*, 448 U.S. 56 (1980).

22. Baum, p. E-1.

23. Cathy Spatz Widom, *The Cycle of Violence* (Washington, D.C., U.S. Government Printing Office, 1992), p. 5.

24. Tamar Lewin, "AMA Guidelines Ask Doctors To Help Identify Abuse of Elderly," *The New York Times* (24 November 1995), p. A-10.

25. Ibid.

Index